THE ILLUSTRATED STORY OF

Opera

DAVID NICE

THE ILLUSTRATED STORY OF

Opera

DAVID NICE

CHARTWELL
BOOKS, INC.

This edition published by

Chartwell Books, Inc.

A Division of Book Sales, Inc.

114 Northfield Avenue

Raritan Center

Edison, N.J. 08818

First printing 1994

This printing 1994

Produced by Marshall Cavendish Books

(A Division of Marshall Cavendish Partworks, Ltd)

119 Wardour Street

London W1V 3TD

Senior Editor: Sarah Bloxham

Copyeditor: Corinne Orde

Senior Art Editor: Joyce Mason

Designer: Simon Wilder

Picture Researchers: Mirco Decet and Angela Parman

Production Controller: Inger Faulkner

ISBN 0-7858-0039-5

Printed and bound in China

CONTENTS

It seems hard to believe now that opera was ever under threat. Yet in the 1960s the spokesmen for the avant-garde declared that the only way forward was to tear down every major opera house; the art-form was labelled fit only for museums, its moneyed patrons élitist. Then came the rallying of the media and the communications

iNTRODUCTION

OPERA TODAY

explosion. If you heard an aria on the radio or were intrigued by seeing an opera singer interviewed on television, you could go on to buy the record, video, CD or even laser disc. Operas produced at the very highest level reached millions, televised from opera houses such as Glyndebourne in England, or Wagner's festival shrine at Bayreuth, where the person in the street stood little chance of obtaining a ticket even if he or she could afford it. Other houses – the London Coliseum, home of the English National Opera, for example – set up as affordable competition to

their starry-cast rivals with striking and topical productions that continued to challenge the imagination. Newspaper editors and journalists continued – and, in some cases, continue – to wield the catchphrase of 'élitism', easily producing evidence of top seat prices to support their case. It is easy to answer back, however, that a night at the opera can be enjoyed – at least in London and Vienna – for less than the price of a cinema ticket.

Has the opera boom gone too far? Should operatic voices be used to sell British Airways or to provide a background to an Italian meal (especially since, as any singer who has worked in a restaurant will tell you, singing the best-loved arias for an hour at a stretch is voice-wrecking work)? I can only say that although Pavarotti singing '*Nessun dorma*' may be the extent of many people's interest, if a small percentage goes to see Puccini's *Turandot* (the opera in which the aria appears) as a result, then popularization will have served its purpose. No research, to my knowledge, has been carried out on where the potential opera buff goes next – whether '*Nessun dorma*' has ever led to an interest in more 'difficult' modern composers, such as Berg and Britten.

The usual basis for interest is a gut response to the melodic richness of an Italian aria, resulting in the discovery of some of the most miraculous musico-dramatic structures ever created (I am thinking especially of Puccini's perfectly paced *Bohème* and *Tosca*). I also know theatre-goers whose familiarity with the tough drama of plays by Ibsen, Strindberg and Shakespeare has enabled them to appreciate the dramatic impact of such operas as Berg's *Wozzeck* or Strauss' *Elektra* on a first-time visit. Many long-term opera buffs still have problems with Wagnerian length – invariably citing Rossini's maxim, 'wonderful moments but dreadful quarters of an hour' – yet the symbols and the potent mythology of the *Ring* cycle, as well as the physical theatre of Patrice Chéreau's breathtaking production, captured a million viewers when the Bayreuth centenary *Ring* was shown on television.

THEN AND NOW

Just as there are no hard-and-fast rules as to where to start enjoying opera, so there is no such thing as straight-line historical progress in this art form – old works sometimes foreshadow later developments, new works sometimes draw on past traditions. So, for instance, the music dramas of Monteverdi, the first great operatic composer, may strike us as lean in the strictly operatic sense,

with arias inserted only when the context demands them, all in the cause of telling the story clearly and powerfully. In many ways this approach mirrors that of modern music theatre. Mozart's comedies, too, can seem closer to our way of thinking than the sometimes florid display pieces of the early 18th and 19th centuries. This book aims to help opera-goers of all levels tread a path through these myriad developments in style and content by telling the story of opera chronologically from its origins through to the present day.

HERE AND THERE

Grouping operas by their region of origin is a useful way of broaching the subject, and I have organized two of the four sections in the book in this manner. The differences in operatic style and taste between nationalities are, however, far less fixed than a superficial summary might suggest: Wagner and his contemporaries learned a great deal from the Italian art of *bel canto*, and the Italians returned the compliment in the later part of the 19th century; even Verdi, in *Otello* and *Falstaff*, incorporated some of Wagner's discoveries in the field of music drama, though he would maintain – probably rightly – that he was still antipathetic to the atmosphere engendered in

Wagner's operas. Even in our own century, the procedures that were adopted by Britten in his operas would not have been the same without the example of Wagner, whom he professed to detest. Stravinsky's melting-pot of styles in *The Rake's Progress* emphasized the usefulness of operatic traditions at a time when composers were claiming to break entirely with the past. That era of arid intellectualism and novelty for its own sake has passed; once again, tradition and reference are vital components in new opera.

PRODUCTION VALUES

Even now, fashions go in cycles. Reactionary critics complain of 'produceritis' or 'directoritis', clamouring for traditional values and 'What The Composer Wanted' – which, in many cases, is neither possible nor desirable, since opera must have meaning for us today and aesthetics change. Wagner's 'naturalistic' demands for live rams and horses on stage or Verdi's kitsch exotica would look ridiculous. Yet it is also true that some directors have superimposed their own vision on a work to such an extent that the original dramatic meaning is distorted and the musical values are submerged; in such cases, a return to first intentions is certainly desirable.

Ultimately, though, the visual aspect a production is more properly the province of the designer; and the theatrical world has acknowledged that it rarely matches opera designs for fantasy and imagination. The director's role is to establish the chemistry between singers – the body language of relationships and real teamwork. Such things are not always possible on the international circuit, when a star singer flies in the day before the performance.

Even if the director has rehearsal time at his disposal, will his singers always be equal to his dramatic demands? We know that, generally speaking, more is expected of the opera star than in the past: good looks, a trim figure, stage presence and flexibility in a wide repertoire are prerequisites of the aspiring young singer. The audience tends to laugh when the fat lady sings. Yet once again, fashion is coming full circle to accept that great voices don't always tally with dramatic credibility. In certain repertoires – notably the *bel canto* operas of Bellini and Donizetti, which are very much back in circulation – the voice has to come first, and recordings can help to emphasize that. In the last analysis, what matters is whether the singer acts with the voice. At that stage, both opera at its most artificial and music theatre at its most compelling share equal honours in the repertoire – one of the richest and most wide-ranging of any artistic treasure stores. Opera buffs beg to differ – for one set, the star voice matters most, and for another, the drama is more important – but the present operatic climate welcomes all shapes and sizes.

OPERAS AND SINGERS

No history of opera, unless it is a dictionary or reference book, can expect to be comprehensive, and inevitably this is a personal guide – though not, I hope, a record of personal biases. I rejected what could have become a check-list of the repertoire in favour of operas that seemed to be most representative of style and striking subject matter.

The outstanding monuments of the operatic tradition are, however, all here – hopefully with some understanding of what makes them great; no-one can expect to fall in love with every aspect of the repertoire, but respect for the true masterpieces is never difficult to find. The number of featured operas is, inevitably, too small, involving some compromise between my own favourites and the cornerstones of the repertoire. There are some notable exceptions: you will find *Aida*, for instance, considered in the main text but not featured in the spreads, because I genuinely believe it not to be one of Verdi's greatest operas; had there been room for *Don Carlos*, *A Masked Ball* and *The Force of Destiny*, they would undoubtedly have come first. On the other hand, I did cross *Idomeneo*, *The Girl of the Golden West* and *The Turn of the Screw* off the short-list simply because the best-loved Mozart and Puccini operas, and Britten's *Peter Grimes*, chose themselves; personal preference came second to popular demand. I make no apologies for ending with a so-called musical – Sondheim's *Sweeney Todd* – for reasons given in the final chapter.

Choosing the all-time greats among the singers, too, was far from easy. To those who nostalgically wonder where the great voices have gone, it is easy to respond with an impressive list of charismatic singers among the younger generation – including bass-baritone Bryn Terfel and mezzo-sopranos Cecilia Bartoli and Anne-Sofie von Otter. Since it remains early days for star potential, however, and since – once again – the choice has to be limited, I have restricted myself to the most impressive long-term careers.

David Nice

LONDON, 1994

9

*The apparatus of baroque opera at its most extravagant in a 1729 production of a
dramatic cantata by Leonardo Vinci.*

bEGINNINGS

Monteverdi's Orfeo, *fast-moving and intensely dramatic, is the first great opera in the repertoire. After Monteverdi, opera branched off into the formal displays of tragic or heroic dramas and frivolous comedy. It was Mozart who brought the two together again in his masterly collaborations with the Italian poet Lorenzo da Ponte. They were* The Marriage of Figaro, Così fan Tutte *and* Don Giovanni, *each a mixture of serious drama and comedy.*

CHAPTER 1

Monteverdi to Mozart: mythology

Opera began as an attempt by a group of intellectual Florentines to revive the principles of Greek drama, which they rightly maintained was an artform set to music. Monteverdi's *Orfeo* survives as the first profound expression of those principles. The characters of Greek mythology continued to feature in the lavish entertainments at the French court and in the London theatres, where Handel courted a wider public with his brilliant vehicles for star singers. In 1767 Gluck changed operatic history with his call for a return to uncluttered dramatic expression, and Mozart followed Gluck with an elaborate but dramatically powerful experiment in his serious masterpiece, *Idomeneo*, and with the strange hybrid of his final year, *The Magic Flute*.

Early-19th-century design by German romantic Schinkel for the entry of the Queen of the Night in The Magic Flute.

Claudio Monteverdi in 1640 – portrait by Bernardo Strozzi. It was at this late stage in his life that Monteverdi composed The Return of Ulysses *and* The Coronation of Poppea *for the Venetian public theatres.*

The myth of Orpheus, who with his music charmed the beasts and hell itself, makes a helpful starting-point for the story of opera. It provided the basis for a kind of pagan miracle-play in mid-15th-century Florence, in which singing played only a small part. It was also one of the subjects approved by the late-16th-century *camerata*, the circle of Florentine composers which played its part in the humanist ideals of the Italian Renaissance by attempting to revive the musical drama of Greek tragedy. Then, in 1607, the Cremona-born composer Claudio Monteverdi took the story to heights of dignified expression that have never been surpassed.

THE FIRST OPERAS

The fact that Monteverdi's *Orfeo* happens to be the first great opera now seems less important than its ability to move an audience. His use of dramatic recitative – declamation which employs singing as a kind of heightened speech – was not new. It had already appeared in operas by Peri and Caccini, who had both set the libretto of *Orfeo* to music. Yet their operas seem stilted by comparison. Monteverdi's greatest gift was not so much his technical originality as his deep involvement with human emotions – no mean achievement for a man who thought of himself first and foremost as a writer of sacred music. In a letter to his librettist, Striggio, in 1616, the composer rejects a 'chorus of winds' in a proposed 'maritime fable': 'How can I by such means move the passions? Ariadne moved us because she was a woman, and similarly Orpheus because he was a human being, not a wind'.

Orpheus and Ariadne, the Cretan princess whose sad lament is all that remains of Monteverdi's opera based on her legend, played

out their dramas before privileged audiences that were connected with the Gonzaga court at Mantua, where the composer served for 23 years of his long musical career. By the time of Monteverdi's next surviving masterpiece in 1641, the opera craze had travelled to Rome (where Pope Clement IX gave it his blessing) and on to Venice. The Renaissance had given way to the baroque era. Opera on mythological subjects thrived in Paris under the patronage of Louis XIV,

following the presentation in 1647 of another Italian *Orfeo* by the composer Luigi Rossi.

The pioneer of this highly stylized French development of the form – the *tragédie lyrique* – was Jean-Baptiste Lully; his solemn music for dancing, singing and extravagant processions strikes us as rather square and unadventurous by comparison with that of his colourful successor, Rameau, who produced daring harmonies and lavish invention.

A wider gulf separates the operas of the two composers we have come to regard as the leading lights of early opera in England. Henry Purcell's *Dido and Aeneas*, first produced at a Chelsea girls' school in 1689, shows a direct and truthful approach to match that of Monteverdi, but time has moved on and the heroine's starkly moving lament, 'When I am laid in earth', is closer to what we now think of as an aria than the heightened recitative of Monteverdi's Ariadne. Like

Continued on page 18

Kathleen Ferrier

AS GLUCK'S ORFEO, SHE IMMORTALIZED THE ARIA *'CHE FARÒ SENZA EURIDICE?'* OR 'WHAT IS LIFE?' AND BECAME BRITAIN'S BEST-LOVED SINGER. SHE PROBABLY REMAINS SO DECADES AFTER HER UNTIMELY DEATH FROM CANCER IN 1953. SHE LEFT SCHOOL AT 14 TO BECOME A TELEPHONIST AND DID NOT TAKE UP A PROFESSIONAL SINGING CAREER UNTIL THE AGE OF 25, BUT THE NATURAL QUALITY OF HER DEEP, RICH CONTRALTO VOICE WAS IMMEDIATELY RECOGNIZED: MANY HAVE TRIED TO IMITATE IT, BUT NONE HAS SUCCEEDED. KATHLEEN FERRIER SPENT MORE TIME ON THE CONCERT PLATFORM THAN ON THE OPERATIC STAGE – HER RECORDING OF MAHLER'S *DAS LIED VON DER ERDE* (*THE SONG OF THE EARTH*) IS AS FAMOUS AS THAT OF GLUCK'S *ORPHEUS AND EURYDICE* – BUT SHE CREATED ONE GREAT TRAGIC FIGURE IN OPERA: BRITTEN'S HEROINE IN *THE RAPE OF LUCRETIA* (1946). SHE SANG ORFEO IN HOLLAND, AT GLYNDEBOURNE, ENGLAND, AND IN ONLY TWO PERFORMANCES AT COVENT GARDEN, LONDON, SHORTLY BEFORE HER DEATH.

Orfeo (Laurence Dale) leading Euridice (Marie Angel) out of Hades in David Freeman's stark and physical production for English National Opera.

ORFEO

WHO'S WHO

MUSIC *(Soprano)*
Prologue

ORFEO *(Tenor/Soprano)*
A Poet

EURIDICE *(Soprano)*
His Wife

MESSENGER *(Soprano/Mezzo)*
Bearing News of Eurydice's Death

HOPE *(Soprano)*

CHARON *(Bass)*
Ferryman to Hades

PROSERPINE *(Soprano)*
Queen of Hades

PLUTO *(Bass)*
King of Hades

APOLLO *(Tenor/Baritone)*
God of Music & Father of Orfeo

NYMPHS, SHEPHERDS & SPIRITS

The original description of *Orfeo* as an art-form was '*favola in musica*', 'fable in music'; the term 'opera' was first applied more than 20 years later (to Cavalli's first work). First performed at the court of Duke Vincenzo Gonzaga I of Mantua, Monteverdi's patron, in February 1607, *Orfeo* was not staged in England until 1925, nor in America until 1929.

The short introduction is one of the most impressive in opera. Monteverdi calls on the sumptuous orchestra the Duke of Mantua put at his disposal, with its impressive array of brass instruments, to usher in the court before the entertainment proper begins. Music (La Musica) appears for the Prologue. Between six orchestral *ritornelli*, or repeats of a dance-like theme which reappears later in the opera,

she announces her powers and paves the way for Orfeo's story; the style of declamation, a kind of recitative which puts the meaning of the words before any vocal display, typifies Monteverdi's attempt at a natural expression in music.

ACTS ONE & TWO

Nymphs and shepherds mark the wedding of Orfeo and Euridice with dances, solos and duets of thanksgiving, and madrigals typical of the late Renaissance. Their celebrations embrace the first of Orfeo's great solos, '*Rosa del ciel*' ('Rose of Heaven') and Euridice's simple response. Two shepherds encourage Orfeo to express his happiness further in song and dance at the beginning of Act Two, the perfect calm before the storm. A messenger arrives and, true to the principles of Greek tragedy which Monteverdi and his contemporaries sought to revive, solemnly unfolds an offstage tragedy: Euridice has been bitten by a viper while walking through a flowery meadow and has died in an instant.

Orfeo's response is the first of the plaintive laments at which Monteverdi excelled, ending with a line of pure despair realized in the simplest musical terms – 'Farewell earth, farewell to the sun and the heavens, farewell' – and crowned by a chorus of grief that is almost frightening in its directness.

ACT THREE

Encouraged by La Speranza, the figure of Hope, Orfeo resolves to reclaim Euridice from Hades, the Underworld. The first challenge he encounters comes from Charon, oarsman across the river Styx, whose character as guardian of the nether regions Monteverdi emphasizes by allocating the role to a bass (the voice-type of Pluto, too, in the following scene).

Trombones mark a new solemnity in the action, and Orfeo uses all his powers as a singer to gain entry. 'When the sense does not demand it, leave aside every ornament,' wrote Gagliano (a contemporary of Monteverdi) in the preface to his *Dafne*, 'so as not to act like the painter who knew how to paint cypress trees and therefore painted them everywhere.' Here is a marvellous example of a scene which does indeed call for ornamentation of the vocal line, and the set piece is a formidable challenge to the technical skill and coloratura resources of the leading tenor (surprisingly, Monteverdi also provided a simpler, alternative version).

Charon enjoys these musical blandishments, but it takes a simpler, more touching request from Orfeo to send him to sleep, leaving Orfeo to row himself across. A solemn chorus of spirits brings this pivotal act to a close.

ACT FOUR

Proserpine, the nymph who was snatched from the light to bring comfort to Hades as Pluto's wife, makes a sympathetic plea for Euridice's return to earth. The stony, solemn Pluto finally agrees, but only on condition that Orfeo, when leading his wife out of Hades, should not look back at her. In the course of his rapturous song, Orfeo breaks the condition and Euridice reproachfully slips away from him. The spirits lament and, as might be expected, draw a moral from Orfeo's lack of self-discipline.

ACT FIVE

The orchestral *ritornello* that was first heard in the Prologue introduces a now inconsolable Orfeo, who wanders about the plains of Thrace while being pursued by an echo, until Apollo appears to tell his son that he will see Euridice again among the stars.

Striggio, the opera's librettist, originally followed in part the traditional conclusion to the Greek myth, in which Orpheus is torn to pieces by Thracian maenad women (followers of the wine-god, Dionysus) and his singing head floats on to the island of Delos; but courtly tastes in Mantua did not welcome such gruesomeness on stage. The revised libretto of Monteverdi's *Orfeo* at least avoids the compromise of Gluck's opera on the same subject, which was written a century-and-a-half later and in which Eurydice is finally restored by the god of love. In Monteverdi's version of the story Apollo and Orfeo ascend heavenwards, extravagantly duetting as they go, to the accompaniment of harps; the earthly chorus rejoices with singing and dancing.

Orfeo (Anthony Rolfe Johnson) celebrates the power of music in English National Opera's 1981 production.

George Frideric Handel at the height of his fame as an operatic composer. Handel wrote a rich and varied sequence of 35 operas for the London stage.

Monteverdi, Purcell also showed remarkable individuality in adding ornamentation to a plain vocal line if the situation so demanded.

HANDEL

By the time the German-born composer George Frideric Handel came to London in 1710, embellishment was an expected part of the singer's accomplishments. The vehicle for display was the *da capo* aria, in which the singer would perform the basic melody of the aria unadorned, then proceed to a middle section (usually in contrasting mood) and finally return to the principal theme (*ritornello*), this time embellishing it with as many vocal fireworks as he or she could muster. Alessandro Scarlatti was the figure who introduced the form (in his 1693 opera *Teodora*), but few companies stage his works today, while the Handel revival is proof of Handel's skill at characterization within a convention. Nicholas Hytner's production of *Xerxes* at the English National Opera in 1986 established just how many dramatic situations can be extracted from the *da capo* aria.

Many worthwhile Handel operas still await revival; after early days in Hamburg, Florence and Venice, he wrote no fewer than 35 works for the London stage, all to Italian texts. *Alcina* and *Semele*, two of the most popular, are

Senesino

'IN MY DAY,' SINGS OLD DR BARTOLO IN A WITTY
ENGLISH TRANSLATION OF *THE BARBER OF SEVILLE*,
'OPERA WAS OPERA AND THE SOPRANOS WERE MEN.'
MORE TO THE POINT, THEY WERE *CASTRATI* WHOSE
PURE, TREBLE VOICES WERE PRESERVED BY AN
OPERATION BEFORE PUBERTY. THE CREATOR OF
MONTEVERDI'S *ORFEO* WAS A *CASTRATO*, AND IN THE
18TH CENTURY THE SPECIES' BRILLIANCE AND VIR-
TUOSITY COMMANDED HIGH FEES. SENESINO, BORN
FRANCESCO BERNARDI IN SIENA, WAS HANDEL'S
FAVOURITE AND THE COMPOSER WROTE THE LEADING
ROLES IN 15 OPERAS SPECIALLY FOR HIM. HE WAS
CRITICIZED FOR COMPORTING HIMSELF LIKE A STATUE
ON STAGE, MAKING INAPPROPRIATE GESTURES, BUT
HIS CELEBRATED FLEXIBILITY IN VOCAL DISPLAY WAS
WHAT THE AUDIENCE CAME TO HEAR.

typical examples of his sensuous and light-hearted approach to fantasy and mythology.

GLUCK TO MOZART

But the fashion for florid vocal display could only go so far at the expense of the drama. In 1767 Christoph Willibald von Gluck provided a backlash against empty display in the preface to the first version of his opera *Alceste*. He wanted to strip Italian opera of its long-standing abuses, 'to restrict music to its true office of serving poetry by means of expression and by following the situations of the story, without interrupting the action or stifling it with a useless superfluity of ornaments.'

Gluck was no young icono-clast when he wrote those words, but a sober-minded man in his fifties who had composed a number of operas in the florid Italianate style. The turning-point had come in 1762 with *Orpheus and Eury-dice*, but he put his principles most effectively into practice with two late masterpieces that dealt with the events framing the Trojan war: *Iphigenia in Aulis* (1774) and *Iphigenia in Tauris* (1779). His pared-down treatment of Greek tragedy can be dramatic and thrilling, as the conductors Sir Charles Mackerras and John Eliot Gardiner have recently proved. Even so, nothing in Gluck quite

prepares us for what Mackerras describes as the 'great cornucopia of effects and instrumentation' in *Idomeneo*, Mozart's first opera of genius, which he wrote in 1781 for the Munich court at the age of 25. His earlier experiments in the style of 18th-century *opera seria*, with its heroic gestures, formal arias and spectacular transformations, had been stiff and formal, but with *Idomeneo* he broke the rules with a shattering self-confidence. The story of the Cretan king forced to sacrifice his own son takes on an unprecedented urgency as orches-tral storms break across unfinished formal arias and characters drop their masterful poses to reveal human weakness and doubt.

Idomeneo is a young man's opera – at odds with the world – as Mozart's serene last experiment in the dying form of *opera seria* is not. He wrote *The Clemency of Titus* to celebrate the Prague coro-nation of Leopold II as King of Bohemia in September 1791. It is certainly easier to categorize than the opera he was working on more or less simultaneously, *The Magic Flute* – part *Singspiel* (a German form of opera with spoken dia-logue), part heroic opera. Here, it is in the noble figures of the prince, Tamino, and the heroine, Pamina, that Mozart took up the torch of Gluck and his belief in a 'beautiful simplicity'. The age of enlighten-ment's quest was far from over.

Mozart's comic bird-catcher, Papageno, as portrayed in the late 18th century.

THE
*m*AGIC *f*LUTE

As always, Mozart had a specific company in mind when he created *The Magic Flute* – in this case that of the actor-impresario Emanuel Schikaneder. More significantly, Mozart and Schikaneder were freemasons, and the opera is full of masonic symbols.

WHO'S WHO

TAMINO *(Tenor)*
Prince of Egypt

PAMINA *(Soprano)*
His Future Wife

THE QUEEN OF THE NIGHT
(Soprano) Pamina's Mother

THREE LADIES *(Sop. & Mezzo)*
In Attendance on the Queen

THREE BOYS *(Trebles)*
Benign Spirits

SARASTRO *(Bass)*
Priest of Isis & Osiris

THE SPEAKER *(Bass)*
A Priest in Sarastro's Service

MONOSTATOS *(Tenor)*
A Moor in Sarastro's Service

PAPAGENO & PAPAGENA *(Bar. & Sop.) A Bird-catcher & His Mate*

The freemasons' favourite number three plays a key part in the overture. As with the opera, however, no inside knowledge is necessary and the orchestra's curtain-raiser can be enjoyed as a colourful summary of the hero's journey from light to darkness before finally steering back to the light again.

ACT ONE

Enter Tamino, a tenor with heroic tendencies, pursued by a serpent. He faints; three mysterious ladies save him and, in close harmony, stop to admire his prostrate figure. Papageno, bird-catcher to the Queen of the Night, appears to take the credit and the ladies, who also turn out to be in the service of

the Queen, padlock his mouth in the first stretch of spoken dialogue. They tell Tamino of the Queen's daughter, Pamina, who is trapped inside the castle of a wicked demon, and hand him her portrait. Musing on it, he sings one of the most rapturous of all Mozart arias.

The Queen herself appears in the guise of wronged mother. Her slightly stilted lament almost wins our sympathies until sadness turns to fire, and a flashy, if brilliant, display of vocal pyrotechnics alerts us to potential villainy (the role, though short, is one of the most taxing in the repertoire and calls for a coloratura soprano of considerable power).

During a light and airy quintet the three ladies release Papageno from his padlock and send him to join Tamino in the quest for the lovely maiden, with supernatural assistance in the shape of a magic flute for the prince, a set of bells for the bird-catcher and three benign spirits – boy trebles – in a flying machine.

In the domain of the high-priest, Sarastro, Papageno comes face to face with Pamina's guardian, the lecherous Monostatos. Each thinks the other must be the devil and they run off in opposite directions. Fortunately, it is the bird-catcher who returns to take Pamina away with him, but not before praising the joys of love in a serene, strictly platonic, duet.

Meanwhile, the three boys have led Tamino to Sarastro's temples of Wisdom, Reason and Nature, leaving him with another three-fold piece of advice: 'Be silent, patient and persevering'. In an impressive stretch of accompanied recitative a priest (known as the Speaker) tells Tamino of Sarastro's essential goodness and the Queen's falsehoods. 'A woman has beguiled you?' he asks Tamino, adding, 'a woman does little, chatters much', with a strong element of masonic mysogyny, which, as it eventually transpires, Mozart and Schikaneder, his librettist, do not share. Bewildered in this realm of

Papageno padlocked for chattering by the Queen of the Night's ladies in Nicholas Hytner's 1988 ENO production.

'endless night', Tamino dispels the gloom with music, like Orpheus, and makes the beasts dance to the tune of his magic flute. The bells work even more effectively for Papageno and Pamina when they are cornered by Monostatos and his minions, who turn from violent threats to childlike docility on hearing the soothing strains.

Finally, all three travellers find themselves before Sarastro. Pamina and Tamino swiftly and ecstatically greet each other before being separated, but Sarastro turns out to be no tyrant (except to Monostatos), and Tamino, with an unwilling Papageno in tow, agrees to undergo the initiation trials of this brotherhood.

ACT TWO

The second act begins by confirming the noble intentions of Sarastro's circle, as it invokes the Egyptian gods, Isis and Osiris, and exposing the malicious frivolity of the three ladies as they attempt to sabotage the trial of silence undergone by Tamino and Papageno. While Papageno plays the fool, in long stretches of dialogue that were clearly intended for the pantomimic talents of Schikaneder (who created the role), Tamino remains steadfast. Though she has not so far been allowed to play a part in the ritual, Pamina is undergoing trials of her own. She is besieged

by Monostatos and her mother, the Queen of the Night, who, in a crucial stretch of dialogue before her manic second aria, reveals that her late husband had passed on the 'sevenfold circle of the sun', symbol of his authority, not to her but to Sarastro. Rebelling against his authority, she has come to retrieve the circle for her own purposes. This narrative explains why the Queen and Sarastro were once on the same side, and why the 'bad' assistants should have been in command of 'good' magical properties like the flute and the bells. The Queen's command to her daughter to kill Sarastro is forestalled by the arrival of the leader himself, who consoles Pamina with paternal benevolence in the most reassuring of his arias.

What Pamina cannot endure is the apparent indifference of the silent Tamino; her lament for what she believes to be lost love is the most affecting single number in the opera. The three boys prevent her attempted suicide, reassuring her in a glowing quartet, and she recovers to strike a blow for the previously discredited female sex by leading her prince through the ultimate trials of fire and water, the grave and radiant climax of the opera. They pass the test.

Papageno, who has found and lost the mate he yearned for when she appeared to him in the disguise of an old woman, also

contemplates ending his life. The noose is already around his neck when the boys make another timely intervention. He plays his magic bells and Papagena appears. The bird-like couple greet one another with stammering *Pa-pa-pa*s and express in duet their hopes for a nestful of children. The Queen and her ladies, now in league with

Monostatos, make a final attempt on Sarastro's citadel, but they are shadows of their former selves and their designs are easily overturned.

The chorus sings a hymn of praise to Pamina and Tamino, who are equal vanquishers of darkness, as the new initiates step forward for their consecration in the Temple of the Sun.

The three airborne spirits – little Mozarts in this 1979 Royal Opera production – lead Tamino and Papageno on their quest for Pamina as the three ladies take their leave.

Nero threatens the maid servant Drusilla in the Opera Factory production (1992) of The Coronation of Poppea.

CHAPTER 2

Monteverdi to Mozart: true to life

When Venice's theatres opened their doors to the paying public in the 1630s, opera turned into a more democratic art-form overnight. Monteverdi, now an old man, adapted without compromise and produced two further masterpieces. The frivolous mythological operas of Cavalli introduced comic elements, and comedy finally broke away from its strange role as an *intermezzo* (interlude) in serious operas to become a new Italian genre, *opera buffa*. Its counterparts were the English ballad-opera, the French *opéra comique* and the German *Singspiel*. Collaborating with the Italian poet Lorenzo da Ponte on three operas, Mozart once again turned convention on its head. With *The Marriage of Figaro*, *Don Giovanni* and *Così fan Tutte* they followed Shakespeare's use of the comic art-form as a device for revealing fundamental truths about the human condition.

When the 16th-century Florentine poets and musicians who belonged to the *camerata* (see page 14) drew up the guidelines for a revival of Greek tragedy, they were forced to ignore one important element in the picture: Athens' greatest dramatists in the fifth century BC were writing for audiences of thousands, everyday citizens who took their places in the amphitheatre of Dionysus to weep at the sufferings of Electra and Ajax as well as to laugh at the comic obscenities of Aristophanes' characters. The new form of drama set to music which came to be known as opera, however, provided entertainment for the chosen few.

A WIDER AUDIENCE

The Gonzaga court, which had been so faithfully served by Monteverdi, came to an end in 1630, sacked during the imperial war of succession. Monteverdi had continued to work with his librettist, Striggio, corresponding with him from Venice, where he was master of music to the Venetian republic, with special duties at St. Mark's. Then, in 1637, an event took place in Venice which was to have a momentous significance for the history of opera. The theatre of San Cassiano opened its doors to a paying public for the whole of the carnival season, taking advantage of a wider audience's enthusiasm

Montserrat Caballé

THE SPANISH SOPRANO'S ABILITY TO SING SOFTLY AND TO SPIN LONG, SMOOTH LINES WITH EFFORTLESS BREATH CONTROL HAS GIVEN HER A GOOD REPUTATION IN MOZART, THOUGH HER REPERTOIRE IS WIDE (AS WAS ESPECIALLY EVIDENT DURING THE EARLY YEARS FOLLOWING HER DÉBUT IN 1956, WHEN ROLES RANGED FROM AIDA AND TATYANA IN *EUGENE ONEGIN* TO SALOME AND RENATA, THE POSSESSED HEROINE OF PROKOFIEV'S *THE FIERY ANGEL*). AT GLYNDEBOURNE, ENGLAND, SHE SANG THE COUNTESS IN *THE MARRIAGE OF FIGARO* AND THE MARSCHALLIN IN *DER ROSEN-KAVALIER*. AT THE SAME TIME, IN THE MID-1960S, SHE ALSO CREATED A SENSATION IN NEW YORK AS THE SCHEMING HEROINE OF DONIZETTI'S *LUCREZIA BORGIA*, AND, AS A RESULT, HAS SPECIALIZED IN THE *BEL CANTO* REPERTOIRE OF DONIZETTI, BELLINI AND ROSSINI. HER CHARM AND HUMOUR WERE ASSETS IN THE ROYAL OPERA'S 1991 PRODUCTION OF ROSSINI'S *THE JOURNEY TO RHEIMS* AT COVENT GARDEN, LONDON, WHERE SHE ENCOURAGED A LIVELY REPARTEE WITH THE CONDUCTOR. MONTSERRAT CABALLÉ EVEN MADE A CELEBRATED VENTURE INTO POP WITH THE LATE FREDDIE MERCURY IN *BARCELONA* – A TRIBUTE TO THE CITY WHERE SHE WAS BORN IN 1933.

for opera as the craze arrived fresh from Rome. Dependent on good box-office returns and subscriptions from the richer citizens of Venice, the art-form became simpler. The emphasis was now, more than ever, on the individual and the development of character. Elaborate orchestrations, such as Monteverdi had been able to provide with the Duke of Mantua's resources, were shorn away in favour of the barest of accompaniments to the singing (probably only a handful of instruments), and choruses gave way to a whole host of minor roles.

VENETIAN OPERA

In the early years of Venetian opera mythological subjects were still the order of the day, though now they included fair helpings of comedy. Ludicrous old nurses (sometimes played by male singers in drag) or greedy, lascivious servants provided a counterpoint to the more serious lead roles. This frivolous, ornamental approach to the Greek myths is epitomized by the operas of Francesco Cavalli, a disciple of Monteverdi at St. Mark's, whose first work for the stage, *The Marriage of Peleus and Thetis*, was produced two years after the opening of the San Cassiano opera-house, and was the first entertainment of its kind officially to bear the name of 'opera'.

Most surprising of all, perhaps, was Monteverdi's willingness to be part of the new movement. He was in his seventies, even older than Gluck at the time of his call for reform a century later, when he composed his celebrated Venetian operas, *Il Ritorno d'Ulisse in Patria* (*The Return of Ulysses to his Native Land*) in 1640 and *L'Incoronazione di Poppea* (*The Coronation of Poppea*) in 1641–42. The two works could hardly be more different in tone, and taken together they provide perfect examples of the move from heroism towards new emotional realities.

Il Ritorno d'Ulisse is an opera in praise of constancy – that of Penelope, who has waited on the island of Ithaca for her husband, Ulysses, during the ten years of the Trojan War and the further ten years of his trials on the homeward journey. She has even withstood the insistent pleas of the suitors who eat away at the resources of the palace. Yet despite her classic patience, Penelope is a figure very true to life – first full of doubts, and later, in a duet of recognition which is the crowning glory of the piece, unable or perhaps unwilling to believe that the man who stands before her after all this time is her husband. There is lively contrast in the gallery of minor characters – the good and bad servants, the light-hearted maid and her lover, and a trio of importunate suitors.

In *L'Incoronazione di Poppea* the moral message is eroded and more earthy values hold sway. It seems clear from the obligatory allegory contained in the Prologue that Fortune and Virtue will stand no chance against the power of Love – or perhaps we should say Sex or Passion hand in hand with naked Ambition, since these are the means by which the heroine wheedles her way towards the crown of imperial Rome. Poppea is a remarkable figure in the story of opera; it is not until Marc Blitzstein's *Regina* (1949) that we come across a woman of such flamboyant resourcefulness – and Regina's victory is by no means complete. Poppea overcomes the opposition of Nero's discarded wife and his stoical tutor, Seneca, to achieve her aim, finally joining with Nero in the most sensuous and caressing of all Monteverdi's climactic duets.

The point of the overlapping phrases of the duet, finally joining on the same note, is lost if the role of Nero is taken by a tenor. Monteverdi's Nero would have been a male soprano or *castrato*; and since most of the present-day male altos or counter-tenors find that the vocal part lies too high, it makes sense to dress a soprano or mezzo-soprano in male clothing. Arnalta, Poppea's mildly comic nurse, was probably sung by a tenor – an option more often avoided today. More controversial

is the question of the right size and type of orchestra to accompany the singers. There are two manuscripts of the opera that have survived – a Venetian score apparently 'edited' by Cavalli to suit a particular cast and a Neapolitan version with some different music and four, rather than three, lines of music for the players in the purely instrumental sections; neither can claim to be 'authentic' in terms of what the Venetian audience at the first performance actually heard. What now seems certain is that the lavishly orchestrated edition prepared by the conductor Raymond Leppard for a 1962 production at Glyndebourne, England, is out of keeping with the minimal scoring used by Monteverdi to keep the spotlight firmly on the singers.

THE *INTERMEZZO*

Like Mozart's three operas to texts by Lorenzo da Ponte, the two late operas of Monteverdi defy categorization: most of human life is included, parading before us in bewildering succession. It was perhaps inevitable that the different genres of opera after Monteverdi should gradually become more inflexible until Mozart, the next genius of the highest order, came along to loosen the boundaries. Monteverdi would no doubt have been bewildered, had he lived beyond 1643, to see the themes of

Continued on page 28

Cherubino, accompanied by Susanna, tempts the Countess with his song in a 1991 production in Santa Fé.

THE
*M*ARRIAGE OF
*f*IGARO

WHO'S WHO

COUNT ALMAVIVA *(Baritone)*
Owner of a Palace near Seville

COUNTESS ALMAVIVA *(Soprano)*
His Wife

FIGARO *(Bass) Valet to the Count*

SUSANNA *(Soprano)*
Maid to the Countess

CHERUBINO *(Soprano) Page*

DOCTOR BARTOLO *(Bass)*

MARCELLINA *(Soprano) Duenna*

DON BASILIO *(Ten.) Music-master*

DON CURZIO *(Tenor) Lawyer*

ANTONIO *(Bass) Gardener*

BARBARINA *(Soprano) His Niece*

In his introduction to the libretto of *The Marriage of Figaro*, first performed at Vienna's Burgtheater on 1 May 1786, Lorenzo da Ponte expresses his hope that 'our desire to offer as it were a new kind of spectacle' will excuse this selective adaptation of Beaumarchais' complex play.

An ideally paced performance of Mozart's overture, in the memorable words of one critic, should be the perfect egg-timer at anything between three and four minutes. Its breezily conspiratorial chatter is an ideal introduction to one 'mad day' in the life of the Almaviva household.

ACT ONE

In two fast-moving duets, Figaro measures up the palace room which is to be his and Susanna's after their impending wedding and is astonished when she points out that the room is in a useful position for the lascivious Count to reach her. Alone, he resolves to make the Count dance to his tune. More trouble looms for Figaro in the shape of Marcellina and Doctor Bartolo, for they intend to make Figaro marry Marcellina unless he can pay a debt he owes her. Susanna and Marcellina exchange

insults in a sly duet which ends with Marcellina worsted.

Cherubino enters, dismissed by the Count for making love to young girls the older man would prefer to have for himself. The role of this teenager at the mercy of his libido is a 'trousers' part for a female singer, and Cherubino's first aria is a miraculous expression of stammering adolescent confusion. Cherubino hides at the sudden entry of the Count, who in turn seeks concealment on the arrival of Don Basilio, the music-master. Angrily, he reveals himself when Basilio gossips about the Countess and Cherubino and, in the trio that follows, uncovers Cherubino as he relates how he discovered him in the room of the gardener's daughter, Barbarina. To remove him from the scene, the Count gives Cherubino a post in his regiment; Figaro, while outwardly celebrating military glories in store for the boy (in the famous '*Non più andrai*'), makes sure he does not leave immediately.

Confusion for the Countess, Susanna and Figaro in Peter Sellars' contro-versial Trump Tower setting (1988).

ACT TWO

The Countess laments her loveless marriage, but rallies at Susanna's encouragement and Figaro's plot: he will attempt to expose the Count by sending him an anonymous invitation to the garden at night to witness his wife with a lover and at the same time to meet Susanna. Cherubino arrives to be dressed up as Susanna, first singing the women a courtly ballad ('*Voi che sapete*' or 'Tell me, fair ladies'). The Count arrives, suspecting Cherubino's presence, but the page escapes through a window and Susanna takes his place, occasioning an apology from the Count to his wife.

Complications ensue over the origins of the mysterious letter, which the valet obstinately refuses to acknowledge, and the bluster of the gardener Antonio, whose geraniums have been crushed by a man jumping out of the window – Cherubino, of course, but Figaro attempts to shoulder the blame. His marriage prospects look still bleaker when Marcellina, Basilio and Bartolo complete the line-up claiming breach of contract.

ACT THREE

Susanna agrees to meet the Count in the garden, so long as he settles Figaro's debt to Marcellina, and her casual slips fail to arouse his suspicions. He does, however, hear her aside to Figaro – 'We've won our case without a lawyer' – and rages against his intended decei-vers in a powerful aria. In the sextet that follows, his plans are upturned again by the revelation that Marcellina is Figaro's mother and Bartolo his father.

The Countess, alone, sings the most moving of her set pieces before joining Susanna in a new plan for the garden: they will dress up as each other. The Count now has to bless the marriages of two couples, Bartolo and Marcellina as well as Figaro and Susanna, but secretly gloats over his assignation.

ACT FOUR

Barbarina laments over the loss of the pin which sealed the Count's reply to Susanna. Figaro, who is unaware of the new plan, thinks that Susanna really intends to cuckold him; she finds out and teases him with a sensuous aria of seduction to the Count. Almaviva enters and begins to make love with the woman he believes to be Susanna – the Countess in disguise.

Figaro meets the supposed Countess, realizes she is Susanna, and pays her back by going on with the charade and pretending to flirt with his 'mistress'. Confusions are unravelled, the Count makes his second apology within 24 hours – and everyone rejoices in a happy end to the crazy day.

Act One, Scene One: Susanna (Janis Kelly) takes advantage of her Figaro in the exuberant produc-tion by London's Opera Factory.

27

Mozart at the piano: an unfinished oil-painting of the composer in 1782 or 1783 by Joseph Lange.

Greek and Roman tragedies stiffen into *opera seria*, with its emphasis on ornament for ornament's sake and rigid posturings. Yet even within the convention, a curious division was taking place. In the later Venetian operas, and more especially in the new Neapolitan branch of the art, it was customary to provide an *intermezzo*, during which comic characters, descendants of the masked Harlequins seen in Italian *commedia dell'arte*, mocked the heroic figures in a separate entertainment. Richard Strauss's 20th-century chamber opera, *Ariadne on Naxos*, is a witty backward glance at this period in operatic history, in which the real fun of Hugo von Hofmannsthal's libretto begins when the rich patron demands that the *opera seria* and the harlequinade should be played at one and the same time.

In the early 18th century the whimsical world of the *intermezzo* found a home of its own as a separate category: *opera buffa* or comic opera. One celebrated specimen, Pergolesi's opera, *La Serva Padrona* (*The Maid as Mistress*, 1733), actually began life as an *intermezzo* within an *opera seria*, though the grander work is not performed today. Pergolesi's light and graceful manner lived on in the charming, deliberately superficial *opere buffe* of Cimarosa and Paisiello. The former's 1792 opera

Il Matrimonio Segreto (*The Secret Marriage*) is the last flourishing of an 18th-century innocence to survive in the repertoire.

Other nations developed their versions of *opera buffa*, usually employing spoken dialogue to further the action between numbers rather than the rapid recitative with harpsichord accompaniment, which was so much part of Italian comic opera. In France, the *opéra comique* became the fashion by the mid-18th century. Gluck made a few contributions to the style early in his career when Vienna briefly took up the craze, but the most characteristic examples are by Philidor and Grétry. Tchaikovsky further developed the genre in his Pushkin-based ghost story with an 18th-century setting, *The Queen of Spades* – though the number he actually quotes is from a more ambitious work, *Richard Cœur de Lion* – as did the conductor Sir Thomas Beecham, who regularly included the delicate ballet music from Grétry's *Zémire and Azor* in his stock of encores.

England's version of *opera buffa*, the ballad-opera, was the most populist of all. John Gay's libretto for *The Beggar's Opera* (1728) sets well-known tunes of the day (arranged by the German-born composer Pepusch) to texts featuring political satire and celebrations of London low life; two centuries later, it provided the impetus for

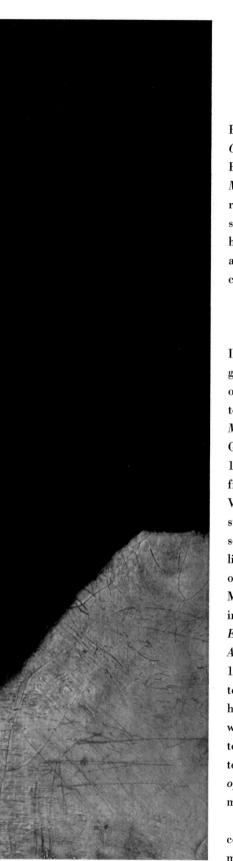

Brecht and Weill's *Threepenny Opera*. This was without doubt the Broadway musical or the *Les Misérables* of its day, and called rather for good actors who could sing well enough than for finely honed operatic voices, though it also took a swipe at the florid conventions of serious opera.

MOZART

It was the ballad-opera which truly gave birth to the German *Singspiel* or song-play when Charles Coffey's texts for *The Devil to Pay* and *The Merry Cobbler* were translated into German and set to new music in 1750. The *Singspiel* craze moved from Leipzig to Berlin and later to Vienna where it turned, slowly but surely, from trivial comedy into a serious form of national opera and lived on in the German romantic operas of Weber and Marschner. Mozart payed a neat, orchestrally inventive tribute to the form in *Die Entführung aus dem Serail* (*The Abduction from the Seraglio*) in 1782, before linking the *Singspiel* to serious purposes at the end of his life in *The Magic Flute*. There was no genre that Mozart left untouched or unchanged: in operatic terms, the arts of *Singspiel* and *opera seria* could never have moved on without him.

It was in the realm of Italian comic opera, however, that he made his richest and most complex contribution. His talents as a young prodigy, though rightly celebrated, never quite amounted to genius. Both Mendelssohn and Bizet as teenagers produced compositions of phenomenal inventiveness, while Mozart's first experiments in *opera buffa* – *La Finta Semplice* (*The Feigned Simpleton*), written in 1769 at the age of 13 – and in *opera seria* – *Mithridates, King of Pontus* (1770) – carefully followed the formulas of the times. There are hints of darker undertones to come in *La Finta Giardiniera* (*The Counterfeit Garden-Girl*, 1775), in which a stock plot contrasts with a musical characterization that plumbs surprising depths.

If Mozart had died at the age of 22, we should think of him as only one of the leading opera composers of his generation, fit to rank alongside his contemporary, Joseph Haydn (whose mastery of the symphony and string quartet is indisputable and always surprising, but whose modest if prolific achievements in the operatic field are surely being placed at too high a value at present). Yet he went on to become the confident master who within two years poured a wealth of melodic and instrumental ingenuity into two very different opera scores – *Idomeneo* and *Die Entführung*. Nothing could be further from the image, perpetrated by Peter Shaffer in his play, *Amadeus*, of the rather foolish young composer whose inspirations fall from the sky than the correspondence between Mozart and his father at the time of the work on *Idomeneo*. It shows Mozart as a supreme craftsman and man of the theatre, testing new ideas again and again until he is satisfied that they will actually work in practice. Certainly, there was inspiration on the road to *The Marriage of Figaro, Don Giovanni* and *Così fan Tutte*, but above all a great deal of hard work and learning by experience.

FIGARO

In 1782, commissioned to write an *opera buffa* for Vienna, Mozart met one of the Italian poets who had just settled at the court there, Lorenzo da Ponte, who impressed the composer by his creation of real human characters in a series of libretti based on French plays. It was at Mozart's suggestion that, three years later, they decided to turn into an opera the inflammatory, almost revolutionary comedy *The Mad Day or The Marriage of Figaro* by the French playwright, Beaumarchais. The latter's first play to feature the characters of Figaro and the Count Almaviva, *The Barber of Seville*, had already been successfully transformed as an opera by Paisiello – and, of course, would be immortalized by Rossini some years after Mozart's

Continued on page 32

Seduction in the old-fashioned manner: Don Giovanni (Maurice Renaud) takes the hand of Zerlina (Bessie Abbot).

Da Ponte based his version of the Don Juan legend on an already existing libretto, as was customary, though he also referred to plays by Tirso de Molina, Molière and Goldoni. The opera was first performed in Prague on 29 October 1787.

DON GIOVANNI

DON GIOVANNI *(Baritone)*
A Licentious Young Nobleman

LEPORELLO *(Bass)*
His Servant

THE COMMENDATORE *(Bass)*

DONNA ANNA *(Soprano)*
His Daughter

DON OTTAVIO *(Tenor)*
Betrothed to Donna Anna

DONNA ELVIRA *(Soprano)*
A Lady of Burgos, Deserted by Don Giovanni

ZERLINA *(Soprano)*
A Country Girl

MASETTO *(Bass/Baritone)*
Betrothed to Zerlina

COUNTRY FOLK & MUSICIANS

Don Giovanni's status as a comic opera with serious elements, or *dramma giocoso*, rather than a straightforward *opera buffa*, is announced in the opening hell-fire of the overture – the hair-raising music to which the statue of the Commendatore arrives at Don Giovanni's supper. The music then relaxes into more familiar comic chatter before leading straight into the first scene of the opera.

ACT ONE

Leporello bemoans the boredom of his employment – keeping watch by night while his master takes his pleasure inside the house of the Commendatore. Don Giovanni runs out, pursued by the furious Donna Anna (did she yield just a little before making her protest – or did she really believe the man in the darkened room was her fiancé, Don Ottavio, as she later says?). A trio of reactions – the lady's indignation, the would-be seducer's pique and the servant's observations – breaks off at the entrance of the Commendatore, who draws his sword on his daughter's assailant. Giovanni fatally wounds him in the ensuing duel, and master and servant make their escape. The grief-stricken Anna is comforted by Don Ottavio and together they swear vengeance on her father's murderer.

The scene changes to a nearby street. Comic-opera badinage between Don Giovanni and Leporello is interrupted as the libertine catches the scent of a woman. It is Donna Elvira, who has journeyed to find the man who abandoned her. Don Giovanni's self-interested consolation stops short as he realizes that he is the object of her search. He leaves her to the counsel of Leporello, who in the celebrated 'Catalogue aria' cruelly lists his master's conquests – a grand total of 2,065, of which 1,003 happen to be Spanish.

Near Don Giovanni's villa outside Seville peasants celebrate the approaching marriage of the charming Zerlina and her swain, Masetto. The tactics of the seducer swing into action for the first time as Giovanni gets rid of the fuming fiancé and takes hold of the girl's hand in the duet *'La ci darem la mano'* – proof that his reputation is well-founded. But in the course of the opera he is destined to be unsuccessful: Elvira arrives to sweep the yielding Zerlina away.

Anna and Ottavio converse amiably with Giovanni – whom, of course, Anna did not recognize in the dark. When Elvira arrives to make further trouble, Giovanni passes her off as insane, though the other couple are convinced by her pleas and Anna suddenly recognizes the voice of her father's assassin. Her narrative of that night's events, accompanied by full orchestra, and the aria that follows call for a soprano of heroic stamina. Ottavio's gentle response – 'Dalla sua pace' ('Upon her peace of mind') – was written for the Vienna revival as a replacement for the florid aria in Act Two, though both are often sung in productions today. It contrasts with Giovanni's libidinous celebration of wine, women and song – the misnamed 'Champagne aria'.

In the garden of Giovanni's villa Zerlina charms the jealous Masetto into submission ('Batti, batti'). The masterly finale eventually brings all the characters together for the first time. After a rapid conflict between Giovanni, who is still chasing the half-willing Zerlina, and Masetto, three masked guests arrive for the libertine's party: Ottavio, Anna and Elvira, now in league. Their prayer for heavenly guidance is the first touch of the sublime which Giovanni will find himself increasingly confronting. To ingenious writing for three stage bands – each playing dances appropriate to the different social orders represented in the opera – Giovanni finally manages to make off with Zerlina, but her screams alert the assembled company and they form a league of vengeance.

ACT TWO

High drama is followed by comic relief in the form of the familiar master–servant routine and a light-hearted trio in which the credible Elvira begins to feel renewed sympathy for her seducer. But he is after her maid and serenades her while Leporello plays the master and spirits Elvira away from the scene. Masetto and friends are out to murder Giovanni, who meets them in Leporello's guise and sends the henchmen off in different directions before giving Masetto a thrashing. Zerlina once more has to provide sweet consolation to her belaboured fiancé in the aria 'Vedrai, carino'. Leporello is less fortunate: cornered by the five vengeance-seekers, he is forced to reveal his true identity, but soon manages to make his escape. Don Ottavio's original aria reveals him as a substantial agent of good, and

the set piece that Mozart gave his Vienna Elvira in 1788, 'Mi tradì', is the crowning glory of her role.

Fooling in a nearby church-yard, Don Giovanni and Leporello are startled by the solemn voice of the Commendatore's statue, which Giovanni, nothing daunted, invites to supper. It accepts, and after an interlude, which hopefully puts us back on the side of the angels by

virtue of Donna Anna's long, exquisite and richly ornamented second aria, we see the results. Leporello comments on the familiar tunes played by the serenading wind-band at Don Giovanni's supper, Giovanni rejects Elvira's renewed pleas with flamboyance and the Commendatore's statue makes its appearance. To the sound of icy, rushing scales from

the orchestra, the Commendatore asks his murderer to repent, but Giovanni – a Byronic figure before his time – refuses and is dragged to hell by demons. Many Mozart lovers think the opera should end here, but Mozart does his best for the good folk left behind. In a final sextet the survivors moralize on the fate of wrong-doers in time-honoured comic-opera style.

Don Giovanni (Ruggero Raimondi) feels the icy grip of the Commendatore's statue in Joseph Losey's film, which is perhaps the most successful cinematic treatment of opera yet.

death – but *The Marriage of Figaro* was rather more controversial since it had run into censorship problems in several European courts, including that in Vienna. The challenge to Mozart and da Ponte was to slip past their operatic rivals at the intrigue-laden Viennese court and have the ban on this potential box-office hit lifted.

TWO MORE OPERAS

They were victorious, but only after Mozart had pleased the Emperor Joseph II with a short and sweet satire on the backstage business of opera, *Der Schauspieldirektor* (*The Impresario*), and da Ponte had used his special influence with the Emperor to make a diplomatic plea for the new work. *The Marriage of Figaro* achieved a modest success in Vienna between May and December of 1786, but fared even better in Prague at the hands of the chief Italian company there. It was as a result of that triumph that Pasquale Bondini, the manager of the company, commissioned Mozart and da Ponte to write a new opera for Prague to mark the wedding celebrations, in October 1787, of the Emperor's niece, Maria Theresa, with Prince Anton Clemens of Saxony. That new opera was *Don Giovanni*, and more than two centuries later it was performed at the same theatre in Prague, the newly restored Tyl

(or Stavovsky) Theatre, to mark the bicentenary of Mozart's death. The last of the Mozart–da Ponte operas, *Così fan Tutte*, was also commissioned following a brilliantly successful *Figaro* – this time back in Vienna, in 1789, when the Emperor finally capitulated to the charms of the first court masterpiece in a revised version and asked for more.

The respective atmospheres of the three operas could hardly be more different, and their official descriptions go some way towards defining the mood intended. While *Figaro* was termed a '*commedia per musica*' – a comedy for music, the description that was also used by Strauss and Hofmannsthal in 1911 for their 'second Figaro', *Der Rosenkavalier* (*The Knight of the Rose*) – both *Don Giovanni* and *Così* go by the name of '*dramma giocoso*', which neatly sums up their mixtures of comedy and serious drama. In *Don Giovanni* Mozart makes the most daring contrasts between figures from the world of *opera seria*, like Donna Anna and her courtly suitor, Don Ottavio, and characters from *opera buffa*, such as the servant, Leporello, and the country-girl, Zerlina; in *Così* the composer and his librettist follow Shakespeare's example by taking an artificial situation and drawing from it a deeply human and occasionally disturbing drama as the opera progresses.

Even so, the operas of Mozart and da Ponte have much in common. In all three Mozart's brilliant and instinctive setting of the Italian language is as important in the recitatives – stretches of rapid sung dialogue with harpsichord accompaniment between numbers – as it is in the arias, ensembles and finales. When he came to write *The Clemency of Titus* in the last year of his life, he farmed out the writing of the recitatives to a pupil, Süssmayr, but the recitatives of *Figaro*, *Don Giovanni* and *Così* are authentic Mozart from first note to last. According to the Italian conductor Riccardo Muti, 'there is nothing more perfect than the recitative of Mozart–da Ponte; the relationship of words and music is absolutely miraculous'.

Mozart always devised his roles with specific singers in mind, and, inevitably, the skills of the Prague company forged links between *The Marriage of Figaro* as performed by Bondini's troupe and *Don Giovanni*. Luigi Bassi, the Count Almaviva in the Prague *Figaro*, created Don Giovanni at the tender age of 22, a point worth remembering when we see so many seasoned roués in the role. Felice Ponziani, the first Prague Figaro, again played the servant to Bassi's master as Leporello, so in the scene where Leporello hears the on-stage wind-band for Giovanni's supper playing Figaro's Act One aria, the

words 'I know this tune all too well' have an added meaning, since he had been singing the aria only a season earlier.

CASTING

The composer was careful to tailor the vocal demands of the arias to the singers' abilities. He adored Nancy Storace, the English soprano, who created the role of Susanna, as testified by the two light and delectable arias he gave her. But by the time of the Vienna revival in 1789, she had returned to England. Her place was taken by da Ponte's mistress, Adriana Ferraresi del Bene, and Mozart obliged the lady, whom he respected but hardly loved, with two florid and comparatively formal replacement arias, which are not used today. Ferraresi was also the first Fiordiligi in *Così fan Tutte*, and it was clearly her pride in an extraordinarily wide vocal range which Mozart exploited to the full in Fiordiligi's Act One aria, her showy set piece of protest against the 'new' suitors.

We now think of Mozart's leading ladies as light or coloratura sopranos, dramatic sopranos and mezzo-sopranos, all sharing the honours: the role of Cherubino is as much prized by mezzos as that of the Countess is by sopranos. So it can be disconcerting to learn that differentiation in Mozart's time was made not by voice-type but by order of importance. The *prima donna* of the company sang Susanna (for long considered a more important role than the Countess), Zerlina (an even more extraordinary first choice) and Fiordiligi; the second soprano played the Countess, Donna Anna and Dorabella; and the third lady, hardly cast in the shadow, was destined for the roles of Donna Elvira, Cherubino, and Despina.

Our present-day star system, in which the great names fly to an international opera house for one rehearsal, is alien to the Mozart–da Ponte style – which is probably why only smaller houses with long rehearsal periods, such as Glyndebourne, can do justice to these works, for they are true ensemble operas, which can only truly succeed if all the singers are prepared to work with each other. After Mozart, Rossini would provide the last specimens of the ensemble-opera before the demands of Italian audiences brought the star to the forefront again. In opera, as in history, everything proceeds in cycles, and the 19th century would also find its Mozarts. Yet for all the advances made over the last century in the cause of true music theatre, the Mozart–da Ponte operas continue to find new productions full of new meanings, and their dramatic and psychological insights remain inexhaustible.

Thomas Allen

THE MOST FAMILIAR DON GIOVANNI OF OUR TIME, THOMAS ALLEN HAS NOW SUNG THE ROLE IN THE WORLD'S MAJOR OPERA HOUSES AND SHOWS NO SIGNS OF RELINQUISHING IT. THE BARITONE, WHO WAS BORN IN COUNTY DURHAM IN THE NORTH OF ENGLAND, HAS BEEN REGARDED AS A COVENT GARDEN 'HOUSE SINGER' SINCE HIS DÉBUT THERE IN 1971. HE WAS FIRST SEEN ON STAGE IN SMALLER PARTS AND PROGRESSED TO BRITTEN'S BILLY BUDD, THE IDEALISTIC RODRIGO IN VERDI'S *DON CARLO* AND ALL THE MAJOR MOZART ROLES – THE COUNT IN *FIGARO*, GUGLIELMO IN *COSÌ FAN TUTTE* AND PAPAGENO IN *THE MAGIC FLUTE*, AS WELL AS DON GIOVANNI – INCLUDED AMONG A GRAND TOTAL OF 36 TO DATE. HE IS ALSO A SUBTLE INTERPRETER OF *LIEDER* AND HIS WARM LYRIC BARITONE AND CHARISMATIC STAGE PRESENCE HAVE WON HIM A LOYAL FOLLOWING.

A novel English rendering of Mozart and da Ponte's virtually untranslatable title for the first production in England of Così fan Tutte.

così *f*an *t*utte

WHO'S WHO

FIORDILIGI *(Soprano)*
A Lady from Ferrara

DORABELLA *(Soprano/Mezzo)*
Her Sister

DESPINA *(Soprano)*
Their Maid

FERRANDO *(Tenor)*
Engaged to Dorabella

GUGLIELMO *(Bass/Baritone)*
Engaged to Fiordiligi

DON ALFONSO *(Baritone/Bass)*
An Old Philosopher

SOLDIERS & SERVANTS

'Così fan Tutte' hardly sounds elegant in translation: 'Thus do all women'. The subtitle is easier – *La Scuola degli Amanti* or *The School for Lovers*. For the première of his third collaboration with da Ponte, Mozart returned to Vienna, where the opera was first performed on 26 January 1790.

On either side of the main comic business in the overture Mozart places strategic references to the phrase used by Don Alfonso in the opera to sum up the inconstancy of women – 'Così fan tutte'. Here, it appears after the initial oboe solo and before the final crescendo.

He wagers that he can prove that their sweethearts are fickle, and the young men accept.

Fiordiligi and Dorabella wax lyrical over their lovers in a garden by the sea. Don Alfonso enters in convincing perplexity to tell them that their men have been ordered immediately to the wars. In the first of the many ensembles which abound in the opera the ladies express grief, their newly arrived fiancés simulate it and Don Alfonso makes ironic asides. A second quintet brings its audience close to heartbreak with its stammered exchanges and a glorious phrase for Fiordiligi. But the men must leave, and their sweethearts' wishes for a calm sea and a prosperous voyage are reinforced, this time with a show of sincerity

ACT ONE

The premise of the opera unfolds in three short, light numbers linked by rapid recitative. In a café in Naples two young officers, Ferrando and Guglielmo, sing their fiancées' praises. Don Alfonso scorns their idealism: the faithfulness of women is like the phoenix, discussed but never seen.

by Alfonso, in the famous flowing trio 'Soave sia il vento'. We then meet Despina, a worldly-wise antidote to her mistresses' theatrical laments. Alfonso bribes her to join the plot, though he does not tell her that Fiordiligi and Dorabella's two new suitors, who are introduced as Albanians, are Ferrando and Guglielmo in disguise; nor does she recognize them when they arrive to press their suit. Fiordiligi is adamant that she will remain faithful, though she protests too much in the deliberately exaggerated leaps, plunges and ornamentations of the display aria 'Come scoglio'.

When the indignant ladies leave, the officers think they have won their bet and Ferrando basks in the security of love with the sweetest of tenor arias, 'Un'aura amorosa'. In an artificial but ever-amusing *opera buffa* finale, the men pretend to take poison for their unrequited love, are revived by a 'doctor' (Despina in disguise) and win a little devotion from their outwardly reluctant targets.

ACT TWO

The siege begins in earnest. Despina persuades Fiordiligi and Dorabella to have a little fun while their officers are away. The lovers are now clearly regrouped, and a careful sequence of arias framed by two contrasting duets shows

how resistances are broken down. Dorabella, the more frivolous of the sisters, capitulates easily to Guglielmo's seduction. Of the four arias, Ferrando's desperate reaction to his girl's unfaithfulness and Fiordiligi's plea for pity ('*Per pietà*'), the still centre of the opera, reveal the two who suffer most and who are perhaps better suited to each other. Fiordiligi prepares to join her lover in the wars, but Ferrando appears at the crucial moment to win her in a duet that has moments of extreme pathos. As always, Mozart reveals depths of feeling before we can tire of comic conventions.

Don Alfonso knows he has won his bet, but he now wants the men to go through with a mock-marriage ceremony. As the couples drink a toast before the signing of the contract, it is Guglielmo who steps savagely out of line to wish the women death by poisoning in an otherwise sublime quartet. Just as the notary – Despina, of course – sets forward the contract, the military chorus that had whisked the men away in Act One is heard in the distance. Ferrando and Guglielmo depart and re-enter as their old selves in no time. Having sufficiently tortured their ladies, they reveal the truth and Despina is as crestfallen as her mistresses. There is a conventional happy ending, but who returns to whom? Producers today prefer to explore the long-term disruption rather than the renewed harmony, and Mozart's music has certainly given them good cause.

Dorabella (Agnes Baltsa) and Fiordiligi (Kiri Te Kanawa) do as the 'doctor' tells them and support their Albanian suitors in the Act One finale at Covent Garden, 1981.

A resistance fighter defending Rome against the French. Garibaldi's campaign led to the short-lived establishment of a Roman republic in 1848: Verdi, true musician of the Risorgimento, marked the occasion with the opera La Battaglia di Legnano *(The Battle of Legnano).*

SOUTHERN EUROPEAN TRADITION

The Italian gift for melody passed from the bottled sunshine of Rossini's comedies and the limpid romanticism of Bellini into the new era of Verdi's powerful dramas and on to the fast-moving music theatre of Puccini. In Paris, grand opera, opera comique (dramatic or sentimental opera with spoken dialogue), and the high-kicking satires of Offenbach vied for attention.

CHAPTER 3

Italian Bel Canto

Rossini revived the tradition of the star singer within the framework of true ensemble comedies, following up the stock situations of *The Italian Girl in Algiers* and *The Barber of Seville* with a 'serious comedy' worthy of Mozart: *La Cenerentola*. He also set heroic subjects to music and his last work, *William Tell*, was a lengthy grand opera to suit Parisian tastes. The torch then passed to Bellini – a pioneer of the long, limpid melody much admired by Chopin – and Donizetti, a prolific manufacturer of vehicles for the divas of the day, who proved his true worth in his facility for comic opera.

Harem girls and eunuchs in Jean-Pierre Ponnelle's opulent production of Rossini's The Italian Girl in Algiers, *Covent Garden, London, 1989.*

Comic perplexity at the ball, with Maria Ewing as Cinderella, in Rossini's opera on Cinderella's story, La Cenerentola (Houston, Texas, 1979).

For the French writer Stendhal, the complex orchestral writing and the deeply human characters of Mozart's operas were worthy of admiration. Yet Stendhal, unlike most of his fellow-countrymen who professed a love of music, was an Italophile and, in 1823, explained why Mozart would never enjoy true success in Italy: '... his music does not reflect the temperamental characteristics induced by the Italian climate; it is emotive music, destined above all to evoke images in a vein of tender melancholy, which fill the soul with memories of sadness and echo the dying languor of the sweetest of passions. But

love is not the same in Bologna as it is in Königsberg; love in Italy is far more dynamic, more impatient, more violent, less dependent upon dreams and imagination.'

Cimarosa and Paisiello, light-hearted Italian masters of 18th-century comedy, were all very well, but it was a composer of the next generation who fitted Stendhal's bill as Italian vivacity personified.

ROSSINI

Gioacchino Rossini was born on 29 February 1792 in Pesaro, the city which still commemorates him with a yearly festival of his operas. His

father was an instrumentalist and his mother a singer, so it seemed natural that he should pursue a musical career. Already an accompanist in Pesaro's opera-house and an operatic composer by the time he was 13, he entered Bologna's College of Music a year later. Towards the end of his life he would make the immortal comment to his maker, 'I was born for *opera buffa*, Thou knowest it well', and the first of his operas to be staged, *La Cambiale di Matrimonio* (*The Marriage Contract*, 1810), shows promise of comic operas to come.

His first great hit, though, was an *opera seria* (or, to give its correct definition, 'heroic melodrama') about Tancredi, the champion of the Sicilians against the Moors. In the first version of *Tancredi* the hero is reunited with his sweetheart, Amenaide, to general rejoicing. But Rossini also provided an alternative ending for a production in Ferrara shortly after the 1813 première: a death-scene for Tancredi, which demonstrates how profoundly simple his approach to tragedy could be. Yet it is hardly surprising that the most popular number from the opera, Tancredi's short cavatina, '*Di tanti palpiti*' ('Pity for such suffering') should be a thing of grace and joy. Stendhal amusingly records how this came to be known as the '*Aria dei risi*' or 'Rice aria'. After the *prima donna* had turned down

the original aria on the eve of the première, Rossini returned despondently to his lodgings and then, between the host's usual question, 'Will you take a plate of rice, sir?' and the presentation of the dish, dashed off the number. If the anecdote is untrue, it still remains pertinent to a composer who took great delight in culinary pursuits.

The early masterpiece that is most characteristic of Rossini's lively temperament is the comic opera *The Italian Girl in Algiers* (1813). The effervescent arias and duets are testimony to just how much virtuosity Rossini expected from his singers. Both the light-voiced type of tenor, the *tenore di grazia*, and the bass who plays the ridiculed Turk, Mustafà, have to deal with as much fast-paced ornamentation in their vocal writing as the mezzo-soprano who sings Isabella, the resourceful Italian girl. The age of the *castrati* may have been over, but the legacy of their vocal displays lived on. It is in the Act One finale, though, that Rossini's comic genius carries the audience to near hysteria: having carefully brought all his characters on to the stage in the manner of Mozart, the composer then ties them in knots with an ensemble of confusion. Bells, hammers, crowing and cannon-fire besiege their brains in an orgy of onomatopoeia. 'In Venice,' Stendhal tells us, 'where this finale was sung by

Paccini, Galli and Madame Marcolini, the audience, by the end, were struggling and gasping for breath, and wiping the tears from their eyes.' This still happens in a good performance.

Some of the formulas were repeated in *The Barber of Seville* (1816) – successfully, as it turned out, after an infamous first night. It was not until *La Cenerentola* – an enlightened treatment of the Cinderella story produced the year after *The Barber* – that Rossini truly progressed in his comic experiments. *La Cenerentola* was classified, along the lines of *Don Giovanni*, as a *melodramma giocoso*, a blend of comedy and seriousness. The latter is touched upon in the portrayal of the heroine's pathos – characterized by her repetitions of a sad ballad – and her magnanimity to her step-father and sisters when she gains the upper hand. The moral subtitle of the opera, 'Goodness triumphant', is in earnest. Hilarity still takes over in many of the numbers – above all in the great Act Two sextet – but there is more than a hint of nastiness about Cinderella's step-father Don Magnifico when he tells the disguised Prince and his valet that the third daughter of the house is dead. Rossini, with his usual perfect sense of timing, marks this shocking turn of events in the comic proceedings with a dramatic silence.

Continued on page 44

Gioacchino Rossini:
a portrait by Camuccini.

THE *b*ARBER OF SEVILLE

WHO'S WHO

COUNT ALMAVIVA *(Tenor)*
A Spanish Nobleman

FIGARO *(Baritone) A Barber*

DOCTOR BARTOLO *(Bass)*
An Old Man

ROSINA *(Mezzo) His Ward*

DON BASILIO *(Bass)*
Her Singing-teacher

FIORELLO *(Bass)*
Servant to Almaviva

BERTA *(Soprano)*
Housekeeper to Bartolo

NOTARY, OFFICIAL, MUSICIANS
& SERVANTS

Rossini's opera was first performed under the title *Almaviva or The Useless Precaution* to avoid invidious comparison with an earlier operatic setting by Paisiello of Beaumarchais' play, *The Barber of Seville*. In spite of a calamitous opening night at the Teatro Argentina, Rome, on 20 February 1816, the second *Barber* – to a libretto by Cesare Sterbini – soon put Paisiello's attempt in the shade, and remains the most often performed of Rossini's operas.

Frequently arranged for anything from brass band to six solo voices, the overture seems to have been tailor-made for the brightly conspiratorial world of Rossini's opera, but was in fact borrowed from earlier, serious works, beginning life as the overture to *Aureliano in Palmira* (a failure) before being repackaged as a prelude to *Elizabeth, Queen of England*.

ACT ONE

Outside Doctor Bartolo's house in Seville, Fiorello and musicians stealthily pave the way for the dawn serenade of their master, Count Almaviva, who is in love with the doctor's ward, Rosina. Almaviva's cavatina, '*Ecco, ridente in cielo*' ('Lo, smiling in the eastern sky'), is another example of Rossini's habitual self-borrowing when appropriate – it, too, is a refugee from *Aureliano*, and provides the tenor with a grateful combination of smooth, legato singing and ornamental flourishes.

When Rosina fails to appear, the Count dismisses his accomplices, with a certain amount of comic business over their noisy departure. Figaro makes a brisk appearance to advertize himself as the most sought-after man in town, to the brilliant patter of the '*Largo al factotum*' – a gift to a baritone with a ringing upper register. Encountering Almaviva, he passes on the useful information that Rosina is merely Bartolo's ward of chancery, not his daughter; then she appears on the balcony and reveals her youthful resourcefulness by managing to drop a note to the Count in spite of fierce interrogation by the possessive doctor. While Bartolo descends to retrieve it, Almaviva serenades Rosina and the scene ends with a brilliant duet in which Figaro offers to help the Count on the promise of money – the guiding force for these not conspicuously lovable characters.

Inside the Bartolo residence, Rosina reveals that the serenader, 'Lindoro', is the man for her and that she has no intention of playing the languishing heroine: 'I can be docile, respectful and obedient, but touch me and I'll be a viper.' The rapid coloratura display of her famous aria suits Rosina's slightly menacing brilliance perfectly. Other members of the household have their own ideas about control. Basilio suggests that Bartolo blacken Almaviva's name: this would be easily achieved once the winds of scandal were suitably fanned; his aria '*La calunnia*' illustrates the process graphically with one of Rossini's celebrated crescendos. And, just when the machinery of the Almaviva plot seems to be going smoothly in a sprightly duet between Rosina and Figaro, Bartolo enters to announce that he won't be fooled. '*A un dot-*

tor della mia sorte' is his great comic set piece, though the rapid delivery can be a problem for a true bass.

The finale begins as the Count enters, disguised as a drunken soldier billeted on Bartolo (the tenor now has to turn comedian). Rosina recognizes him as 'Lindoro', but the Doctor calls for the militia to arrest him. Almaviva takes the chief officer aside to reveal his true identity and the action freezes into one of Rossini's best ensembles – the sextet *'Fredda ed immobile'* ('Awestruck and immovable'). A scene of general confusion brings down the curtain.

ACT TWO

Figaro's plan number two for Almaviva is to send the Count into the Bartolo household as a music teacher – a risky proposition since he has to pretend that Basilio is ill and has sent him as a substitute. He gains access to Rosina by faking a singing lesson. The music Rossini selected for Rosina's vocalizes still exists, and is usually performed today, although he gave his *prime donne* the option of singing 'an air, *ad libitum*, for the occasion'; divas have taken the opportunity to perform anything from Donizetti and Bellini to 'Home, sweet home'.

Figaro finds the keys to the balcony and persuades Almaviva and Rosina to elope at midnight.

Then, as he begins to give Bartolo his daily shave, Basilio makes an untimely entrance; in a quintet with an unctuous 'good night' as its amusing refrain, he is bribed into claiming that he really is sick after all. Bartolo, however, soon overhears the lovers' conspiracy. Once

his rage has subsided, he tries to foil their plot by subtler means, telling Rosina that 'Lindoro' is merely the agent for Count Almaviva. Since she does not wish to marry a stranger, she offers her hand to Bartolo and reveals the plans for midnight.

Rosina (Della Jones) and Figaro (Gwion Thomas) contemplate their next move (Welsh National Opera, 1986).

A thunderstorm breaks, providing the opportunity for an orchestral tone-poem within the opera (there are fine Rossinian storms, too, in *Cinderella* and the overture to his last opera, *William Tell*). The hours have passed: Figaro and Almaviva enter for the midnight elopement. Rosina is delighted to learn the truth about her lover and Rossini, in a glowing trio, makes much of the operatic convention where lovers carry on singing even though time is pressing. Figaro, meanwhile, is urging haste. They cannot make their escape – Bartolo has removed the ladder to the window – but Figaro swiftly arranges for the notary (procured by the doctor for his wedding to Rosina) to conduct a marriage on the spot, with Basilio bribed to be witness.

Bartolo enters, once again demanding an arrest, and again Almaviva reveals his true identity – this time publicly. At this point in the opera he has a big, florid scene, which is often cut in production, usually because its coloratura demands are too much for the average tenor (Rossini reworked some of the music into Cinderella's aria of forgiveness in his next comic masterpiece, to better effect). Finally, Bartolo is appeased by the prospect of receiving the dowry. The three victors celebrate their happiness in a short and sweet finale.

Maria Malibran

HER COLOURFUL LIFE AND VOLATILE TEMPERAMENT MADE MARIA
MALIBRAN A LEGEND IN HER OWN LIFETIME AND A WORTHY SUBJECT
FOR DRAMATIC TREATMENT: THE BROADWAY ORCHESTRATOR AND
COMPOSER ROBERT RUSSELL BENNETT EVEN WROTE AN OPERA ABOUT
HER IN 1935. TRAINED BY HER FATHER, THE SPANISH TENOR MANUEL
GARCÍA, SHE SANG WITH HIS NEW YORK COMPANY IN 1825, GOING ON
TO BECOME A FAMOUS NORMA AND A TEMPESTUOUS CREATOR OF THE
ROLE OF DONIZETTI'S MARIA STUARDA IN THE OPERA OF THAT NAME.
HER VOICE WAS A DEEP CONTRALTO WHICH WAS ALSO CAPABLE OF
IMPRESSIVE FORAYS INTO THE SOPRANO REGISTER.

Beethoven's advice to Rossini in 1822 was: 'Never try to write anything but *opera-buffa* ... give us plenty of *Barbers*.' Comic numbers abound in *The Journey to Rheims* (1825), the 'stage cantata' that was written for the coronation of Charles X of France, and in a delightful offshoot that uses much of its music, *Count Ory* (1828).

Yet Rossini also continued to cultivate the serious side of opera in *Semiramide*, the last of his Italian works, and *Moses in Egypt*. He made a final, supremely ambitious attempt to capture the imaginations of the northern Europeans in 1829 with a four-hour epic on the exploits of William Tell. Its deep seriousness won the approval of Berlioz, who was otherwise hostile to Italian opera, and of Wagner, who in 1860 praised Tell's plea to his son to be still while he aims for the apple on the boy's head as reaching 'the highest summits of lyric expression'.

William Tell may well, in the words of the hard-to-please critic Eduard Hanslick, have marked 'a new era for opera ... and not only in France.' In fact, it turned out to be Rossini's last work for the stage. Charles X was deposed in 1830 and the new government decided not to honour the contract which would have commissioned four more new operas from Rossini. He lived on until 1868, composing two significant religious works and innumerable smaller pieces to which he referred as 'sins of my old age' and which were invariably incorporated into the fascinating programmes of his fashionable soirées.

BELLINI

In Italy, the operatic torch passed at first to two of Rossini's great admirers, Bellini and Donizetti. Vincenzo Bellini developed the limpid, lyrical side of Rossini's style to far-reaching effect. In his three greatest operas – *La Sonnambula* (*The Sleepwalker*, premièred in 1831, two years after *William Tell*) and the less idyllic dramas of *Norma* and *I Puritani* (*The Puritans*) – melody reigns supreme. Bellini often gives the melody to a solo woodwind instrument above a simple accompaniment in an introduction of variable length; then the voice takes over, sometimes ornamenting the line in strict accordance with Bellini's score. This *cantabile* is the essence of romantic song; its influence can be heard in the piano music of Chopin as well as the operas of Wagner. The supreme examples are the aria '*Casta diva*' ('Chaste goddess') and the duet '*Mira, o Norma*' ('See, Norma') in *Norma*, Elvira's mad-scene in *I Puritani*, and the sleepwalker Amina's proof of her innocence, '*Ah! Non credea mirarti*', in *La Sonnambula*.

Amina's words in that aria, 'I never thought you would die so soon', took on a special poignancy with the death of Bellini at the age of 34 in 1835: they were engraved on his tomb. Handsome, much loved and inclined to melancholy, Bellini fulfilled one qualification of the romantic type by taking his leave at the peak of his career. That left the Italian stage free for the man he clearly perceived as his rival, Gaetano Donizetti, whose first mature success in 1830, *Anna Bolena*, provided the spur that Bellini had needed to produce *La Sonnambula*.

DONIZETTI

Unlike Bellini, Donizetti was a prolific composer of more than 60 operas, with all the lapses and repetitive formulas that a capacity for over-production might suggest. When dealing with serious subjects, he rarely rose to Bellini's melodic heights, and it is not always his best work which has survived. *Lucia di Lammermoor*, for instance, though a formidable test of the leading soprano's dramatic and coloratura talents, is patchy in inspiration; many of its scenes are furnished with music which might just as well be set to texts with a completely different meaning. We are back in the world of display opera, where the talents of the leading singers count for more than plot or drama. In recent years sopranos like Maria Callas and Joan Sutherland have found more dramatic truth in these works than earlier generations suspected, though once again, the task still seems to be both easier and more worthwhile with Bellini's work.

Where Donizetti excelled was in comic opera, and he kept the Rossinian comic spirit alive well into the 1840s with the delightful *Don Pasquale*. It hardly matters that he added nothing new, though *The Elixir of Love* admits more sentiment than Rossini might have permitted and *The Daughter of the Regiment* makes a bow in the direction of the French *opéra comique*. By the time of *Don Pasquale*, Verdi had arrived on the scene; but his first attempt at *opera buffa* was a failure and it was not until 1893 that he returned to comedy with his operatic swan-song *Falstaff*. By then, the age of innocence in Italian comic opera was over and a new, dramatic sophistication had taken its place.

Joan Sutherland

ALTHOUGH SHE HAD SUNG MANY ROLES WITH LONDON'S ROYAL OPERA SINCE JOINING THE COMPANY IN 1952, THE AUSTRALIAN SOPRANO ACHIEVED FAME IN A NIGHT WITH HER PORTRAYAL OF DONIZETTI'S LUCIA DI LAMMERMOOR AT COVENT GARDEN IN 1959. HER BRILLIANT COLORATURA AND STRONG TECHNIQUE MADE HER A PERFECT EXPONENT OF THE ITALIAN *BEL CANTO* REPERTOIRE AND TOGETHER WITH HER HUSBAND, THE CONDUCTOR RICHARD BONYNGE, SHE ENSURED THE REVIVAL OF NEGLECTED OPERAS BY BELLINI AND DONIZETTI; SHE ALSO SURPRISED HER CRITICS IN THE 1970S BY EXTENDING HER REPERTOIRE TO INCLUDE THE TAXING ROLES OF MASSENET'S ESCLARMONDE AND (ON RECORD) PUCCINI'S TURANDOT. SHE MADE HER STAGE FAREWELL IN A GALA PERFORMANCE OF *DIE FLEDERMAUS* (*THE BAT*) AT THE END OF 1990, AND NOW GIVES REGULAR MASTER-CLASSES.

NORMA

WHO'S WHO

NORMA *(Soprano)*
High-priestess of the Druids

POLLIONE *(Tenor)*
Roman Proconsul in Gaul

ADALGISA *(Soprano/Mezzo)*
Virgin of the Temple

OROVESO *(Bass)*
Archdruid & Norma's Father

CLOTILDE *(Soprano)*
Norma's Confidante

FLAVIO *(Tenor)*
A Centurion

DRUIDS, BARDS, PRIESTESSES, GALLIC WARRIORS & SOLDIERS

Bellini's eighth opera was first performed at La Scala, Milan, on 26 December 1831, and was clearly conceived as a vehicle for the great soprano Giuditta Pasta. Bellini had written to her in September of that year, telling her how effective his librettist Romani considered the subject – 'just right for your encyclopaedic character, since Norma's character is the same.' It remains for sopranos a supreme test of *bel canto* and owes its revival to the dedication of such singers as Rosa Ponselle, Maria Callas and Joan Sutherland.

ACT ONE

The year is 50 BC, and the place is Roman-occupied Gaul. Druids gather to cut the mistletoe on the night of the new moon. Their high-priest, Oroveso, hopes that their god Irminsul will speak the words necessary to break their treaty with the Romans and to send them into war. The Roman Pollione tells his friend Flavio that he is the lover of Norma, Oroveso's daughter, and father of the two children she has borne him in contravention of her priestess' vows. Now, however, he loves Adalgisa. The two men hide as the Druidical rites

begin. Norma arrives, crowned with verbena and carrying a golden crescent. In heroic recitative she tells the assembly that it is not yet time for an uprising against Rome. Then, cutting the mistletoe, she prays to the moon in the aria *'Casta diva'* ('Chaste goddess'), the ultimate test of smooth, expressive *bel canto* singing. Little wonder that this piece should have served as an inspiration for some of Chopin's nocturnes; in both the aria and the piano music the ornamentation is attached to the melody like pearls on a string. In the aria's more rapid concluding passage (known as the cabaletta) Norma expresses a public hope for vengeance and a private prayer to the goddess for the return of her unfaithful lover.

Pollione, alone with Adalgisa, persuades her to leave with him for Rome before the scene changes to the home which Norma shares in secret with her two children. In conversation with her confidante, Clotilde, Norma reveals her mixed emotions as a mother. This is one of several scenes which suggest the dramatic integrity of Bellini and his librettist Romani. They have created a central character whose sense of conflict owes something to the heroines of Greek tragedy.

Adalgisa enters and begs Norma to free her from her sacred vows. The high-priestess, remembering her own folly in love, is sympathetic to her plea and agrees to release Adalgisa in the first of their great duets together. It is only when Pollione enters that

Norma (Margaret Price) embraces her children while Adalgisa (Alicia Nafe) looks on (Covent Garden, 1987).

Norma learns the identity of her friend's lover. Her own past is revealed and Adalgisa turns against Pollione, vowing support for the vengeful Norma. The sound of the temple gong is heard and the women warn Pollione of the threat to the Roman occupation.

ACT TWO

Norma's sons are sleeping in the secret forest home they share with their mother. In a recitative, which is closer to dramatic monologue, she contemplates killing them to save them from being taken to Rome with their father, but her maternal feelings are too strong and she drops the knife – unlike Medea in the Greek tragedy by Euripides, whose speeches Bellini and Romani may have had in mind. Norma asks Adalgisa to take the children with her and to live happily with Pollione, but again she meets with a refusal. In the most moving of all their duet numbers, *'Mira, o Norma'*, Adalgisa asks Norma to take pity on her own children. The quicker section of the duet which concludes this masterly scene, *'Sì, fino all'ore estreme'* ('Until the final hour') is another confirmation of female solidarity: clearly the great confrontations in this opera are not between the lovers but between two women. Neither the tenor nor the bass in the opera has music to com-

pare with that of Norma's solo scenes or either of her great duets with Adalgisa.

The final scene takes place in another part of the wood. The Gauls are eager for battle, waiting for Norma's verdict. When she learns that Adalgisa has failed in her mission – to see Pollione and plead with him to return to his old love – she dramatically proclaims war against the Romans and un-leashes a strikingly barbaric chorus with a gentler aftermath. Pollione has been discovered within the sacred precinct; the penalty is death. At last the tenor and soprano face each other in duet. In their first scene together the furious Norma threatens to punish Pollione by sending Adalgisa to the flames. But before the assembled company the per-jured priestess whom she offers as sacrifice in Pollione's place is her-self. She entrusts her children to Oroveso and rises to the heroic challenge – both musically and vocally – as she prepares to mount the sacrificial pyre. Pollione, his love rekindled, joins her in the flames. A noble trio accompanied by chorus ends the opera.

CHAPTER 4

Verdi

Verdi made his name as a stirring spokesman for Italian patriotism with the Chorus of the Hebrew Slaves from *Nabucco*, his first great triumph, and with an opera that was written specifically to celebrate the short-lived triumphs for Italy in 1849, *La Battaglia di Legnano* (*The Battle of Legnano*). Following the one-off innovations of *Macbeth*, Verdi's true masterpieces began in the 1850s with *Rigoletto* and *La Traviata* (*The Woman Gone Astray*), the latter a landmark in the operatic treatment of realistic subjects. He then went on to cover an astonishing emotional and dramatic range in the succession of operas which ensued and, after the 14-year silence which followed the Egyptian première of *Aida* in 1871, he crowned a long career with two very different tributes to Shakespeare – *Otello* and *Falstaff*.

Conventional Pharaonic splendour in English National Opera's 1982 production of Aida.

Giuseppe Verdi was born in 1813, the same year as Wagner, at a time when Rossini was achieving his first major successes with *Tancredi* and *The Italian Girl in Algiers*. By the time Verdi first made his mark in Milan with his opera *Oberto* (1839), everything had changed. Rossini had lapsed into silence on the operatic front after *William Tell* – a silence that would continue until the end of his life – and Bellini was in the ascendancy, with his long-limbed romantic melodies and his restriction of vocal display to the leading soprano role. Tenors were expected to be romantically tearful, heroic even, rather than light and gracious, and basses no longer had to compromise their sonorous instruments with nimble and florid ornamentation.

Critics like the Frenchman Fétis would argue that Bellini had brought about the demise of good singing and that Verdi, demanding great stamina from his soloists in the name of dramatic forcefulness, simply took opera further on the road to ruin. Donizetti was surely more perceptive when he wrote in 1844, four years before his death, that 'the world wants something new. Others have ceded their places to us and we must cede ours to still others…I am more than happy to give mine to people of talent like Verdi.' By then, three Verdi operas had been produced in Milan and a fourth, *Ernani*, which

was premièred in Venice, firmly established the composer's international reputation: even the notoriously hard-to-please Eduard Hanslick, a renowned critical opponent of Wagner, admired *Ernani's* colossal energy.

NABUCCO

It was clear, right from the start, that Verdi was a powerful force in the world of Italian opera – and it seemed to the public that they could also depend on him for an emotional response to the issue of Italy's independence. The young man from Bussetto had arrived in a Milan that was very much under the thumb of Austria, with strong police surveillance and its opera house, La Scala, as the status symbol of Austrian rule. For the libretto of his second opera to be produced at La Scala Verdi turned to the powerful poet and avowed patriot Temistocle Solera, whose father had been imprisoned for revolutionary activity, and, according to his early biographer, Folchetto, 'began – I would say instinctively at first – to serve political ends with his music.'

It all began when the impresario Merelli urged him to read a libretto by Solera which had been turned down by the German composer Nicolai because he found 'interminable raging, bloodshedding, reviling, striking and

murdering…no subject for me'. According to Verdi's romantic anecdote, he took the libretto home and 'The book had opened in falling … Without knowing how, I gazed at the page that lay before me and read the line: Fly, thought, on golden wings [*Va, pensiero, sull'ali dorate*]. I ran through the lines that followed and was much

A fanciful souvenir postcard of Verdi in later life, pondering composition of Otello, by Balestrieri (1915).

moved, all the more because they were a paraphrase from the Bible, the reading of which had always delighted me ... Unable to sleep, I got up and read the libretto not once, but two or three times, so that by the morning I knew Solera's libretto almost by heart.'

The subject was Nabucco, based on the Old Testament story of the Babylonian tyrant, and 'Va, pensiero' became the Chorus of the Hebrew Slaves – perhaps the most famous melody from any Verdi opera and the first evidence of his ability to touch a wider audience than any of his contemporaries. Milan audiences at the early performances of the work in 1842 clearly heard it as an expression of Italy's 'enslavement' by Austria, and it was sung – and staged – only recently as a plea for freedom in the former east Germany and in Bucharest under Ceausescu's régime. Political circumstances obviously lend an extra dimension to the piece, but listeners in free democracies have always found the long, soaring theme moving in itself. 'With Nabucco my career can be said to have begun,' wrote Verdi much later. 'Since then I have never lacked for commissions.' The première was also auspicious in another, less obvious way: Giuseppina Strepponi, the *prima donna* playing the tigress Abigaille, seems to have been in terrible voice, but Verdi must have warmed

to her. When she retired in 1847 to teach singing in Paris, he lived with her there, and they married 12 years later in 1859. She was his second wife; the first, Margherita Barezzi, died of an unknown disease in 1840, shortly after the deaths of their two infants. We can only imagine what impact these losses had on the characterizations of frail heroines and filial relationships in Verdi's later operas.

THE EARLY OPERAS

Solera provided Verdi with three more stirring librettos: *I Lombardi* (The Lombards, 1841), *Giovanna d'Arco* (Joan of Arc, 1845) and *Attila* (1846). Although the plots were far from simple embodiments of a nation's struggle to independence – there are villains and heroes on both sides in *I Lombardi* and *Attila* – there was always a phrase, a line or a number to which Italian patriots could respond. 'The public found allusions everywhere,' writes Folchetto, 'but Verdi had spotted them first, and set them to inspired music which often stirred revolution in the theatre.' Included in *I Lombardi* is another striking chorus – this time of crusaders and pilgrims who remember their native Lombardy – which a newspaper critic described as moving the public 'to orgasm'; and *Attila* features a virile baritone villain who rises to a single moment

of glory when he sings to the Hun, 'You may have the universe, but leave Italy to me.' The musical phrase is typical of the kind of striking vocal lines, rising and falling in a generous arch, which Verdi favoured throughout his composing life, though the context is representative only of early Verdi in the vigorous but crude orchestration.

There is one striking exception to the raw vitality and vocal primacy of Verdi's early operas. He sought out exotic subjects as well as those with a national tinge – the clash of Incas and Spaniards in *Alzira* (1845), for example, or the romantic tales of *I Masnadieri* (*The Brigands*, 1847) and *Il Corsaro* (*The Corsair*, 1848), based, respectively, on Schiller and Byron – but he realized he was heading for 'something new' as he worked on an operatic adaptation of Shakespeare's *Macbeth*, with an effectively condensed libretto by Francesco Maria Piave. 'This tragedy is one of the greatest creations of the human spirit,' he told Piave in 1846. 'If we cannot make something great out of it, let us at least do something out of the ordinary.'

Central to the new approach was the acting ability of the baritone Felice Varesi, who created the role of Macbeth. Verdi's correspondence with the baritone is full of instructions to be as faithful as possible to Shakespeare and to

colour the words. The result was Verdi's finest piece of dramatic writing so far, Macbeth's hair-raising soliloquy ('Is this a dagger I see before me?') as he prepares for the murder of the king.

Side by side with such superb experiments, operatic conventions sometimes jar in Macbeth, but the form of the cantabile aria followed by the vital cabaletta certainly suits Lady Macbeth's overweening ambition; and her sleepwalking scene is another masterpiece of dramatic intensity. The orchestral colours are often dark and chilling – a perfect equivalent to Shakespeare's blackest night – and the fusion of words and music comes closer to Wagner's ideals of a 'total work of art' than anything else in Italian opera so far – closer, perhaps, than anything Wagner himself had produced by this time. Verdi was to revise the opera for Paris in 1865, but nearly all the most original gestures belong to the first version.

PUBLIC TO PRIVATE

Macbeth was a triumph at its first performance, which was given in Florence in March 1847, but there were those, like the Italian patriot Giusti, who urged Verdi to leave a foreign theme and turn his attention back to 'that high and solemn sorrow which fills the heart of the Italian nation.' Events played their

Continued on page 54

rIGOLETTO

THE DUKE OF MANTUA *(Tenor) A Young Libertine*

RIGOLETTO *(Baritone) His Court Jester*

GILDA *(Soprano) Rigoletto's Daughter*

SPARAFUCILE *(Bass) An Assassin*

MADDALENA *(Mezzo/Contralto) His Sister*

GIOVANNA *(Mezzo) Gilda's Duenna*

COUNTS MONTERONE & CEPRANO *(Bass & Baritone)*

COUNTESS CEPRANO *(Mezzo)*

MARULLO *(Baritone) A Courtier*

BORSA *(Tenor) A Courtier*

COURTIERS, NOBLES, PAGES & SERVANTS

'I have in mind another subject which, if the police would allow it, is one of the greatest creations of the modern theatre,' wrote Verdi to his librettist Piave. Based on Victor Hugo's play *Le Roi s'amuse*, it underwent changes due to censorship before becoming *Rigoletto*, but the opera proved immediately popular on its first performance at Venice's La Fenice Theatre on 11 March 1851.

The pervading atmosphere of gloom is established with a short prelude based on the music of Monterone's curse, which pursues Rigoletto throughout the opera.

ACT ONE

A brilliant fête is in progress at the ducal palace, featuring Verdi's favourite device of a stage-band playing cheap music in the next room. The Duke confirms his reputation as a ladies' man by telling his courtier Borsa of an unknown charmer he has seen in church and simultaneously pursuing the wife of Count Ceprano. His philosophy and his featherlight insouciance are reflected in the short aria *'Questa o quella'* ('This one or that one'). Rigoletto encourages him in his amorous escapades and Count Ceprano plans vengeance on the hunchbacked buffoon – a punishment which will involve the girl the courtiers believe to be Rigoletto's mistress. Count Monterone rails against the Duke for seducing his daughter and Rigoletto goes too far in his mockery; the Count curses him, and he reels in terror.

At night, in the street outside Rigoletto's house, the jester meets Sparafucile, a professional assassin who, to more darkly-orchestrated 'nocturnal' music, offers his services. Rigoletto soliloquizes on his kinship with this man, who uses his sword while his own weapon is a spiteful tongue. He is still haunted by the curse, but the mood changes as Gilda rushes to meet him. In one of the touching father–daughter duets that are a Verdi speciality, he asks her duenna to take good care of her. But Giovanna is susceptible to bribery and admits the Duke, who plays the part of an ardent young student and wins Gilda's love. Alone, she muses rapturously and innocently on this new lover in the aria *'Caro nome'* ('Dear name') – the purity of which is powerfully contrasted with the stealthy arrival of the courtiers, bent on carrying off Rigoletto's 'mistress'. The jester appears; they pretend that they have come to abduct the Countess Ceprano and persuade him to join them, blindfold. He does so and, too late, hears Gilda's offstage cries for help. The curse has already begun to work.

ACT TWO

Back at the palace, the Duke momentarily wins our sympathy by expressing his sense of loss (in the aria *'Parmi veder le lagrime'*) at discovering that Gilda has gone from Rigoletto's house. His mood instantly changes, however, when he finds out that she is the girl his courtiers have just brought in.

The rape takes place offstage as Rigoletto arrives in search of his daughter, with a masterly dissimulation of feeling before he bursts out in a furious attack against the courtiers. Gilda comes out of the Duke's room, dishevelled, and tells her father the whole story; he comforts her. Briefly reminded of the curse once again by Monterone's appearance, he goes on to swear his own father's vengeance in the violent last stages of the duet. It is a short act, but one which requires tremendous stamina and intensity from the principal baritone.

ACT THREE

The scene, an inn by the banks of Mantua's river, shows the inside of the building as well as its desolate location. Sparafucile uses his gypsy sister, Maddalena, to lure men to the inn to be robbed or murdered. Rigoletto has brought Gilda, still in spite of everything infatuated with the Duke, to witness his faithlessness. The Duke's aria, *'La donna è mobile'* ('Woman is fickle') is a bouncing, devil-may-care tune which suits the unrepentant libertine to perfection.

The Duke attempts to seduce Maddalena, leading the famous Quartet in which the reactions of the four participants are perfectly characterized – the Duke and the flighty gypsy within the building, the jester and his distraught daughter standing outside. Rigoletto has hired Sparafucile to kill his master, but wants the pleasure of throwing the sack with the body in it into the river himself. Gilda is to go home, change into man's clothing and leave with him for Verona, but she returns to the hut as a storm brews and overhears Maddalena pleading with her brother to spare the life of the handsome stranger. Gilda listens carefully to their bargain: if another man comes to the inn before midnight, he will be killed instead. In a dramatic trio at the height of the storm, she resolves to sacrifice herself and steps through the door.

Rigoletto takes delivery of the sack and drags it towards the river as he hears the Duke's familiar song – an ironic reprise of *'La donna è mobile'*. Untying the sack, he discovers his daughter, scarcely breathing but just able to take her part in a last, pathos-filled duet before she dies. Rigoletto is left alone with a corpse and the final reminder of Monterone's curse.

Jonathan Miller's mafia-style production of Rigoletto at English National Opera, London, in 1982. Arthur Davies' 'Duke' serenades Jean Rigby's barmaid Maddalena.

part in persuading Verdi to follow that advice. In March 1848 the Risorgimento movement in Italy reflected the revolutionary fervour that seethed all over Europe: after five days of fighting on the streets, the Austrians were driven out of Milan and Venice declared itself a republic. An exhilarated Verdi wrote to Piave that this was the hour of Italy's liberation: 'it is the people that wills it, and when the people wills there is no absolute power that can resist.' Although not a fighter, he nonetheless wrote a battle hymn to support the campaign of Sardinia's Carlo Alberto against the Austrians, which, as it turned out, was the first failure of the Italian cause.

Yet if the north was now in trouble, there was always central Italy, where the freedom-fighter Giuseppe Garibaldi joined Rome's revolutionary government and drove back both the French and the royalist Neapolitans. It was in Rome that Verdi's most overtly patriotic opera yet, *La Battaglia di Legnano* (*The Battle of Legnano*), was first performed in January 1849; the theme, which dealt with the defeat of Frederick Barbarossa by the Lombard army in the 12th century, took on even more powerful overtones when Rome was declared a republic two weeks later. Then political affairs quickly took a turn for the worse. A second invasion of Lombardy by Carlo

Alberto ended in defeat at the hand of General Radetzky's Austrians, who then pressed south to take Rome and Florence. Garibaldi fled to America, only to return and eventually succeed when Italy's fortunes rose again in the late 1850s. Verdi would play his part again, too, when the time came. For now, he could only despair that 'force still rules the world,' as he wrote to a friend, and change his operatic tactics from national to personal themes.

Verdi's style now seemed to become more intimate, less elemental, and there are two fine domestic dramas to prove the point – *Luisa Miller* (1849) and *Stiffelio* (1850). What really stops us from casually labelling this as Verdi's 'second period' is the fact that he fully intended to write an opera on King Lear and was prevented only by the failure of his librettist to finish the adaptation in time. No theme could be further removed from the bourgeois worlds of the two operas he did write. Yet *Stiffelio*'s subject is still a remarkable one: the dilemma of a Protestant priest over whether or not to forgive his adulterous wife (he finally does so in church). The opera has proved worthy of recent revival, though it is hardly surprising that it should have been cast in the shade by the even more extraordinary plot and music of its immediate successor, *Rigoletto*. As in *Macbeth*, the mix-

ture of old and new methods is astonishing, never more so than in the last act, where two famous set pieces, '*La donna è mobile*' ('Woman is fickle') and the Quartet, are followed by the longest stretch of sustained dramatic writing so far in Verdi's output.

By comparison, *Il Trovatore* (*The Troubadour*, 1853) seems like a crude return to older methods with its barrel-organ accompaniments and blood-and-thunder confrontations. The style, however, suits the subject: a dark melodrama full of ballad-style reminiscences and confused plotting, which is easily caricatured (and parodies of the gypsy Azucena, a woman so unhinged that she threw her own baby on to a bonfire by mistake, have been plentiful). *Il Trovatore* is decisively the odd one out in so-called 'middle-period' Verdi, having been written between *Rigoletto* and *La Traviata* (*The Woman Gone Astray*).

LA TRAVIATA

During his time in Paris before he returned to his new Italian home at Sant'Agata to work on *Il Trovatore*, Verdi had been to see a new play by Alexandre Dumas the younger, *La Dame aux Camélias* – 'a subject for our time,' he enthusiastically announced once he had decided to write an opera on the subject. He chose relaxed, easy-

going Venice to host the first performance of *La Traviata*, since the sympathetic portrayal of a French courtesan destroyed by hypocritical society would hardly have been likely to pass the censors elsewhere. In fact, the première, on 6 March 1853, was one of the most celebrated failures in operatic history – not because the audience was shocked by the contemporary relevance of the piece (contrary to Verdi's wishes, the production was set in the early 18th century), but perhaps because they wanted more in the way of old-fashioned flamboyancy. The role of Violetta remains a problem for many sopranos because the first act calls for extreme brilliance, whereas its successors require much more in the way of dramatic subtlety. Few singers can offer both, and the first Violetta, Fanny Salvini-Donatelli, was an accomplished display artist suitable for Act One, but evidently no languishing consumptive. The opera's reception at the first run of performances did not improve. 'My fault,' queried Verdi, 'or that of the artists? Time will tell.' It did so within the year, and in the same city; *La Traviata* has remained popular ever since.

'An opera for the Opéra is enough work to fell an ox,' wrote Verdi as he worked on his first five-hour entertainment for Paris in 1854. The French expected spectacle on a grand scale, including a

Enrico Caruso

ENRICO CARUSO FIRST EXCITED LONDON AUDIENCES WITH THE ARIA *'LA DONNA È MOBILE'* ('WOMAN IS FICKLE') IN 1902, EIGHT YEARS AFTER HIS DÉBUT IN HIS HOME TOWN OF NAPLES, ITALY, AT THE AGE OF 21. THE LEGEND OF HIS RICH TENOR VOICE, WITH ITS HINT OF BARITONAL WEIGHT, HAS ONLY BEEN MATCHED IN RECENT YEARS BY THE FAME OF LUCIANO PAVAROTTI, THOUGH THOSE WHO HEARD HIM SING CLAIM THAT THERE IS NO COMPARISON. HE GAVE MORE THAN 600 PERFORMANCES, THE MOST FAMOUS BEING HIS DRAMATICALLY CONVINCING INTERPRETATIONS OF THE DUKE OF MANTUA IN VERDI'S *RIGOLETTO* AND CANIO IN LEONCAVALLO'S *PAGLIACCI* (*CLOWNS*).

lengthy ballet by way of *divertissement*, and that was exactly what Verdi provided with *The Sicilian Vespers*. It hardly remained in the Paris Opéra's repertoire like the crowd-pleasers of Meyerbeer or Rossini's *William Tell* (surviving by virtue of dramatic licence and butchery). Even so, its reception was good enough to ensure that the Parisians welcomed further Verdi operas, and he was happy to adapt *Il Trovatore*, *Macbeth* and, later, *Otello* to French purposes; the additional ballets are rarely performed today.

He returned to Italy for the unsuccessful première (1857) of his next work, *Simon Boccanegra*, the first of the middle-period Verdi operas to take on the Shakespearean theme of the ruler and his conscience, the public and private aspects of a leader. Much later, in 1881, he would try to clarify the historical outlines in this confusing slice of Genoese history, but there are many effective scenes in the original version, not least another poignant father–daughter duet in which the careworn Doge Boccanegra comes to recognize his long-lost daughter Amelia.

As pure, unremitting drama, however, *Un Ballo in Maschera* (*A Masked Ball*, 1859) is a more powerful study of a king and his cares. The subject, based on the assassination of Gustave Adolf, King of Sweden, in 1792 at a masked ball, was a controversial one, especially when the Bourbon tyranny still held sway; mention of Sweden or, for that matter, changing the location to anywhere in northern Europe proved to be out of the question. Verdi and his librettist, Somma, finally settled on Boston at the time of the English occupation. Politics, as it turns out, are of less importance in this opera than in *Simon Boccanegra*. The central triangle is an eternal one with interesting complications. The king loves the wife of his private secretary; although their relationship remains unconsummated, the love duet features Verdi's most passionate writing for soprano and tenor. Even more unusual is the irony in the contrast between the king's devil-may-care buoyancy and the threat of the conspiracy against him: a French lightness of touch is continually undermined by darker strains. *Un Ballo in Maschera* divides loyalties: for many enthusiasts, it is Verdi's most consistently inspired opera.

Verdi did not consider his latest opera to be any kind of nationalist manifesto, even though his name was used as a disguised hymn of support for the Italian king of Sardinia: when Neapolitan crowds chanted *'Viva V.E.R.D.I'*, they meant 'Long live Victor Emmanuel, King (*Re*) of Italy (*d'Italia*). Once again, the question of Italian independence led to war,

Continued on page 58

A young Luciano Pavarotti as Alfredo at Violetta's party, Act One, in a Covent Garden production.

LA *t*RAVIATA

WHO'S WHO

VIOLETTA VALÉRY *(Soprano)*
A Courtesan

ALFREDO GERMONT *(Tenor)*
In Love with Violetta

GIORGIO GERMONT *(Baritone)*
His Father

FLORA BERVOIX *(Mezzo)*
Violetta's Friend

BARON DOUPHOL *(Baritone)*
Violetta's Admirer & 'Protector'

MARQUIS D'OBIGNY *(Bass)*

GASTON DE LETORIÈRES *(Tenor)*

ANNINA *(Soprano)*
Violetta's Maid

DOCTOR GRENVIL *(Bass)*
In Attendance on Violetta

GUESTS, DANCERS & SERVANTS

Verdi's sympathetic treatment of the play *La Dame aux Camélias* by Alexandre Dumas the younger was not a success at its first run of performances. Opening at Venice's La Fenice Theatre on 6 March 1853, *La Traviata* achieved success a season later, and has remained popular ever since.

Some producers, including Franco Zeffirelli in his film of the opera, have accompanied the prelude's depiction of the 'woman led astray' (a literal translation of the title) with images, going on to present Acts One and Two as flashbacks in the memory of the ailing Violetta. Her consumptive state is illustrated by *pianissimo* strings, followed by a long melody which is a pathetic treatment of her great outburst in Act Two: 'Love me, Alfredo, as much as I love you.'

ACT ONE

Violetta is holding a lavish party in the luxurious Parisian home furnished by her current 'protector', Baron Douphol. Among the rapid introductions effected during the opening party scene is the presentation of Alfredo by his friend Gaston, who tells Violetta that the young man has long admired her and came to call daily during her recent illness. The Baron, angered by his attentions, refuses to propose a toast; Alfredo takes it up instead, leading Violetta and the guests in the famous *Brindisi* or drinking-song.

When they are alone together, Alfredo tells Violetta that he has loved her for the past year. She says she can only offer him friendship, but his expansive love-song, *'Di quell' amor'*, takes effect: her rejoinder is a touch flippant at first, but she eventually joins him in duet and, left alone after the departure of the guests, repeats the refrain in the first part of her aria *'Ah, fors'è lui'* ('Perhaps this is true love indeed'). Once again, Verdi turns an operatic convention to his own advantage: the second, faster section or cabaletta is a dazzling and slightly manic expression of Violetta's determination to enjoy Paris' 'whirlpool of earthly pleasures', though Alfredo's off-stage song provides her with further pauses for thought.

ACT TWO

Three months have passed, and Violetta has abandoned her courtesan's existence for a quiet life in the country with Alfredo. He sings of his happiness with her, but on learning from Violetta's maid that she has sold her worldly goods to maintain the country house, leaves for Paris to raise money.

Alfredo's father arrives unexpectedly. His first disapproving comments are met with dignified responses from Violetta, and the long, elaborate duet which is the centrepiece of the opera begins. He tells her of Alfredo's sister, 'pure as an angel', and how her impending marriage will be ruined if Violetta does not break off her 'scandalous' liaison with his son. She tells Germont in agitated, broken phrases, that the shock will exacerbate her disease and kill her, but capitulates, asking Germont to tell his daughter of the sacrifice she has made. Her dignity is compounded by tremendous pathos in the melody of *'Dite alla giovine'* ('Tell the young girl').

Germont leaves. Violetta, in tears, prepares to leave for Flora's party that evening and, accompanied by sorrowful clarinet, writes a letter to Alfredo telling him that she is returning to her old life without giving the reason why. But. Alfredo, having already returned. enters, and she declares her love in the opera's most powerful moment before rushing out. Moments later. he receives her letter and falls into his father's arms. The baritone. whose music so far has been remarkably sympathetic for one so

fectly characterizes the moods and feelings of the three different principals: the father's indignation, his son's shame and Violetta's heartrending protests that she loves Alfredo still – if only he understood the reason for her actions.

ACT THREE

The Prelude begins like its counterpart at the start of the opera, but reaches greater heights of pathos as the curtain rises on Violetta's sickbed. The doctor reassures her that she will recover, but tells Annina that she only has a few hours to live.

To a solo violin reminiscence of Alfredo's *'Di quell' amor'* from Act One, she reads a letter from Giorgio Germont, telling her that Alfredo fought a duel with the Baron, learnt of her sacrifice and is coming to see her. 'Too late', she cries, and sings a fragile aria of despair. At last, Alfredo arrives and they join in a final, gently optimistic duet. But she knows that she is too ill to live much longer. When Alfredo's father appears, she forgives him and gives Alfredo her portrait, asking him to show it to his bride if he should marry. In a last poignant echo of *'Di quell' amor'* she declares that she feels better. But it is only the strange easing of pain sometimes experienced by the dying, and she falls back lifeless on the sofa.

bound by convention, has a tender aria as Germont reminds his son of his native Provence. But Alfredo is not to be calmed. He sees Flora's invitation and leaves in a fury, followed by his father. The scene changes to a brilliant gathering at Flora's house. Fashionable entertainments of 'gypsies' and 'matadors' are followed by the arrival of Alfredo, who settles down to a game of cards as Violetta enters on Baron Douphol's arm. He challenges the Baron and wins. When they are alone together, Alfredo forces Violetta to lie that she loves the Baron. In front of all the guests, he throws his winnings in her face just as Germont *père* arrives. His accusations initiate a rich ensemble in which Verdi per-

A token of Verdi's worldwide popularity as the composer of a 'good tune': arias from his three most popular middle-period operas 'with piano accordion parts', published c.1900.

which happened to break out only two months after the Rome première of *Un Ballo in Maschera* in February 1859. Victories of the combined French and Piedmontese troops led to the treaty of Villefranca, whereby Austria was to give up Lombardy; this was not enough for Verdi, who had expected more from the return of the exiled Garibaldi. In 1860 his wish was partly granted: Garibaldi and his troops liberated Sicily and Naples, paving the way for the state of Italy. This time Verdi served his country through actions rather than music. Elected parliamentary candidate for the local borough of Borgo San Donnino, he wrote, 'during the early days I frequented the chamber up till the great day in which Rome was declared Capital of Italy' (in 1871).

He came out of this short retirement from composition at the request of the Roman tenor Enrico Tamberlick, who was singing at St Petersburg's Imperial Theatre throughout the 1860–61 season. As a result, *The Force of Destiny* was created for an opera house which we tend to associate more closely with the fairy-tale extravaganzas of Rimsky-Korsakov or Mussorgsky's *Boris Godunov*. It is curious to speculate that Mussorgsky may have been influenced by Verdi's opera in his wide-spanning picture of life under a corrupt tsar. Certainly, Verdi had never written

58

anything quite like this harrowing depiction of fate pursuing the principal characters far beyond the boundaries of their native Spain, stretching the epic canvas to include tavern scenes, battles, camp revelry and a peasantry stricken by its country's devastation. As in *Boris*, leading characters vanish for whole scenes and re-emerge to demonstrate the cruelty of passing time: Leonora, haunted by her lover's accidental killing of her father and hounded by her vengeful brother, seeks refuge in a monastery at the end of Act Two and does not appear again until the second scene of Act Four; in the meantime, the brother, Don Carlo, gradually learns the true identity of the lover, Don Alvaro, in a sequence of duets which even tenors and baritones of exceptional stamina find murderously taxing.

The original ending, in which Alvaro commits suicide after the deaths of Leonora and Carlo, is bleakly powerful; Italian religious sensibilities called for a different solution when the opera was staged at Milan in 1867, and for all its beautiful new music, the replacement trio in which the dying Leonora and the Father Superior of the monastery reconcile Alvaro to God can only be a compromise.

Operatic life in Verdi's home country was now fraught with problems for a composer who tended to build, however freshly,

on lessons learned in the 1840s. A new generation of young Italian composers declared that Italy should learn from the example of Wagnerian music drama, where the singing shared equal honours with the orchestral expression of the drama. The leader of the group, the firebrand Arrigo Boito, was also a fervent nationalist and wrote the text to Verdi's *Hymn of Nations* for London's Great Exhibition of 1862. Otherwise, in the 1860s, the two men were at stylistic loggerheads and had nothing to say to each other; they would draw closer in time.

DON CARLOS & AIDA

After St Petersburg, Verdi devoted himself afresh to Parisian projects – the revised *Macbeth* for the Théâtre Lyrique and another large-scale work, *Don Carlos*, the dimensions of which would outstrip those of both *The Sicilian Vespers* and *The Force of Destiny*.

Schiller's play is a mighty amalgamation of true history – the shadow of the Inquisition in 17th-century Spain and the war with Flanders – with romance in the shape of the supposed love between Don Carlos, son of King Philip II of Spain, and his father's wife, Elisabeth of Valois. Together with his French librettists, Verdi had problems in condensing the play, even given the requirements of

French grand opera: some of the music, all of fine quality, had to be cut before the first performance on 11 March 1867. Two years later, there was a staging in Milan for which Verdi removed the first act (which had been set in the grounds of Fontainebleau in France before the action shifted to Spain) and accordingly revised the second. In either version – and there have been productions that restore not only the first act but all the extra music – the cumulative effect of this epic remains overwhelming.

The sense of powerful forces gradually engulfing private concerns reaches chilling heights in the meeting between Philip and the Grand Inquisitor – old and blind but still an evil force to be reckoned with in the pitch-black music Verdi gives him. In *Don Carlos*, the finest in the line of sombre dramas that began with *Ernani* and continued with *Macbeth*, Verdi was following his own tradition, as he pointed out when he was accused of being a 'perfect Wagnerian' by the French press.

Scenes of public ceremony and private confrontation are a feature of Verdi's next opera, *Aida*, which was commissioned for the recently opened Cairo Opera House and premièred during its 1871–72 season. Invariably, the ceremonial aspect takes the upper hand in lavish productions which can afford elephants, dancing-girls

and hundreds of slaves for the triumphal scene in Act Two. That is perhaps unfortunate, for Verdi achieves an exotic intimacy in Act Three, where the Ethiopian princess Aida encounters her father by the banks of the Nile and is persuaded by him to betray her Egyptian lover Radames.

There is a strange beauty, too, in the final scene, in which Aida joins Radames to die in the subterranean vault where he has been buried alive, while above them the jealous Amneris repents of the actions which have led to the incarceration; the final farewell, '*O terra, addio*' is the most ethereal of Verdi's duets. It might not have been out of place in the *Requiem* which Verdi wrote to commemorate the death of the Italian poet, novelist and patriot Alessandro Manzoni in 1873. Like Manzoni, Verdi was no believer, and it was a powerful response to the loss of a man he admired which led him to take up portions of an earlier work; he had written the '*Libera me*' ('Deliver me') in 1868 for a requiem which he had suggested should be a composite tribute from the leading composers of the day to Rossini, who had died that year. Debate continues as to whether Verdi's *Requiem* is, as the German pianist and conductor Hans von Bülow put it at the time, an opera 'in ecclesiastical robes'; surely all that matters is that it is a sincerely

Continued on page 62

OTELLO

Finally reaching the stage nearly sixteen years after *Aida* (Verdi's previous opera), *Otello* was the first product of an operatic collaboration with the librettist Arrigo Boito (also a composer). The subject was broached in 1879, but work did not begin in earnest until September 1885; the first performance took place at La Scala, Milan, on 5 February 1887.

Pen, watercolour and gouache maquette of Otello's *Venetian–Cypriot setting. Design by Chaperon for the Paris Opéra première in 1894.*

WHO'S WHO

OTELLO *(Tenor)*
A Moor, General in the Venetian Army

DESDEMONA *(Soprano)*
His Wife

IAGO *(Baritone) His Ensign*

CASSIO *(Tenor) His Lieutenant*

EMILIA *(Mezzo)*
Iago's Wife, in Attendance on Desdemona

LODOVICO *(Bass)*
Venetian Envoy

MONTANO *(Bass)*
Otello's Predecessor as Governor of Cyprus

RODERIGO *(Tenor) A Venetian*

HERALD, SOLDIERS, SAILORS, VENETIANS & CYPRIOTS

ACT ONE

Boito's libretto dispenses with Shakespeare's Venetian first act, landing us in Cyprus at the height of a storm, and Verdi plunges straight into the action with one of the most dramatic opening gestures in the history of opera. Otello's ship reaches harbour. The Moor bids celebration of his victory over the Turks in a short, impressive declamation ('*Esultate*'). Iago, his ensign, quickly confides his dislike of Otello to the weak-willed Roderigo, in love with Otello's wife Desdemona. Iago claims to hate young Cassio for usurping the rank that should be his. Following a nimble bonfire chorus, Iago prepares to make Cassio drunk and disgrace him, which he does easily in a rapid drinking-song. Roderigo provokes Cassio to a fight, but it is Montano, former governor of Cyprus, who is wounded, and Otello appears at the height of the brawl. Cassio is then dismissed and Iago takes his place.

A solo cello introduces the love scene between Otello and Desdemona. This is less a duet than a sequence of solo narratives set to a glowing series of ecstatic melodies. To a significant phrase, Otello asks for 'a kiss… a kiss … another kiss' and leads Desdemona into the castle.

ACT TWO

In a room on the ground floor of Otello's castle, Iago continues his plotting, suavely suggesting that Cassio should ask Desdemona to plead with Otello for his reinstatement. Iago's lone '*Credo*' is an invention of Boito's, not Shakespeare's, and reveals the villain as a nihilist. Shakespeare's temptation scene is simplified: his Othello does not rise to the bait as easily as that of Boito and Verdi, but the music is powerful and fluent. The poison of Iago's insinuation begins to take effect when Desdemona, all innocence, begs mercy for Cassio. Bewildered by the vehemence of Otello's response, she leads a quartet during which Iago manages to snatch her handkerchief from his wife Emilia to initiate the next stage of the drama.

Otello is now on the rack. His farewell to peace of mind is heroic, but he is further undermined by Iago's claims to have heard Cassio moaning 'Desdemona' in his sleep and to have seen him with the handkerchief Otello gave to Desdemona. Otello swears vengeance and a duet of shattering vehemence brings down the curtain.

ACT THREE

Ambassadors are expected in the palace's great hall; they are to recall Otello to Venice. Before they arrive, the screw turns in a sequence of unnerving scenes. Desdemona continues to plead for Cassio and is astounded when Otello rages about the handkerchief and condemns her as a whore. His desolate monologue is interrupted by the return of Iago, who stage-manages a conversation with Cassio. This revolves around Cassio's mistress, Bianca, but is contrived so that Otello, in hiding, will think it concerns his wife. He even persuades Cassio to flourish the handkerchief. The music, like a rather sinister scherzo in a symphony, winks and leers along with Iago. Cassio leaves and Iago urges Otello to strangle Desdemona in her bed that evening while he despatches Cassio.

The ceremony begins in which Otello is to hand over the governorship. When he learns that the Ducal decree appoints Cassio in his place, his control snaps and he forces Desdemona to the ground. Her sorrow initiates a vast ensemble – one of the few points in the opera where old operatic con-ventions are resplendently called into action. Ordering the crowd to leave and cursing Desdemona, Otello suffers a fainting fit as an offstage chorus sounds his praises. The irony is not wasted on Iago, who stands triumphantly over his general's prostrate body.

ACT FOUR

Woodwind conjure the dim light in Desdemona's bedchamber, leading to the mournful pathos of her 'Willow Song'. Her foreboding is expressed in a heart-rending farewell to Emilia; then muted strings accompany her in an ethereal 'Hail Mary'. The music sinks to the double-basses as Otello enters stealthily. To a recall of the 'kiss' theme of the love-duet, he wakens Desdemona, but the mood changes as he confronts her with his accusations and the tension rises in a steady crescendo. Ignoring her cries for mercy he smothers her.

Emilia rushes in, crying that Cassio has murdered Roderigo. Hearing Desdemona's dying gasps and calls for help, she reveals in front of Otello, Cassio, Montano and Lodovico the saga of the handkerchief and Iago's villainy. Otello now holds centre-stage, regaining much of his dignity before he stabs himself and moves towards the body of his wife. The music of the love duet is recalled once more as Otello asks for a kiss before dying.

The murder of Desdemona: Mario Del Monaco, a famous Otello, and Raina Kabaivanska in 1962.

felt, magnificently constructed homage from one of Italy's leading figures to another – operatic in style, religious in feeling.

Although Verdi was far from idle in his sixties, the fact remains that not a single completely new opera of his was seen on stage between 1872 and 1887. He continued to feel the pressure of new movements in opera, and he could not bring himself to write either in the post-Wagnerian style favoured by some of the younger composers or in the newly emergent fashion of *verismo* (blood-and-thunder realism). This new trend, however, did not flourish fully until 1890, the year of Mascagni's *Cavalleria Rusticana* (*Rustic Chivalry*).

BOITO

Verdi could not understand the novelties of Boito's opera on Faust, *Mefistofele*, which opened in 1868, the same year as the première in Paris of *Don Carlos*; he was unpleasantly struck by how the harmonies of Boito's 'Prologue in Heaven' were 'almost all based on dissonances'. This did not prevent him from finding unexpected common ground with the younger composer in the spring of 1879. Despondent at the initial failure of his *Mefistofele*, Boito had turned translator and librettist; at a dinner in Milan, Verdi's publisher, Ricordi, casually spoke of Boito

and Shakespeare. 'At the mention of *Othello* I saw Verdi look at me with suspicion but with interest,' Ricordi later told his biographer. 'He had certainly understood and had certainly reacted.'

Yet Verdi did not act on Boito's libretto – not, at any rate, for some time. The procrastinations of the older composer, who was full of self-doubt and self-criticism, and the ebullient insistence of the younger Boito are in themselves the stuff of drama and have been the subject of a stage-play by Julian Mitchell, *After Aida*. Verdi's caution was understandable in the face of Shakespeare's masterly tragedy – besides, he had felt the same about *King Lear* in the 1850s, long-standing plans for which were never carried into action.

The turning-point with Boito came in 1881, when the inspired rhetoric of his new Council Chamber scene for *Simon Boccanegra* spurred Verdi to new heights: Boccanegra's plea for peace between Genoa's rival factions and the vehement cursing of the unknown villain who abducted his daughter are great moments in the opera, which make the revised version an essential choice for producers today. It served as a kind of protoype for some of the *Otello* music: and in fact, Francesco Tamagno, the tenor who sang the part of Gabriele, and Victor

Placido Domingo

PLACIDO DOMINGO'S STUDIO RECORDINGS RARELY DO JUSTICE TO THE INTENSITY AND MAGNETISM OF THE SPANISH TENOR'S PERFORMING STYLE. HE TOOK ON HIS MOST CELEBRATED ROLE, OTELLO, IN 1975, AND HAS WRITTEN OF THE OPERA THAT 'EVERY TIME I COME TO THE LAST SCENE...I FEEL AS IF I HAVE LIVED THROUGH THE MOST TRAGICALLY BEAUTIFUL STORY EVER TOLD'. HIS SINCERITY, AS WELL AS HIS STAMINA, IS EVIDENT IN PERFORMANCE. HIS REPERTOIRE IS ENORMOUS AND RANGES FROM WAGNER – HE HAS SUNG LOHENGRIN, PARSIFAL AND TANNHÄUSER WITH GREAT SUCCESS – TO THE SPANISH MUSICAL KNOWN AS ZARZUELA. IT WAS IN ONE OF THESE ROLES THAT HE MADE HIS DÉBUT IN MEXICO IN 1957. HE BEGAN AS A BARITONE, NOT A TENOR, AND HIS TRUE VOCAL STATUS IS STILL NEEDLESSLY DEBATED. DOMINGO HAS ALSO CONDUCTED MANY OPERAS, REFLECTING HIS ORIGINAL TRAINING BEFORE HE TURNED TO SINGING.

Maurel, a magnificent Boccanegra at that 1881 'revival' would go on to create, respectively, the roles of Otello and Iago.

Before the collaboration on *Otello* could truly take wing, Verdi undertook the four-act version of *Don Carlos* for La Scala. There was also a misunderstanding in which Boito was represented in a Neapolitan newspaper as saying that he would have liked to have set *Othello* to music himself. Boito himself set the record straight with Verdi in the spring of 1884, but – apart from sending him the text for

Iago's 'Credo of evil', which Verdi gratefully accepted as being 'very powerful and wholly Shakespearean' – was unable to persuade the composer any further until September 1885. Verdi wrote the miraculous Act-One love duet the following February and Otello's heroic entrance in May, completing the score by November 1886.

At the beginning of that year he took the decision to change the title from *Iago*, the name of the opera's villain, to *Otello*; he had hesitated to use the second title for fear that his own work might be

and speeches from the historical plays *Henry IV Part One* and *Henry IV Part Two*; those two plays, after all, offer the richest insights into Shakespeare's glorious creation of the fat knight Sir John Falstaff.

With the brilliant fugue ('Everything in the world's a jest') that brings down the curtain on *Falstaff*, Verdi ended his operatic career, managing to pay tribute as he did so to a score that held pride of place in his home at Sant'Agata – Mozart's *Don Giovanni*.

He still had two of his *Four Sacred Pieces* to complete, this time closer to the world of church music than opera, and with proceeds from *Otello* he oversaw the construction of a rest-home for retired musicians in Milan; the Casa Verdi still fulfils its function and was recently the subject of a documentary which revealed its inmates living out old performing days with relish.

Verdi lived on to the grand old age of 87, and at his funeral in January 1901, 28,000 bystanders broke into the Chorus of the Hebrew Slaves. He left behind a host of early works whose values are now being appreciated, season by season, at London's Covent Garden, a few pioneering experiments and at least half-a-dozen of the greatest operas in the repertoire. No other operatic composer begins to match the breadth or the consistency of his achievement.

compared unfavourably with the beautiful but dramatically insubstantial opera on the subject by Rossini. As he wrote to Boito, he now preferred people 'to say "he wanted to fight with a giant [in other words, Rossini] and was crushed" rather than "he wanted to hide behind the title of Iago".' The comparisons did not, as it happened, arise. The first performance of *Otello* took place on 5 February 1887 at La Scala, Milan. It was an international triumph, though some visiting music critics were puzzled by the

new, fast-flowing musical style – a dramatic condensation of so much that Verdi had already achieved.

There were no comparable delays in the composition of Verdi's comic swansong, *Falstaff*, though in a touching letter to Boito in July 1889 the 75-year-old composer paused for thought: 'In outlining *Falstaff* did you never think of the enormous number of my years?...Supposing I couldn't stand the strain? And failed to finish it?...Have you a sound argument to oppose to mine...if you can find one for me, and I

some way of throwing off ten years or so, then...what joy, to be able to say to the public: Here we are again!! Come and see us!'

Needless to say, Boito found the right answers, and three days later Verdi gave his wholehearted agreement: 'We'll write this *Falstaff*, then. We won't think for a moment of obstacles, of age, of illness!' Nor is there any trace of them in this nimblest of comedies, an opera which has the distinction of improving on Shakespeare's often leaden *The Merry Wives of Windsor* by incorporating lines

Dietrich Fischer-Dieskau, an unlikely candidate for the laundry basket at Covent Garden in 1967.

ƒALSTAFF

Verdi's last opera, and his only comedy apart from *Un Giorno di Regno* (*King for a Day*), which was written more than half a century earlier, was given its first performance at La Scala, Milan, on 9 February 1893. The title role was taken by Victor Maurel, who had impressed in the 1881 revival of *Simon Boccanegra* and had created the role of Iago in *Otello*.

ACT ONE

A room in the Garter Inn, Windsor (the *'Giarrettiera'* in the Italian). Falstaff has just finished sealing two letters when Doctor Caius bursts in, accusing him and his two drinking companions – the red-nosed Bardolph and his accomplice, Pistol – of bad behaviour. He exits to mock-sanctimonious 'Amens' from the two henchmen. Falstaff complains about the corrupt company that is reducing him to a state of penury and turns to amatory schemes: will Bardolph and Pistol carry love-letters to two of Windsor's 'merry wives', Alice Ford and Meg Page? Certainly not; they are honest men. So he sends his page instead, lecturing the two men on the meaninglessness of honour. The librettist, Boito, here introduces the fine speech from Shakespeare's *Henry IV Part One*, and Verdi rounds it off with an expansive treatment of the melody. Falstaff then chases the scoundrels round the room.

In the garden of Ford's house the two wives, accompanied by Mistress Quickly and Nannetta, Alice's daughter, laughingly compare identical letters from Falstaff and vow revenge. The men are grouped around Ford, who has been warned by Bardolph and Pistol that Falstaff has designs on his wife. Fenton and Nannetta meet twice, lightly parrying words of love in a nimble duet, and finally join the most brilliant comic ensemble since Rossini, in which the four women and five men sing in different metres. The woman have the last laugh over Falstaff's pomposity before the curtain falls.

ACT TWO

Back at the inn, Falstaff receives two visits. The first of these is from Mistress Quickly, who bows with exaggerated servility and countless utterances of *'Reverenza'* ('Your worship'). With comic obsequiousness she tells Falstaff that Alice can see him between two and three o'clock in the afternoon (the phrase is a memorable touch of musical comedy).

The second visitor is one Master Brook (Signor Fontana) – none other than Ford in disguise, who claims to love Alice and wants Falstaff to woo her on his behalf, enticing him with the promise of gold. In this way he discovers Falstaff's own intentions. When Ford is left alone, the comedy gives way to a reminder of *Otello* as the jealous husband muses over what he believes to be his wife's infidelity. Then Falstaff returns and, with exaggerated politeness, they depart arm in arm.

Inside Ford's house the four women plot the downfall of Falstaff. We learn in passing that Nannetta is sad because her father wants her to marry the old fool Caius, not Fenton. Falstaff arrives and Alice begins to play the lute. She receives glowing praise from Falstaff, who, in a featherlight miniature aria, less than a minute long, remembers the days when he was a slip of a lad and page to the

Duke of Norfolk. Just before Ford enters Falstaff manages to hide behind a screen, while Ford's men turn the house upside down as they search for Falstaff.

The women finally conceal Falstaff inside an enormous laundry basket, piling the dirty linen on top of him. Nannetta and Fenton take Falstaff's place behind the screen, only to be discovered by an astonished Ford. The ensuing confusion gives Alice time to order the emptying of the laundry-basket out of the window and into the river Thames. Ford, seeing Falstaff struggling through the water, joins in the laughter.

ACT THREE

Once more at the Garter Inn, Falstaff suffers a very Shakespearean touch of melancholy, until hot wine revives him and a joyous woodwind trill spreads through the whole orchestra. Quickly's extraordinary powers of persuasion force him to agree to another meeting with Alice – this time at Herne the Hunter's Oak in Windsor Forest at midnight. He leaves with Quickly; the whole atmosphere is shot through with fairy magic – Verdi knew his Mendelssohn and his Berlioz – as the ladies look forward to their roles as witches and spirits, and Ford resolves that Caius shall be betrothed to Nannetta that evening. The scene ends in an orchestral whisper – pure enchantment.

The magic continues at Herne's Oak with a romantic aria for Fenton and an exquisite number for Nannetta who, as Queen of the Fairies, is the first to haunt Falstaff – dressed up, as Quickly commanded him, as Herne the Hunter, with horns on his head.

Fairy antics turn to devilment as Falstaff is persecuted with much pinching and kicking, until he recognizes Bardolph's red nose among the 'spirits' and the game is up. He tries to turn the tables by arguing that his 'wit is the cause of wit in others', and he has the last laugh on Ford when a 'masked' wedding turns out to have matched Nannetta with Fenton – and Caius with Bardolph. Blessings ensue, and Verdi bows out with what is traditionally an academic form, a fugue, endowed with colossal good humour as each of the characters takes up the thread, 'All the world's a jest'.

Sir Geraint Evans, one of the most popular of all Falstaffs.

Chinese ritual colourfully realized with designs by Sally Jacobs for the Royal Opera production of Puccini's Turandot at Covent Garden, London, in 1984. Dame Gwyneth Jones' ice princess lays down the law to the unknown prince (Placido Domingo).

CHAPTER 5

Puccini

At the London première of *Manon Lescaut*, the first of Puccini's operas to hold a place in the repertoire, George Bernard Shaw hailed him as the true heir to Verdi. He adapted the fast-moving techniques of the Italian composers who favoured subjects drawn from real life, the *verismo* school, to his own ends in *La Bohème* (*The Bohemians*) and *Tosca* before turning to realistic story-lines set in exotic locations, such as *Madam Butterfly* (which takes place in Japan), and perfecting his often subtle art of orchestration to an astonishingly high level in *The Girl of the Golden West*. His last opera, *Turandot*, was left unfinished at his death in 1924 and was completed by his colleague Alfano. It is the last well-known opera of the 20th century to offer a large-scale, romantically optimistic happy ending.

It was with reason that Verdi feared the Wagnerization of Italian opera in the 1880s, and his long-delayed response, *Otello*, certainly played its part in stemming the Germanic tide that threatened to overwhelm a younger generation of Italian composers. It is in a way ironic that the only Verdi operas that many ardent Wagnerians can stomach are *Otello* and *Falstaff*; yet however much Verdi may have followed the example of Wagner in terms of orchestral sophistication, he adapted his methods to ends that served the very Italian, fast-flowing nature of his two late masterpieces. For without the dramatic telescoping in *Otello* of events that are often violent, the movement which came to be known as the *verismo* school – and which Verdi did not at first welcome – would certainly not have developed in the way that it did.

The first cues originated from across the Alps. What the Italians defined as drama drawn from real life (*vero*, meaning 'true', gives us *verismo*) was nothing more than a translation of French realist principles in literature. The first generation of French realist writers, who were suffused with romanticism, included the younger Alexandre Dumas – whose play *La Dame aux Camélias* gave rise to a *verismo* rose by another name and before its time, Verdi's *La Traviata* – and Henri Murger, the author of the partly autobiographical *Scenes of Bohemian Life* that would capture the imaginations of both Giacomo Puccini and Ruggiero Leoncavallo nearly half a century after they were originally published.

Among the later realists were Gustave Flaubert, Émile Zola, and Prosper Mérimée, whose novella *Carmen* was selectively dramatized in Bizet's opera – the first to feature a violent murder on stage (as Don José stabs Carmen outside the bullring in the final scene). Zola's comments on the genre of the realistic novel, which he himself took to extremes in his purposefully grim portraits of ordinary people, serve just as well in the context of *verismo* opera. He writes that 'the sole object is to register human facts, to lay bare the mechanism of body and soul. The plot is simplified; the first man one comes across will do as hero; examine him and you are sure to find a straightforward drama which allows full play to the machinery of emotion and passion.'

LEONCAVALLO & MASCAGNI

Ruggiero Leoncavallo, acting as his own librettist, put very similar words into the mouth of Tonio the Clown as he introduces the action in the Prologue to *Pagliacci* (*Clowns*): 'The author has sought … to show you a glimpse of life. He has only one conviction, that the artist is a man – and it is for men that he must write. With the truth he would inspire you … consider our souls, because we are men of flesh and bones, and in this inhospitable world, just as you do, we breathe the air!'

Leoncavallo's briskly paced masterpiece often has the good fortune to share a double-bill with Mascagni's *Cavalleria Rusticana* (*Rustic Chivalry*) – a shakier work dramatically, but of great importance historically, since it has always been taken as the starting-point of *verismo* opera and was a runaway success for its 26-year-old composer at its first performance on 17 May 1890. He based the one-act work on a dramatized tale of Sicilian peasant life that had been included by the author, Giovanni Verga, in a collection of stories a decade earlier (evidence of how far ahead 'realistic' literature was of its musical counterparts). The opera's subject matter is indeed violent – Alfio, a carter, murders neighbour Turiddu in a fight with knives, having been told of Turiddu's relationship with his wife by the rejected Santuzza – but it takes an introduction, serenade and chorus for the plot to get under way, and the mechanics of Italian operatic convention break across the developing action. Even so, *Cavalleria Rusticana* is rich in good tunes, as Verdi realized when he played through the score and told his publisher, Ricordi, that 'evidently the tradition of Italian melody is not yet exhausted'.

Early success did not necessarily work in Mascagni's favour. 'It was a pity I wrote *Cavalleria* first,' he remarked in later life. 'I was crowned before I was king.' He soon abandoned the school of *verismo* and exchanged rustic chivalry for rustic comedy in *L'Amico Fritz* (*Our Friend Fritz*, 1891) – the harmonic modernism of which disconcerted Verdi – and turning to Japanese exotica long before Puccini with *Iris* (1898), which contains some lavish orchestral passages. He lived until 1945, but disgraced himself by his association with the Mussolini régime and died in poverty.

Cavalleria Rusticana, in the meantime, has to withstand the comparison in performance with *I Pagliacci*, a work of greater dramatic impetus and some subtlety. Leoncavallo leaned both ways – towards *verismo* as well as the Wagnerian school – and it was only the failure of *I Medici*, the first in a projected *Ring*-style trilogy on the Italian Renaissance, which steered him back to realist subjects.

Yet neither of Leoncavallo's most striking later operas – *La Bohème*, which suffered inevitably (though on its own terms unfairly) from comparison with Puccini's very different treatment of the same subject, and the pleasingly sentimental *Zazà* – have rivalled the often performed *Pagliacci* (1892) for a place in the repertoire.

The elegant pastiche of the play-within-a-play scenes provided by the strolling 'clowns' (*pagliacci*) of the title adds an extra dimension to the opera, but elsewhere it contains all the trademarks of the true *verismo* opera: a coarse confrontation between Nedda, the *prima donna*, and Tonio, the disfigured clown who lusts after her; the most celebrated of all obligatory sob-scenes, or *arie d'urlo*, for the tenor, Canio – '*Vesti la giubba*' or 'On with the motley'; and finally, a full-throttle orchestral repetition of the great tune after the wronged Canio has murdered the unfaithful Nedda on stage.

PUCCINI

Puccini would adopt these *verismo* hallmarks and turn them to his own ends in his most famous operas. Yet the natural 'son and heir' of Verdi did not begin his operatic career as a follower of *verismo*. Born in Parma in 1858, his youth coincided with the heady days of the artistic and intellectual circle which included as its members the young Boito and Amilcare Ponchielli (the composer of *La Gioconda* or *The Ballad Singer*, another opera with a libretto by Boito, Verdi's collaborator on

Continued on page 72

Puccini in his Bohemian youth.

LA *boHÈME*

WHO'S WHO

RODOLFO *(Tenor) A Poet*

MIMI *(Soprano)*
A Seamstress

MARCELLO *(Baritone)*
A Painter

MUSETTA *(Soprano)*

SCHAUNARD *(Baritone)*
A Musician

COLLINE *(Bass)*
A Philosopher

BENOIT *(Bass) A Landlord*

ALCINDORO *(Bass)*
A State Councillor

PARPIGNOL *(Tenor)*
A Toy-seller

STUDENTS, SHOPKEEPERS,
SOLDIERS, WAITERS & CHILDREN

Puccini's librettists,

Giuseppe Giacosa and Luigi Illica, based their slice of Parisian life on Henri Murger's novelized anecdotes about the city (1851). The opera's first performance was given at the Teatro Reggio, Turin, Italy, on 1 February 1896 and was conducted by Arturo Toscanini.

ACT ONE

To a rumbustious theme drawn from an early orchestral work by Puccini, *Capriccio Sinfonico*, the curtain rises immediately on an attic in the Latin Quarter of Paris. It is Christmas eve *circa* 1830. Marcello, who is painting a large canvas of the Red Sea crossing, is extremely cold, and Rodolfo suggests they burn his latest play in an effort to keep warm. Colline joins them, with pseudo-philosophical banter. Schaunard then strides in, bearing unexpected food supplies; he gives a lengthy account of how he came by them, but no-one seems to be listening (and the audience, too, usually misses this quick, witty tale of a troublesome parrot despatched by poisoned parsley).

Benoit, the landlord, arrives for the rent but, easily inebriated, is evicted by the friends, who feign indignation at his extra-marital escapades. They leave to celebrate

Christmas eve at the Café Momus – except for Rodolfo, who stays to finish an article.

There is a knock at the door: an apologetic neighbour has come to beg a light for her candle. The climb up the stairs has exhausted her; she faints, rests a moment, and as she is about to leave her candle flickers out again. She asks Rodolfo to help her look for her key. He touches an ice-cold hand in the dark and a kind of love duet begins with exchanges of confidence in two sweet and tender arias. Rodolfo, not yet the passionate wooer, tells the young girl a little about himself ('*Che gelida manina*' or 'Your tiny hand is frozen'). In return she says that though her real name is Lucia, everyone calls her Mimi ('*Mi chiamano Mimi*'), and sings about her simple life as an embroiderer of flowers. The moonlight catches her, and they declare their love ('*O soave fanciulla*'). In the magical closing bars of the duet, they leave together to join Rodolfo's friends.

ACT TWO

Originally planned as a finale, the Momus scene is brilliant and fast moving. Scenes of Parisian street life are cunningly interwoven with vignettes of the principal characters: Schaunard testing an out-of-tune horn, Rodolfo buying Mimi a pink bonnet. Marcello's faithless

mistress, Musetta, appears with a current admirer at her heels, the old councillor Alcindoro.

In Murger's novel, and in Leoncavallo's alternative operatic treatment, Musetta is the most serious female character; Puccini merely hints at greater depths of feeling beneath the soubrettish exterior as she attempts to win

Mimi returns to die in Rodolfo's arms. Act Four in a production by England's Opera North.

brittle quarrels of Marcello and Musetta; after this great quartet's climactic phrase, the acrimonious couple spits insults, while Rodolfo and Mimi resolve to stay together until the spring returns.

ACT FOUR

Several months later, to the same music as the beginning of Act One, Marcello and Rodolfo are attempting to work, but neither can concentrate and they reveal their true feelings about their lost loves in a nostalgic duet. They resume the usual horseplay with their friends, but Musetta appears in the doorway. She has met Mimi in the street and brought her back, at her request, to be with Rodolfo at her death. It is Mimi who tries to console the stricken group of friends.

Musetta tells Marcello to sell her earrings in return for money to buy medicine and Colline gravely addresses the overcoat he intends to pawn ('Vecchia zimarra').

Left alone with Rodolfo, Mimi sings passionately for one last time before the lovers sink into reminiscences; the smiling delicacy with which Puccini recalls the events of Act One steers clear of false sentimentality. The others return, but it is too late: Mimi dies while Musetta is praying and the medicine is prepared. Rodolfo realizes the truth from his friends' silence and breaks down, crying Mimi's name.

back Marcello with the famous Waltz Song ('Quando me'n vo' soletta'). Musetta sends Alcindoro off to find her a better-fitting pair of shoes and falls into Marcello's arms. The Bohemians march out on the heels of a passing band, leaving Alcindoro to pay for their meal at Momus. He returns to find only the bill.

ACT THREE

Time has passed. In the February dawn, by a tollgate to the city, Mimi has come to find Rodolfo in the tavern where Marcello and Musetta are working. Racked with coughing, Mimi tells Marcello of Rodolfo's jealous and irrational behaviour. When he comes out of

the tavern, she hides and hears him complain to Marcello of her flirting before he reveals the truth – Mimi is so sick that the impoverished life they lead is bound to kill her. He hears her weeping, and, as Marcello dashes into the tavern to deal with Musetta, Mimi sings her lover a gentle farewell. Their duet is interrupted by the

Otello). Eagerly welcoming all things German (and, by implication, hostile to Verdi) the group became known as the *Scapigliatura Milanese*, the Bohemians of Milan (the name derives from the verb *scapigliare*, to rumple). Much as they hero-worshipped Wagner, they were as slow as the rest of Italy to catch up with the developments in musical drama that were taking place with *The Ring*; during the late 1870s and early 1880s their tastes ran instead to the demonic romanticism of Wagner's early operas – *The Flying Dutchman* and *Tannhäuser* – and, by implication, the German supernatural tale that was fashionable during the first half of the 19th century.

Boito's contribution was an ambitious treatment of the Faust legend, *Mefistofele*, which fell flat at its first performance in 1868 (a revival in 1875 proved to be more successful), while the 25-year-old Puccini took his first steps in opera with a ghost-story, *Le Villi*. The plot is based on the folk-legend of the Willis, or spirits of girls who die before their wedding day; the first man they meet is forced to dance with them until he dies of exhaustion. Adam's ballet *Giselle* has kept the myth alive, and there is plenty of dance in Puccini's short opera, too. He wrote it for a competition which was devised by the publishing house of Edoardo Sonzogno; although Puccini's work

did not receive so much as an honorary mention, it was hailed by the critics when it was staged in Milan at the end of May 1884. They noted traces of French refinement (the influence of Bizet and Massenet) which was to play an important part in *La Bohème*, but *Le Villi* is most striking for its generous melodies and vocal writing. In that respect, it is very different from the romantic operas of Catalani, who was dealing with much the same subjects in the 1880s, but who was far more faithful to Wagnerian principles in the importance which he attached to the orchestra.

Catalani made a last brave bid to keep the romantic spirit alive in the face of the new *verismo* with *La Wally* (1892). This Tyrolean tragedy, complete with a 'Song of the Edelweiss', survives by virtue of its touching heroine – Toscanini called his daughter Wally in her honour – whose aria, '*Ebben? Ne andrò lontana*' ('So, I shall depart') was immortalized as representing the essence of Italian opera in the French film *Diva*.

'THE HEIR OF VERDI'

Having toyed with the essence of romanticism in his first opera, Puccini plunged headlong into the sphere of blood-and-thunder melodrama with *Edgar* (1889). Ferdinando Fontana, a fellow-

Beniamino Gigli

ENTHUSIASTS OF THE TENOR VOICE TEND TO FAVOUR EITHER THE ARDENT, BARITONAL TONES OF CARUSO OR THE LIGHTER, SWEETER CHARMS OF GIGLI (WHEN HE WON AN INTERNATIONAL COMPETITION AT PARMA IN 1914, ONE OF THE JUDGES MADE THE FAMOUS CLAIM 'WE HAVE FOUND *THE* TENOR'). HE WAS A LESS ACCOMPLISHED ACTOR THAN CARUSO, AND HIS PORTRAYALS OF MORE MELODRAMATIC ROLES COULD BE UNNECESSARILY VULGAR, BUT HE WAS THE MOST ARDENT AND FRESH-TONED OF ALL RODOLFOS IN *LA BOHÈME* (*THE BOHEMIANS*), AS A MARVELLOUS 1936 RECORDING DEMONSTRATES. HE WAS STILL SINGING RODOLFO AT COVENT GARDEN IN 1946; THE MIMI WAS HIS DAUGHTER, RINA. HIS FINE VOCAL TECHNIQUE ALLOWED HIM A LONG PROFESSIONAL CAREER; HE RETIRED IN 1953 AND DIED FOUR YEARS LATER.

member of the *Scapigliatura*, had provided the libretto for *Le Villi*, but in the plot of *Edgar* he went disastrously beyond the limits in attempting to graft a moral of redemption on to a simple, squalid triangle of love. He did at least stretch his composer to write music that was suitable for such passionate confrontations, and the opera has one interesting character – Tigrana, a Carmen with pathological tendencies (as suggested by her name) and the only major mezzo-soprano role in Puccini's output.

Critical verdicts have to be taken with caution, and the mature Puccini was granted his fair share of false predictions (including the famous judgment that *La Bohème*, 'even as it leaves little impression on the minds of the audience, will leave no great trace upon the history of our lyric theatre.') Yet the critics seem to have been right when *Manon Lescaut* appeared on the scene in 1893, and Italian enthusiasm was backed up by George Bernard Shaw at the opera's Covent Garden première the following year: 'I feel that it is Puccini, more than anyone else, who is likely to become the heir of Verdi'. Puccini had, admittedly, taken a risk with an operatic setting of the Abbé Prévost's novel when Massenet's opera, *Manon*, had already achieved considerable success (though not, at the time, in Italy). He was drawn to the char-

acter of the fallible Manon, who wants to do good but always falls victim of her frivolous nature; her death in the New Orleans desert was the first manifestation of the full-blooded relish Puccini seemed to take in the destruction of his heroines. He had been clear on how his opera would differ from Massenet's: 'Massenet will feel it as a Frenchman, with powder and minuets; but I shall feel it as an Italian, desperate with passion'.

In fact there is plenty of powder in the 18th-century drawing-room of Manon's protector, which provides the setting for Puccini's Act Two; like his contemporary, Richard Strauss, he proved adept at neatly-scored pastiches of a past age and minuets also feature in *La Bohème* and *Tosca*. Yet the hopeless love of the young man, Des Grieux, is indeed 'desperate with passion', and his second-act duet with Manon combines harmonic languishing in the manner of Wagner's *Tristan and Isolde* with true Italianate vocalizing. The Tristan touch continues in the *intermezzo* before Act Three, a chance for Puccini to bring to the fore his colourful and often subtle orchestral writing.

It is above all in *Manon Lescaut*'s skilful ensembles, fast pacing and compactly presented set pieces that Puccini anticipates his first exercise in the *verismo* style, *La Bohème*.

For the critics, the first performance on 1 February 1896 signalled a sad fall from grace. 'We wonder what could have started Puccini towards the degradation of this *Bohème*,' declared the *Gazzetta del Popolo* and warned the composer, 'you have today conceived the whim of forcing the public to applaud you where and when you will. That is all very well for once, but for once only.'

LA BOHÈME

It seems incredible now that anyone should have missed the warmth and wit of Puccini's most perfect score. The quick-witted Luigi Illica and the first-rate playwright Giuseppe Giacosa provided their first libretto-from-scratch for Puccini (having stepped in at the last minute to sort out *Manon Lescaut*) and the text of *La Bohème* is a masterpiece in its own right – a clever, detailed selection and adaptation of Murger's Parisian sketches, which welds the chosen incidents into a coherent whole. Puccini for his part responded with orchestral detail to match the words: the flaming of the fire in the grate as Rodolfo prepares to burn his manuscript for warmth, for example, or the two solo violins whose pizzicato notes illustrate his sprinkling of water on the face of the unconscious Mimi. The situations, too, though oper-

atic, are established with all the immediacy of a good play: what could be more real than the behaviour of Rodolfo and Marcello as we see them at work at the very beginning of the first act?

More realistically inclined in the depiction of his heroine's death than Verdi in *La Traviata*, who has Violetta responding loudly and strongly right up until the moment she breathes her last, Puccini made sure that Mimi sings her most taxing phrases long before she succumbs to half-voiced reminiscences of the past. Thanks to his orchestral tact and subtlety, she dies smiling with a sigh (although the full-force orchestral repetition of a phrase from her last aria to bring down the curtain is a concession to the cruder side of Italian *verismo*).

Puccini's greatest triumph of all was to have incorporated arias for three of the principal characters that, far from holding up the action, actually enhance it. It seems entirely appropriate that Mimi and Rodolfo should get to know each other in Act One by exchanging confidences, or that Musetta should attempt to win back Marcello with the 'Waltz Song' in Act Two, and yet these slices of operatic life can work equally well out of the context of the opera as set pieces for singers. In *La Bohème* the balance between drama and display of fine singing is exactly right.

Continued on page 76

Ricordi's famous poster for Tosca: *the diva observes religious decorum over Scarpia's body.*

tosca

WHO'S WHO

FLORIA TOSCA *(Soprano)*
A Famous Prima Donna

MARIO CAVARADOSSI *(Tenor)*
A Painter & Her Lover

BARON SCARPIA *(Baritone)*
Chief of Roman Police

CESARE ANGELOTTI *(Bass)*
A Political Prisoner

SACRISTAN *(Baritone)*

SPOLETTA *(Tenor)*
A Police Official

SCIARRONE *(Bass)*
A Police Agent

GAOLER, SHEPHERD-BOY, CHOIRBOYS, PRIESTS, POLICE AGENTS, SOLDIERS & PEOPLE OF THE CITY

Sardou's highly successful play *La Tosca*, a vehicle for the actress Sarah Bernhardt, was the second subject which Giacosa and Illica turned into a libretto for Puccini. Since its first performance in Rome on 14 January 1900, the opera has had countless stagings, a current favourite being a setting in Rome during the Second World War.

ACT ONE

In what is surely the most exciting curtain-up in all opera, the full orchestra thunders out the three chords of the 'Scarpia motif' – a summing up of the Roman chief-of-police's all-powerful force.

Angelotti, former consul of the ill-fated Roman Republic, rushes into the Church of Sant' Andrea della Valle. Having escaped from prison in the Castel Sant' Angelo, he finds the key to the Attavanti chapel which his sister, the Marchese Attavanti, has hidden for him, and enters the chapel.

Mario Cavaradossi, an artist, has been painting the Marchese as she prayed; he compares the features of the blue-eyed woman with the darker beauty of his lover, the singer Floria Tosca (decidedly uppermost in his thoughts as he sings the aria '*Recondita armo-nia*'). As he does so, the sacristan of the church, who is a fervent royalist, complains about this god-less 'Voltairean dog'. When he has gone, Cavaradossi promises to help Angelotti, but before doing so, has to allay the suspicions of Tosca, whose jealousy is easily aroused by the blue-eyed madonna; her doubts interrupt the course of a long and sensuous love duet.

Angelotti tells Cavaradossi about his sister's help – which explains her attendance in church – and Scarpia is mentioned for the first time in the course of their conversation; Cavaradossi sums him up perfectly as 'a bigoted satyr who, under cover of devout practice, intensifies his lecherous desires'. He tells Angelotti he may use the well in his garden as an emergency hiding-place. The sound of a shot from the castle announces

that the prisoner's escape has been discovered. The sacristan and his choir look forward to celebrating the defeat of Bonaparte; at the height of their merriment Scarpia's motif is heard, announcing his arrival. Searching the chapel, he finds a fan with the Attavanti crest on it and uses it to arouse Tosca's jealousy in the hope that she will lead him to Angelotti's hiding place – much as, he says, Iago used the handkerchief to goad Othello. As the *Te Deum* begins, Scarpia sends three police agents to follow her. Looking forward to sending Cavaradossi to the gallows and taking Tosca in his arms, he joins in the prayers of the congregation in the climax to a fast-moving first act.

ACT TWO

Dining in his room at the Palazzo Farnese (now the French Embassy in Rome), Scarpia waits for Tosca to finish her contribution to the royalist celebrations. His henchman, Spoletta, informs him that although Angelotti could not be found, Cavaradossi has been arrested. We hear Tosca offstage singing in the cantata; then she enters, only to find her lover carried off to the torture-chamber. Cavaradossi's anguished cries break down her resistance: she reveals Angelotti's hiding-place – the well in the garden – to Scarpia. Cavaradossi is dragged in and is

The Yugoslavian-born soprano, Ljuba Welitsch, a popular Tosca at Covent Garden, London.

brutally made to realize that Tosca has betrayed him; but at that moment royalist hopes are overturned with the revelation that Napoleon has triumphed, and Cavaradossi's energy returns in ringing tenor cries of 'Victory!'

Scarpia orders his execution and is left alone with Tosca. She pleads for her lover's life and the Baron suavely names his price: to make love to her. In desperation, she agrees, although not before holding up the action with recriminations against an unkind God in the celebrated aria 'Vissi d'arte'. Scarpia promises Tosca a mock-execution for Cavaradossi, saying significantly to Spoletta 'as we did with Count Palmieri', and grants her two safe-conducts. She notices a knife on the table; as Scarpia moves to embrace her, she stabs him and he falls dying. The closing mime of the act is a replica of Bernhardt's dumb-show in the play: the religious Tosca places a crucifix on the dead man's breast and lights two candles before running out of the room.

ACT THREE

Cavaradossi awaits his execution in the Castel Sant' Angelo. The last stars are in the sky before dawn; a shepherd-boy sings in the distance, the bells of Rome ring out and the prisoner sings of Tosca and his thirst for life in the tragic lament 'E lucevan le stelle' ('The stars were shining'). Tosca arrives with the news of Scarpia's death and the mock-execution. Their last duet is fragmented; Puccini and his librettists suggest that Cavaradossi knows that this is only another of Scarpia's tricks and does his best to preserve the illusion of escape for Tosca's sake.

An eery military march marks the arrival of the firing-squad. The soldiers shoot; Cavaradossi falls to the ground as Tosca cries, 'what an artist!' – he has apparently kept his joking promise to simulate death 'like Tosca in the theatre' – but she soon realizes that the shots were for real and, before Scarpia's police can arrest her, leaps to her death from the castle battlements.

Another plausible update from Jonathan Miller: Cavaradossi, a tortured resistance fighter, is dragged out of Scarpia's office, to the distress of Tosca (Josephine Barstow).

For his next opera, Puccini returned to a subject which had attracted him as early as 1889 (a few months after the first performance of *Edgar*). At that time, the popular French master of the well-crafted melodrama, Victorien Sardou, had not been willing to entrust operatic treatment of his historical shocker, *Tosca*, to a little-known name in Italian music.

Seven years later – after Verdi, of all composers, had considered setting *Tosca* to music and refused, pleading old age and not lack of interest as the reason – the subject reverted to Puccini, Giacosa and Illica. Now it was the composer who had doubts. He told Sardou that he would do better to find a French composer, but the playwright's response was that a Roman theme needed an Italian's touch (interestingly, the Paris of Puccini's *La Bohème* had been praised by Debussy as the most authentic portrayal of the city he knew). Another of the composer's objections was that the impulsive and passionate Tosca was a very different character from the more gentle Manon and Mimi – to which Sardou is supposed to have retorted that 'women in love all belong to the same family'

As it happened, Puccini had no problems with the new realism: scenes of torture, attempted rape and on-stage murder fired him to outdo the *verismo* masters in terms

of musical tears and sweat, though with an almost classical perfectionism, he ensured that the most refined scoring offset the brassier confrontations. *Tosca* is a far more original score in terms of striking orchestral effects than that of the near-contemporary opera *Andrea Chénier* by another follower of the *verismo* school, Umberto Giordano (whose next opera, *Fedora*, was also based on a Sardou play).

TOSCA

Like Sardou, Puccini was concerned to reflect as closely as he could the atmosphere of the June 1800 setting; although he did not include the play's humorous scenes in which Floria Tosca treats with diva-like disdain the composer and music master Paisiello, one of several real historical figures thrown by Sardou into the melodramatic melting-pot.

Typically, Puccini proved a stickler for correctness of background. As a youthful organist in Lucca he had become familiar with the rites of the Roman Catholic Church, yet he still consulted a priest of his acquaintance on a suitable prayer to be murmured by the congregation before the *Te Deum* at the end of Act One, and a campanologist enlightened him on the correct pitches of the Roman bells which sound the call to Matins in the dawn of Act Three.

In other respects, the sophistication of *Tosca* is closer to the works of Wagner than to *verismo*. Puccini's use of leading themes moves away from the mere reminiscence which plays such an important part in the last act of *La Bohème* and closer to the world of Wagnerian leitmotif – though the pace, of course, is faster than in the operas of Wagner.

MADAM BUTTERFLY

For his next opera, *Madam Butterfly* (1904), Puccini attempted something completely new – an eventful first act followed by an intense psychological study of a single character in the second. Like Wagner's Brünnhilde in *Götterdämmerung*, Butterfly waits endlessly for the return of her American husband, using every resource at her disposal to keep hope alive. So her suicide, when she finally learns the truth of her betrayal, approaches genuine tragedy – the only case in Puccini's output where the term can be applied.

The touching geisha girl of the one-act play by David Belasco becomes a tragic heroine through the power and dramatic intensity of Puccini's music. Few sopranos are able to characterize successfully both the teenage child-bride of Act One and the more mature waiting woman of Act Two, but on the other hand, few can fail to

make Butterfly's predicament profoundly moving. For the first time in a Puccini opera, touches of realism (in this case furnished by the American naval presence in Nagasaki in around 1900) rub shoulders with an exotic setting.

Puccini was thorough in his research of authentic Japanese melodies and folk-songs, incorporating several of these into the score (the best-known also appears in Gilbert and Sullivan's *The Mikado*); he was to do the same with Chinese songs in *Turandot*. In *Madam Butterfly* the Japanese element is neatly assimilated into the composer's own personal style, and while it is sometimes used for local colour, there is none of the irritating quaintness found in the novel by John Luther Long which formed the basis of Belasco's play and Puccini's opera. (A typical example is Butterfly's way of talking in the novel: 'I'm mos' bes' happy female woman in Japan – mebby in that whole worl'. What you thing?')

Tosca and *Madam Butterfly* are skilful adaptations of successful plays, and Puccini repeated the formula with another Belasco adaptation, this time for an American audience. The première of *La Fanciulla del West* (*The Girl of the Golden West*) took place at New York's Metropolitan Opera on 10 December 1910, and the demand for seats was so great that

Continued on page 80

Maria Callas

ALTHOUGH SHE CLAIMED THAT SHE FELT LITTLE SYMPATHY FOR THE CHARACTER, TOSCA REMAINED CALLAS' MOST CELEBRATED ROLE, AND TWO FILMS OF THE OPERA'S SECOND ACT REVEAL THE DRAMATIC AND EXPRESSIVE RANGE OF HER CHARACTERIZATION. THE GREEK SOPRANO (BORN IN NEW YORK) COVERED A VERY WIDE REPERTOIRE DURING THE 1940S, WHICH INCLUDED THE ROLES OF BRUNNHILDE, ISOLDE AND TURANDOT; BUT LIKE JOAN SUTHERLAND, SHE MADE HER NAME IN A *BEL CANTO* ROLE, SINGING ELVIRA IN BELLINI'S *I PURITANI* (*THE PURITANS*) IN 1948, A REVELATION IN THE TRUTHFUL FORCE OF THE CHARACTERIZATION. HER TECHNIQUE EXTENDED TO THE ACCURATE EXECUTION OF *COLORATURA* PASSAGES, BUT SHE RIDICULED THE NOTION OF DISPLAY 'FIREWORKS' AND, A GENUINE PERFECTIONIST, ALWAYS TRIED TO BE FAITHFUL TO THE COMPOSER'S TRUE INTENTIONS IN PERFORMANCE – A FAR CRY FROM THE TEMPERAMENTAL, SELF-SERVING DIVA THAT HAS SOMETIMES BEEN SUGGESTED OF HER. AFTER HER RETIREMENT FROM THE STAGE IN 1965, SHE APPEARED IN CONCERTS AND IN 1975 GAVE A SERIES OF MASTERCLASSES AT NEW YORK'S JUILLIARD SCHOOL OF MUSIC, MANY OF THEM BEING MODELS OF GOOD TEACHING AND SOUND ADVICE AS RECORDED FOR POSTERITY. THE DRAMATIC LEGEND OF HER CAREER WAS COMPOUNDED BY HER DEATH IN PARIS IN 1977 AT THE AGE OF 54.

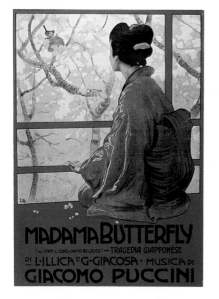

MADAM BUTTERFLY

WHO'S WHO

CIO-CIO-SAN (BUTTERFLY) *(Sop.)*

BENJAMIN FRANKLIN PINKERTON *(Tenor) Lieutenant in U.S. Navy*

SHARPLESS *(Baritone) American Consul at Nagasaki*

SUZUKI *(Mezzo) Butterfly's Servant*

GORO *(Tenor) A Marriage Broker*

THE BONZE *(Bass) Butterfly's Uncle*

PRINCE YAMADORI *(Tenor) A Wealthy Suitor*

KATE *(Mezzo) Pinkerton's Wife*

OFFICIALS, RELATIVES, FRIENDS, SERVANTS & CHILD

The audience's bad

behaviour at the Milan première of *Madam Butterfly*, on 17 February 1904, was supposedly stage-managed by the composer's jealous rivals. He rewrote portions of the opera in time for a successful second performance at Brescia in April of the same year.

ACT ONE

The bustle of Nagasaki is depicted in a vivid prelude, marked '*ruvido*' (rough) in the score. On a hill overlooking the harbour Lieutenant Pinkerton inspects the house that goes with his 'Japanese marriage' to Cio-Cio-San (Madam Butterfly) while the marriage broker, Goro, explains the arrangements.

Sharpless, the consul, arrives and joins Pinkerton in a toast to America (Puccini duly quotes 'The Star-Spangled Banner'). The Lieutenant shares none of his qualms over what this casual marriage might mean to Butterfly; in a duet which is to be recalled with tremendous poignancy towards the end of the opera, when Sharpless' fears have been realized, the tenor ardently proclaims his casual creed and looks forward to marrying a true American wife in the future.

Accompanied by her friends and crowned with a halo of orchestral radiance, Butterfly climbs the hill to the house. She clearly takes the arrangements seriously and has secretly renounced her faith in favour of Pinkerton's; the wedding celebrations take place swiftly and smoothly until the arrival of her uncle, the Bonze, a Buddhist priest. He has discovered Butterfly's conversion to Christianity and commands the assembled family to join him in cursing her. Pinkerton, furious, sends them howling with indignation down the hill.

Slowly and tenderly he calms the anguished Butterfly and the gentle evening music gradually turns into the longest and most opulent of all Puccini love duets.

ACT TWO

Three years have passed. The straitened circumstances of Butterfly's life with her maid Suzuki since Pinkerton's departure are established by the music. Butterfly still believes Pinkerton's promise that he will return 'when the robins nest'. In the first of the great climaxes which demonstrate her strength of will to hope, she vividly imagines his reappearance 'one fine day' ('*Un bel dì*'). As if in confirmation, Sharpless arrives to tell her that Pinkerton's ship is due back in Nagasaki.

He can only deliver half of the lieutenant's message, defeated by Butterfly's wild enthusiasm and the arrival of Goro's latest suitor for her, Prince Yamadori (there is some light comedy in Butterfly's amused rejection of her rich admirer). When Sharpless finally brings himself to intimate to Butterfly that Pinkerton might not return to her, Puccini plays his emotional trump card: Butterfly, indignant, brings in the child that Sharpless and Pinkerton have known nothing about. She tells the consul that he is called Sorrow, but that the day Pinkerton returns, his name will turn to Joy. Butterfly's fury with Goro, caught rumour-mongering that Sorrow has no father, dissolves as a cannon sounds in the harbour, signifying the return of the ship. The orchestra reminds us of 'One fine day' as Butterfly recognizes the ship to be her husband's, and in an ecstatic 'flower duet' she orders Suzuki to fill the room with flowers from the garden. As night falls, she puts on her wedding gown and, with Suzuki and her son beside her, prepares a vigil. The magical 'humming chorus' provides the quiet end to the scene.

Most producers prefer to keep the curtain up during the passionate and initially Wagnerian orchestral interlude that follows, showing Butterfly's hopes and doubts as she sits through the night waiting for Pinkerton. When dawn breaks Suzuki persuades her to go and sleep. Pinkerton and Sharpless arrive; the awful truth of the situation dawns on Suzuki when she sees a strange woman standing in the garden and is told it is Kate, Pinkerton's American wife, who wants to adopt Butterfly's son. A trio gives scope for Pinkerton's overdue remorse before he rushes away, unable to face his victim.

Butterfly has heard voices and rushes in. With great dignity, she manages to control her anguish and agrees to let the child go if Pinkerton will return in half an hour. The death of all her hopes is suggested by bleak chords and long silences. Preparing for suicide, she produces her father's ceremonial sword (inscribed 'to die honourably when one can no longer live honourably') just as Sorrow rushes in. She sings a powerful lament to the child, puts in his hands a doll and an American flag and blindfolds him. Then she goes behind a screen and stabs herself.

The voice of Pinkerton, with his conscience-stricken cries of 'Butterfly!', is heard outside and a brutally inconclusive final chord brings down the curtain.

Diana Soviero as Butterfly arriving for the wedding in the classic Covent Garden production, revived in 1993.

prices were doubled for the second performance. In spite of this, the opera has not achieved the popularity of its predecessors, partly because the orchestral effects are more outstanding than the quality of the vocal writing and partly because the central role proves so difficult to cast. Minnie, the 'girl' of the title, is a curious mixture of the Puccini innocent and the Wagnerian Valkyrie, who has to hurl out top Cs with reckless frequency (her Act-Two duet with the tenor is usually much abridged for that reason). Dick Johnson, the tenor hero, is a kind of Cavaradossi of the wild-west – the 'good guy', even though he is a disguised bandit who woos Minnie under false pretences – and his opponent, Sheriff Jack Rance, turns out to be a transatlantic Scarpia, though Puccini displays a sympathetic understanding of his hard life.

The all-male chorus of Californian gold-diggers shows Puccini at his most advanced in the handling of mob psychology – these homesick miners can be yearning for home one minute and spoiling for blood the next – and the percussive violence of their search for the bandit in Act Three anticipates the sharp edge of *Turandot* (begun 15 years later). The results of his careful study of Strauss' *Salome* and Debussy's *Pelléas and Mélisande* are heard in the opera's endlessly resourceful orchestration.

A TRILOGY

In between the masterly scores of *La Fanciulla del West* and *Turandot*, there were fresh experiments in conjuring new worlds – the faintly charming Parisian operetta, *La Rondine* (*The Swallow*, 1917) and a trilogy (*Il Trittico*) of one-act operas (1918). Here Puccini followed through a scheme along the lines of Dante: the trilogy moves from the Zolaesque inferno of barge-life on the river Seine in *Il Tabarro* (*The Cloak*) – late *verismo* offset by a poetic depiction of Paris' great river – through purgatory in the gentle tale of an errant nun, *Suor Angelica* (*Sister Angelica*) and on to the relative paradise of a Florentine farce, *Gianni Schicchi*.

The dazzling happy ending of the trilogy shows that there was life in the Italian comic opera after *Falstaff*, though to be fair, the cheerful Ermanno Wolf-Ferrari had kept the flame burning with his settings of Goldoni comedies and his delightful *Susanna's Secret*, a one-act period-piece in which a husband suspects his wife of hiding a lover when her only secret vice is smoking (without a hint of health-warning, the pastime is depicted in glowing, sensuous orchestral colours). But *Gianni Schicchi* has it all: a roguish central figure (the character had appeared in Dante's work, in

Luciano Pavarotti

LUCIANO PAVAROTTI BECAME THE BEST-KNOWN SINGER IN THE WORLD WITH THE WORLD CUP PACKAGING OF A FIRM FAVOURITE, THE ARIA 'NESSUN DORMA' ('NONE SHALL SLEEP') FROM *TURANDOT*, ALTHOUGH HE HAD LONG BEEN REGARDED BY OPERA-LOVERS AS THE NATURAL SUCCESSOR TO CARUSO AND GIGLI. HE MADE HIS DÉBUT AS RODOLFO IN *LA BOHÈME* (*THE BOHEMIANS*) AT REGGIO EMILIA, ITALY, IN 1961, AND HIS TENDER, ARDENT TREATMENT OF PUCCINI'S HEROES HAS BEEN A STAPLE OF HIS REPERTOIRE. DRAMATIC VIVIDNESS CAN BE DIFFICULT FOR HIM TO ACHIEVE – HIS OTELLO, RECORDED LIVE IN CONCERT, LACKS INTENSITY – BUT THE GLORIOUSLY RICH QUALITY OF THE VOICE IS USUALLY AMPLE COMPENSATION. HIS RARE APPEARANCES IN LONDON OCCASION RECORD TICKET PRICES.

which he had been consigned to hell for forgery), a pair of sweet lovers (the girl, Lauretta, has the only show-stopping number, 'O mio babbino caro' or 'Oh my beloved father'), and a grotesque gallery of grasping relatives.

TURANDOT

The third part of *Il Trittico* was the first of Puccini's operas to boast a genuinely happy ending; and that was the plan, too, for *Turandot*. Puccini died, however, in 1924, before being able to complete the triumphant final scene of this Chinese fairy-story.

Some critics and producers argue that he simply could not bring himself to write the end of the opera. There is in Puccini's own life a curious parallel with the tale of the ice princess who, in her resolve to avenge the rape of an ancestor, brings about the deaths of many adoring suitors as well as that of the servant girl of the one man who can answer her riddles. In 1909 the persecutions of the composer's insanely jealous wife Elvira resulted in the suicide of his (innocent) maid, Doria Manfredi. The incident preyed deeply on his conscience, as his letters reveal, and some argue that *Turandot* should properly end with the funeral procession of the servant-girl, Liù. Puccini clearly had every intention of finishing *Turandot* in spectacular style. In September 1924 he wrote enthusiastically to Adami, one of his two librettists, that the final confrontation of Turandot and Calaf after the death of Liù 'must be a great duet. These two almost superhuman beings descend through love to the level of mankind, and this love must at the end take possession of the whole stage in a great orchestral peroration'. The following month he received the lines he needed from Adami's collaborator, Simoni: 'they are very beautiful, and they complete and justify the duet'.

A few weeks later, tormented by a throat complaint which was eventually diagnosed as cancer, he travelled to see a specialist in Brussels, taking with him the sketches for the final scene. He died of a heart attack under the strain of the treatment on 24 November. The finale of the opera was completed by his colleague Franco Alfano, but was not performed on the first night (which took place at La Scala, Milan, on 25 April 1926). A reporter from the *Corriere della Sera* gave an eloquent description of the event: 'The opera stopped yesterday at the point where Puccini had had to leave it … The performance, punctuated by frequent applause, ended with a moment of silence, when the little, mangled body of Liù disappeared behind the scenes followed by the procession of the mourning populace … Then, from where he stood as conductor, Toscanini announced in a low voice full of emotion that at that point Puccini had left the composition of the opera. And the curtain was slowly lowered on Turandot … This moment of intense emotion will not be repeated. For at the second performance the opera will be given with the addition of the last duet and the short final scene of which Puccini had merely outlined the music.'

And so it is invariably given today, though Alfano's completion is usually heard in the opera house in an abridged version. It makes a satisfying conclusion to an opera that is full of powerful confrontations. Puccini excelled the dramatic tensions even of *Tosca* in the great scene in Act Two where Turandot sets three riddles for Prince Calaf and he answers them successfully; and there is writing of watercolour-like delicacy for the three courtiers Ping, Pang and Pong, who appear as interested commentators on the action.

'NESSUN DORMA'

Turandot now outstrips even *La Bohème*, *Madam Butterfly* and *Tosca* in the performance stakes by virtue of a single aria. In '*Nessun dorma*' or 'None shall sleep' Puccini remained true to his aims of providing a grateful set piece for one of the leading characters (in this case, the tenor playing Calaf) and furthering the cause of the drama at the same time: in the context of the opera, the aria does not come to a halt to allow for ecstatic applause. It blends beautifully into the slightly sinister nocturne at the beginning of the act and stands as a perfect characterization of Calaf's unquenchable optimism. Even in his last opera the composer maintained a perfect balance between the demands of the singers and the dramatic requirements of his subject matter.

While he remained a romantic at heart, Puccini did not ignore the discoveries of a new generation of composers, and *Turandot* is another step forward in terms of strange, innovative harmonies and exotic, percussive sounds. It completes an impressive line-up of music dramas that are always effective in the opera-house, no matter what the quality of the performance might be.

It is true that Puccini never ranged as far or as widely as Verdi, either in his choice of dramas or in his musical language. Yet he always manages to touch the heart, often by the most subtle and sophisticated means, and his mastery of sentiment is not to be confused with indiscriminate sentimentality. With *Turandot*, the golden age of Italian opera gained an extended lease of life.

Puccini died before having finished the final scene of *Turandot*. At the Milan première, on 25 April 1926, Toscanini laid down his baton at the appropriate moment; the final scene, completed by Franco Alfano, was played at the second performance.

tURANDOT

WHO'S WHO

TURANDOT *(Soprano)*
Princess of Peking

CALAF *(Tenor)*
The Unknown Prince

LIÙ *(Soprano)*
A Slave Girl in His Service

TIMUR *(Bass)*
Calaf's Father & Exiled King of Tartary

THE EMPEROR ALTOUM *(Tenor)*
Turandot's Father

PING, PANG & PONG *(Baritone & Tenors) Turandot's Ministers*

A MANDARIN, GUARDS, EXECUTIONERS, PEOPLE OF PEKING, GHOSTS, WAITING WOMEN & PRIESTS

ACT ONE

The plot of the opera takes place in a legendary China as imagined by the Italian 18th-century playwright Carlo Gozzi, on whose fable the libretto is based.

A Mandarin proclaims that the Prince of Persia, the latest suitor for the hand of Princess Turandot, has failed to guess her riddles and is to be executed. Calaf recognizes his aged, exiled father Altoum in the melée, accompanied by the slave girl Liù, who has risked much for him because Calaf once smiled at her in the palace.

The bloodthirsty crowd is represented by music of startling barbarism and strangeness. In a highly rhythmic and percussively scored chorus, it encourages the executioner to turn his grindstone; then the mood changes to stillness in anticipation of the rising moon.

Calaf is horrified by the execution of the Prince of Persia, but immediately spellbound by the majestic appearance of Turandot. Neither the princess' comic ministers Ping, Pang and Pong, in a sprightly interlude, nor Liù, with her exquisite aria of entreaty, '*Signore, ascolta*' ('Listen, my lord'), can dissuade him – though his reply to the slave-girl is touching and tender ('*Non piangere, Liù*' – 'Do not cry, Liù'). A powerful ensemble builds, at the height of which Calaf rushes forward and strikes the gong three times in readiness for his trials.

ACT TWO

Ping, Pang and Pong reflect on the good times in China before Turandot's bloodthirsty reign and sing nostalgically of the country

residences they will never see again (many a young baritone has made his mark with Ping's solo about his house in Honan). The scene changes to a vast square before the palace. The frail old Emperor unsuccessfully begs Calaf to reconsider. Then, after a dramatic silence, Turandot sings for the first time. She explains ('*In questa reggia*' – 'In this palace') how her actions are a response to the rape and murder of her ancestress Princess Lo-u-Ling; no man shall ever possess her. 'The riddles are three, death is one', she cries, and Calaf, raising the pitch exultantly, responds: 'the riddles are three, life is one'.

The ritual begins. Turandot tensely asks the three questions. What is the phantom invoked by the world, constantly renewed? What flickers like a flame when you dream of conquest? What ice gives fire and makes you a king when it accepts you as a slave? Calaf responds with a confidence inspired by love: Hope, Blood and Turandot are the three answers.

Horrified, Turandot pleads with her father not to give her away like a slave and asks the prince if he wants to take her by force. Calaf, hoping to win her heart, sets her a riddle: if she discovers his name before dawn – a forewarning of the music of '*Nessun dorma*' appears in the orchestra – he will agree to die.

Placido Domingo's Calaf resolves to win Turandot's hand as the Emperor Timur and Liù look on (Covent Garden, 1984).

ACT THREE

In the balmy night, the voices of the heralds resound: 'None shall sleep in Peking tonight'. *'Nessun dorma'*, echoes Calaf, taking over the dreamy orchestral melody with renewed ardour as he looks forward to Turandot's yielding. Immediately, Ping, Pang and Pong are on the scene, pleading with the Prince to give up his quest and to avert the princess' promise of mass bloodshed; they offer him women and jewels in vain. 'Though the skies fall I will have Turandot,' he declares – but then Timur and Liù are dragged in. They were seen talking to the Prince, and torture will surely force them to reveal his name. Liù admits that she knows it, but will never reveal it. The princess, amazed at Liù's power to resist the pain that is inflicted on her asks what gives her such courage. Puccini hints that the ice princess might be melting a little. 'It is love,' Liù explains in two heart-felt arias; at the end of the second she kills herself.

The music of her funeral procession is of the utmost tenderness, and Puccini only scored the opera up to this point. Alfano's completion of the final duet works well and proves exciting enough on stage: Turandot yields to Calaf's kiss, and he puts himself in her power by telling her his name. Before the assembled populace, she declares that she knows the name: it is Love. To a blaze of choral and orchestral light, there is general rejoicing.

Dame Gwyneth Jones as the Ice Princess in Andrei Serban's Covent Garden production (1984), with designs by Sally Jacobs.

CHAPTER 6

French Opera and Operetta

The contrasts of French opera – or rather opera in French, since so many of the notable contributors were outsiders – are extreme. They range from the huge crowd scenes and balletic spectacle of Meyerbeer's extravaganzas for the Paris Grand Opéra to the gentle lyricism of Gounod and the pleasure-seeking satires of Offenbach's operettas. While the demands of the audiences at the Opéra were clearcut – anything long, lavish and loud – the form of *opéra comique* with its spoken dialogue provides examples as diverse as Cherubini's *Medea*, Bizet's *Carmen* and Offenbach's only 'serious' opera, *The Tales of Hoffmann*. In 1902 operatic history was made with the first performance of an opera that was quite unlike anything that had been written before – Debussy's *Pelléas and Mélisande*.

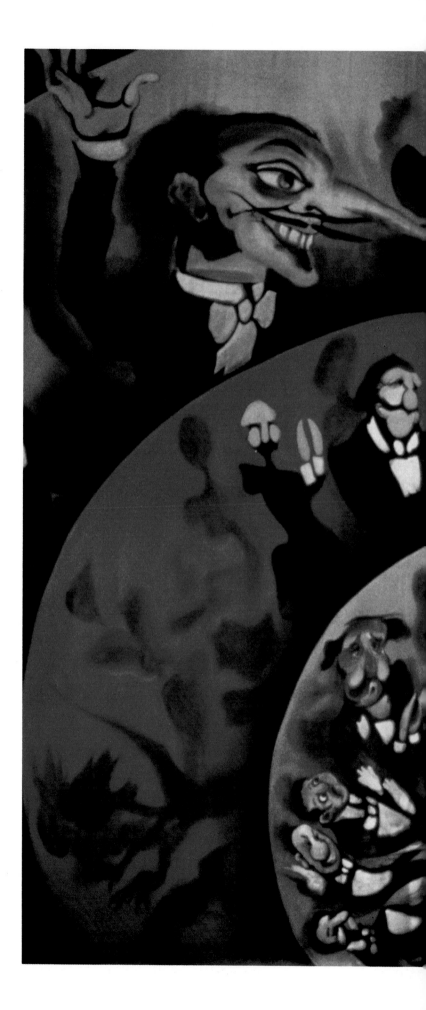

Orpheus fiddles against one of Gerald Scarfe's many dazzling backdrops in the 1985 English National Opera production of Offenbach's Orpheus in the Underworld.

Maquette's design for an invitation to an open rehearsal of Berlioz's The Trojans, *c.1900.*

Académie Nationale de Musique et de Danse

⊚ ⊚ ⊚

RÉPÉTITION GÉNÉRALE

DE

LES TROYENS

Poême et Musique de Hector BERLIOZ

M

Le Directeur,

Never did so many different styles of opera jostle for attention as in Paris during the 19th century. First, there was grand opera, which was established in 1807 by the Italian Spontini with his drama of ancient Rome, *La Vestale* (a statuesque precursor of Bellini's *Norma* that was much admired by Wagner), and taken to its lengthiest, most extravagant heights as a recognizably French art by the German Meyerbeer in the 1830s.

Then there were the genres known as *opéra comique* and *opéra lyrique*. The first was not comic opera, but music drama with spoken dialogue that allowed for a more literary and (eventually) more realistic treatment; and the second was a graceful and elegant compromise between grand opera and *opéra comique*.

Last, but not least, there was *opéra bouffe*, perfected in the late 1850s and early 1860s by Jacques Offenbach, and accepted as pure French naughtiness.

Although several of these operatic variants existed side by side, the form they took was very much dictated by events in French history. And so, when the 'grande bourgeoisie' of the second empire took over the reins of France from Charles X in 1830, grand opera changed; from the hymn to individual liberty that Rossini had made it in his operatic swansong *William Tell*, it turned into a novel art-form, a kind of mighty synthesis which could move the middle classes. That, at least, was how Meyerbeer's *Robert le Diable* (*Robert the Devil*) was perceived at its first performance on 21 November 1831. 'Only when the great choruses of *Robert le Diable* or *Les Huguenots* roared harmonically, rejoiced harmonically, sobbed harmonically, did men's hearts hearken and sob and rejoice and roar in inspired accord,' wrote the German poet Heine, adding that Meyerbeer 'is the man of the epoch, and the epoch, which always knows how to choose its man...celebrates in him its joyous domination.'

In fact Meyerbeer, the son of a German-Jewish banker, turned out to be both a blessing and a bane for the next generation of composers. His structural grasp of the monumental historical sagas provided by the librettist Eugène Scribe was episodic and his inspiration across the long operatic span demanded by the public of the Paris Grand Opéra was fitful. Yet his edifices undeniably contributed to the development of grand opera, with its Shakespearean possibilities for conflict between private conscience and public ceremony, and Verdi's *Don Carlos* (1867) would never have been possible without Meyerbeer.

Both Wagner and Berlioz admired the orchestration, the harmonies and the gigantic forms of *Les Huguenots* (1836), which undoubtedly features Meyerbeer's most powerful music – above all in the fourth-act scene where the Catholic forces swear loyalty to their cause in the forthcoming massacre of the Huguenots.

Moments like these make it clear why Meyerbeer was regarded with awe by his contemporaries and why the young Bizet could talk of him in the same breath as Mozart and Beethoven, claiming that 'Meyerbeer feels as Michelangelo felt.' As the century progressed, however, tastes changed and support for Meyerbeer waned. Wagner looked back on his early enthusiasm with embarrassment, writing to Schumann in 1843 that he didn't know 'what "Meyerbeerish" signifies except a cunning angling for shallow popularity.' And Tchaikovsky, temporarily setting aside the themes of grand opera in the late 1870s for the novel intimacy of *Eugene Onegin*, summed up his feelings on *L'Africaine*, which was Meyerbeer's last opera and ran to six hours at its first performance in 1865, a year after the death of the composer: 'Unfortunate woman! Slavery, a dungeon, death under the poison tree, and the victory of her rival in her final moments – all this is her lot, and yet I did not feel sorry for her at all. And, incidentally, there are stage effects as well: a ship, fights, the whole bag of tricks!'

Such circumstances make it difficult for present-day audiences to accept anything but ironic interpretations of these operas, which is a pity for Meyerbeer's music.

BERLIOZ & GOUNOD

There is, however, one truly grand French opera which survives in the present repertoire: Berlioz's *The Trojans*. Berlioz's aims have been vindicated by time: he wanted to return to the classical world of Gluck, to present noble, heroic characters and their predicaments once more on the French stage rather than mass spectacle, albeit within a form that is the equal in length of a Meyerbeer opera.

Yet Berlioz had great difficulty in finding Parisian acceptance for his powerful adaptation of episodes from Virgil's epic *Aeneid*. Eventually it was the Théâtre Lyrique, patently less well-endowed than the official Opéra or Opéra Comique theatres, which offered some sort of compromise: it would stage the last three of *The Trojans'* five acts as a separate drama of Aeneas' journey to Carthage after the sack of Troy (the subject of the first two acts) and his ill-fated relationship with Dido. Berlioz never lived to see a complete performance of his operatic masterpiece, though he had reason to be grateful to the Théâtre Lyrique.

It was this opera house which did the most to encourage native talent in the face of the Grand Opéra's ostentatious courtship of German and Italian composers. The Théâtre Lyrique had hosted the success of Gounod's *Faust* in 1859. Although light-years away from the atmosphere of Goethe's classic – captured with outrageous modernism by Berlioz in his 'dramatic legend' *The Damnation of Faust* – Gounod's pretty turn of melody and pastel shades distilled the essence of Goethe's story for public consumption, and *Faust* remains one of the most popular operas in the world. The Théâtre Lyrique went on to stage three more Gounod operas – *Philémon and Baucis* (1860), *Mireille* (1864) and *Romeo and Juliet* (1867). Only selected arias from these operas receive regular airings today.

For all its enterprise, the Théâtre Lyrique was outlived by the Opéra Comique, which was established in 1715 as a home for the French version of opera that featured spoken dialogue. The contributions to this genre were remarkably diverse and the flow of inspiration seems to have lasted until the 1890s. No *opéra comique* is further from our assumption that the word *'comique'* must at least embrace concepts of French lightness, than the Italian composer Cherubini's full-blooded Greek tragedy *Medea* (1797).

The status of *opéra comique* as a worthy artistic enterprise was confirmed around this time by Beaumarchais, who complained that at the Opéra, 'fed up at not hearing the words, the audience turns towards the music', which in turn 'gives way to interest in the ballets', and by Goldoni, who proclaimed the immortal truth that 'it is better to hear a well-delivered dialogue than to suffer the monotony of a tedious recitative.'

Nowadays it is all too rare to hear 'a well-delivered dialogue' as Opéra Comique audiences would have enjoyed it, one reason why we rarely see productions of such early-19th-century charmers as Boieldieu's *La Dame Blanche* (*The White Lady*, 1825) or Auber's *Le Domino Noir* (*The Black Domino*, 1837) – though this also exists in a version with recitatives by Tchaikovsky, of all composers, replacing the spoken dialogue.

Auber, like Meyerbeer, wrote epics for the Grand Opéra as well as lighter pieces for the Opéra Comique: the effect of his earnest revolutionary study *La Muette de Portici* (*The Dumb Girl of Portici*) sparked off the Belgian rebellion against the Dutch in 1830. Yet his best music is to be found in the dancing arias and sparkling ensembles of his *opéra comiques*. *Le Domino Noir* deserves to be remembered for more than its charming overture; the sentimental

Continued on page 90

CARMEN

WHO'S WHO

CARMEN *(Soprano/Mezzo)*
A Gypsy

DON JOSÉ *(Tenor)*
A Corporal

MICAELA *(Soprano)*
A Country Girl

ESCAMILLO *(Baritone)*
A Toreador

FRASQUITA & MERCÉDÈS
(Sopranos)
Carmen's Gypsy Friends

DANCAIRO & REMENDADO
(Tenors) Smugglers

ZUNIGA *(Bass) A Lieutenant*

MORALES *(Baritone) A Corporal*

SOLDIERS, SUITORS, CIGARETTE GIRLS, PEOPLE OF SEVILLE, PICADORS & MATADORS

The lukewarm reception of *Carmen* during its first run of performances at the Paris Opéra Comique in March 1875 and the hostility of the critics are thought to have been a contributory factor to Bizet's early death. He did not live to learn of the opera's success in Vienna in October of that year; it has been popular ever since.

The prelude features music that recurs in Act Four, when the crowd is anticipating the bullfight, and the theme of Escamillo's 'Toreador Song'. A dramatic motif against tremolo strings presents Carmen as a *femme fatale*.

ACT ONE

Soldiers idly observe life in a Seville square. Micaela appears, looking for Don José; Morales tells her he is due to arrive with the next company. The changing of the guard takes place, and as the bell of the cigarette factory signals the time to start work, the girls gather, flirting with the local men. Carmen is the centre of attention, declaring seductively in the *Habanera* that she will love the man who does not love her. She throws a flower to the apparently indifferent Don José as her theme resounds for the first time within the opera.

José's confusion is diverted by the return of Micaela, who shyly passes on a letter and a kiss from his mother back in Navarre. The sweet purity of their duet contrasts with the violent scene that follows: Carmen has drawn a knife in a factory quarrel, and Zuniga orders José to guard her arrest. She persuades him to release her: they will meet at Lillas Pastia's tavern, she promises to the vibrant strains of a *Seguidilla*. José lets her escape and is himself arrested.

ACT TWO

Carmen and her friends entertain tavern customers with gypsy song and dance. Escamillo arrives with a tremendous following and captivates Carmen with his narrative of a bullfighter's life (the 'Toreador Song', a perfect character-study). Yet she is – for the moment – 'in love' with Don José, and when the smugglers Dancairo and Remendado announce that they need her along with Frasquita and Mercédès for business, she tells them in a featherlight Quintet that she cannot yet join them.

José arrives fresh from prison and Carmen dances to the accompaniment of distant bugles sounding the retreat. She taunts him for preparing to return to his barracks and he reveals the depths of his love in the exquisite 'Flower Song'. If he really loves her, she retorts, he will join her in a free mountain life. Zuniga makes an untimely appearance. His confrontation with José is interrupted by the smugglers and José realizes he has no choice but to leave with Carmen and her friends.

ACT THREE

Flute and harp lead the second of the orchestral *entr'actes*, an idyllic calm before the storm. Up in the mountains, Carmen has already tired of José and fatalistically accepts that he may kill her. The

Act One: A square in Seville. Set design by Bertin for a 1950s production in Paris.

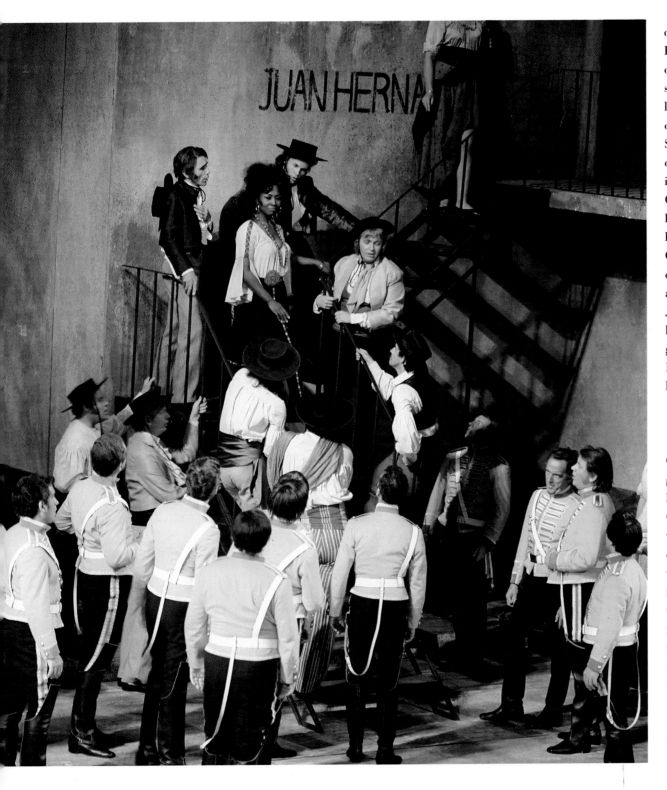

cards which spell good fortune for Frasquita and Mercédès signal only death for her. Micaela has shown much bravery in coming to look for José and her aria is a sign of strength, not mere prettiness. She hides as José, guarding the contraband, shoots at a newcomer; it is Escamillo, who is pursuing Carmen now that she has tired of her soldier. The two men fight with knives, but are interrupted by Carmen, and Escamillo leaves with dignity. Micaela is discovered and announces that she has come to tell José, the man she once loved, that his mother is dying. Despairing, he goes with her while in the distance Escamillo, as if in mockery, sings his signature-tune.

Carmen (Shirley Verrett) is surrounded by admirers on the steps of the cigarette factory, at Covent Garden, London (1973).

ACT FOUR

Outside the bullring a crowd has gathered to watch the procession, headed by Escamillo with a radiant Carmen on his arm. Her friends warn Carmen that José is in the crowd, but she resolves to face him while everyone goes in to watch the fight. José's pleading is in vain. Goaded by her declaration of love for Escamillo as cheering is heard inside the arena and by the contempt with which she throws his ring in his face, he stabs her. As the crowd emerges from the arena and Carmen's motif is heard on full orchestra, he announces that he has killed the woman he adores.

escapism of its plot is, perhaps, another reason for its neglect, and it is certainly typical of the times.

After the Revolution of 1848, the fashion changed to more literary subjects, but the treatments were not necessarily sympathetic to their sources. Berlioz's *Beatrice and Benedict* is a mockery of Shakespeare's *Much Ado about Nothing*, the play on which it was based, but it nonetheless contains three of the most ravishing pieces in the whole of French opera.

Jacques Offenbach was a remarkably late and unexpected convert to the art of *opéra comique*. He died in 1880 with, as he had predicted, 'a tune on the tip of my pen'; but it was not the frivolous tune of the operettas with which he had made his name.

OFFENBACH

A German Jew, like Meyerbeer, he came to Paris to study and first earned his living as a virtuoso cellist. In 1855 he opened his own theatre, the tiny Bouffes Parisiens, and struck gold. His luck as well as his inspiration lasted for more than a decade: the spirit of the age in the Paris of Napoleon III was bent on pleasure, and crowds flocked to enjoy the fresh air of Offenbach's operettas, which combined biting satire with sensuous wit. The first of these was *Orpheus in the Underworld* (1858), partly a reac-

tion to what the composer saw as the frigid classical poses of Gluck, and it was followed by another mythological spoof in which the can-can gave way to French-style waltzing, *La belle Hélène* (1867).

After *The Grand-Duchess of Gerolstein* and *La Périchole* (two of many operettas that came effortlessly off the compositional production line), Offenbach's days as 'the Mozart of the boulevards' were over: with the advent of the Commune in 1870 Paris was no longer the place for such frivolity. Later, he returned to writing operettas, but only as a means of making money while he worked, slowly but surely, on the *opéra comique* that he regarded as his bid for immortality. It was based on three tales by E. T. A. Hoffmann, and Offenbach and his librettists, Barbier and Carré, had the idea of linking the tales with a portrait of the poet as a frequenter of taverns, who recalls three of his lost loves to the assembled company. In his music for the tale of Olympia, the mechanical doll, and, up to a point, in his depiction of the supernatural sensuousness of Hoffmann's infatuation with the Venetian courtesan Giulietta, the composer remained close to the spirit of his operettas. It was with the story of the consumptive Antonia that he scaled the operatic heights with a trio to match Gounod's prison scene from *Faust*.

Offenbach did not miss the parallels between Antonia's melodrama and the fact that he, too, was living on borrowed time as he worked on *The Tales of Hoffmann*. He died four months before the opera's première in February 1881, leaving instructions for the orchestration of the unfinished sections. There was no real excuse for the haphazard presentation at the Opéra Comique, which substituted tedious recitative (not by Offenbach) for much of the spoken dialogue, cut the 'Giulietta' act and transported Antonia from Munich to Venice for the sake of the famous Barcarolle. It has since been proved possible to present *Hoffmann* close to Offenbach's original intentions, but unauthentic hybrids still crop up in many of the world's great opera houses.

CARMEN

On 3 March 1875, six years before the first performance of *The Tales of Hoffmann*, the Opéra Comique gave the première of the first French opera truly to shake the world, if not (at the time) the complacency of the greater part of the Parisian press. Many of the comments make the critical response to Puccini's *La Bohème* in 1896 – another celebrated case of opinion made foolish by the passing of time – seem positively mild. 'Certainly no one will accuse M. Bizet of

melodic prodigality,' wrote Oscar Comettant, in *Le Siècle*. 'I do not mean to say that there are not what are called themes in M. Bizet's music. Unfortunately, as a rule, they are anything but original and they lack distinction.' Others complained about 'this inferno of ridiculous and uninteresting corruption.' The opera, of course, was *Carmen*, and its reception by an audience that was expecting wholesome family entertainment surpassed even the indignant furore over the violent novella by Prosper Mérimée on which, with a fair amount of concession to operatic taste, it was based. Ironically, only the whiff of immorality kept *Carmen* running for a further 45 performances, as well as the fact that Bizet died suddenly, deeply disillusioned, on the night of the 33rd performance. It is amazing that he managed to complete the few operas that he did, given his fierce self-criticism and his consciousness of having to strike a balance between instinct (represented, he thought, by Italian genius) and intellect (exemplified for him by the Germans). He projected, began or half-finished no fewer than 19 operas or operettas as a result. Yet it is also deeply ironic that the two most popular of his seven finished stage works, *The Pearl Fishers* (1863) and *Carmen*, were criticized at the time of their first performances for their 'Wagnerisms' – a cliché used by the French wherever they suspected the use of academic procedures. Bizet's technique was refined, but never at the expense of direct lyrical expression.

Carmen succeeded in Vienna later that year, but with recitatives in place of the *opéra-comique* dialogue – a practice swiftly condemned by Saint-Saëns. Tchaikovsky saw the opera in Paris in 1876 and, according to his brother, had rarely been so deeply moved by a stage performance. The most perceptive of critics, he was one of the first to praise the very French elegance with which Bizet treated a subject from contemporary life, without trivializing the theme: '...I know of nothing in music which has a better right to stand for the element which I call the pretty, *le joli*. It is...delightful from beginning to end, there are plenty of piquant harmonies and completely new combinations of sounds, but that is not the exclusive aim; Bizet is an artist who pays due tribute to his age and his times, but he is fired with inspiration.' Tchaikovsky was a better judge than the snipers at the first performance. 'I am convinced,' he wrote in 1879, 'that in ten years or so *Carmen* will be the most popular opera in the world'. Of course, he was right.

However profound an impact the savage drama of *Carmen* may have had upon the younger generation of operatic 'realists' in Italy,

Continued on page 94

José Carreras

A HANDSOME, AUTHENTICALLY SPANISH DON JOSÉ AND THE MOST CONVENTIONALLY PASSIONATE OF THE 'THREE TENORS', CARRERAS' BRILLIANT CAREER AS AN ARDENT EXPONENT OF VERDI AND PUCCINI CAME TO A HALT WITH HIS MUCH-PUBLICIZED FIGHT AGAINST LEUKAEMIA. THE TURNING-POINT IN HIS CAREFUL RETURN TO THE STAGE CAME IN 1992, WHEN HE CHAMPIONED A RARELY-PERFORMED VERDI OPERA, *STIFFELIO*, WITH RENEWED VOCAL ARDOUR. HE MADE HIS PROFESSIONAL DÉBUT IN 1956 AS A BOY TREBLE IN BARCELONA'S TEATRO DEL LICEO, SINGING IN THE SPANISH COMPOSER MANUEL DE FALLA'S *MASTER PETER'S PUPPET SHOW* AND FOLLOWING THE TOYSELLER IN THE CAFÉ MOMUS ACT OF PUCCINI'S *LA BOHÈME* (*THE BOHEMIANS*). 21 YEARS LATER HE HAD PROGRESSED TO THE ROLE OF RODOLFO IN THE OPERA AND WAS SINGING ON THE STAGE OF LA SCALA, MILAN.

Mary Garden, the first Mélisande, in a classic pose for the journal Le Théâtre *at the time of the opera's première in 1902.*

Debussy chose to adopt Maeterlinck's symbolist drama with very few alterations. The opera has been staged more than 500 times at the Opéra Comique in Paris since its first performance there on 30 April 1902, with the Scottish soprano Mary Garden singing the role of Mélisande.

PELLÉAS ET MÉLISANDE

WHO'S WHO

PELLÉAS *(Tenor/High Baritone) Son of Arkel & Half-brother of Golaud*

MÉLISANDE *(Soprano)*

GOLAUD *(Baritone)*

ARKEL *(Bass) King of Allemonde*

GENEVIÈVE *(Mezzo/Contralto) Mother of Pelléas & Golaud*

YNIOLD *(Treble/Soprano) Golaud's Son by His First Marriage*

A PHYSICIAN, SERVANTS & VOICES OF NATURE

ACTS ONE & TWO

Musically and dramatically, the opera begins shrouded in mystery. Golaud, lost while hunting, finds a maiden weeping by a forest spring. She begs him not to touch her and evades many of his questions. Maeterlinck (and Dukas in his opera *Ariadne and Bluebeard*) later provided the explanation that she was one of Bluebeard's wives who had escaped, but during the course of the opera nothing is learnt of her past life. In a trance-like state the girl, who finally gives her name as Mélisande, agrees to leave with Golaud.

In the castle, Geneviève reads out to her father-in-law, Arkel, a letter from Golaud (her son by her first marriage) to Pelléas (her son by her second husband). The relationships are complicated: both husbands were sons of Arkel and therefore brothers. Golaud wants to bring his enigmatic new wife, Mélisande, by ship to Allemonde, but fears Arkel will disapprove; if the news is good, Pelléas is to shine a light from the tower and he will return home. Pelléas enters: he wants to visit a dying friend, but Arkel says that his sick father (who remains unseen throughout the opera) needs his attentions here.

The third scene is a garden by the sea. Golaud and Mélisande have returned; she finds the castle and its surrounding forest gloomy. With Pelléas and Geneviève she watches the ship that brought her depart on a stormy sea. Pelléas says he is probably leaving Allemonde on the following day, and Mélisande shows the first signs of curiosity towards Pelléas when she asks him why he must go away.

At the beginning of Act Two Pelléas and Mélisande talk inconsequentially by a well in the park. Mélisande plays carelessly with Golaud's wedding ring and it falls into the well. What should they tell Golaud? The truth, Pelléas replies, as the music lightens again. But the childlike pair have not reckoned with Golaud's fury when he sees

no ring on Mélisande's finger. Frightened, she lies to him that she lost it in a grotto by the sea, and Golaud sends her with Pelléas to retrieve it. Debussy conjures the seascape and the moonlit magic of the cave where she must pretend to have lost the ring; the mood changes when Mélisande is frightened by three old beggars, victims of famine, asleep in the cave, and she hurriedly leaves with Pelléas.

ACT THREE

Mélisande sings as she combs her long hair in a window of the tower. Pelléas passes and asks her to let her hair out of the window; as she does so, their music becomes more sensuous. Golaud has been watching in the shadows and rebukes the behaviour of these 'children'. His underlying menace is confirmed as he leads Pelléas to the castle vaults and terrifies him with their atmosphere; light enters the score again as they emerge on to a terrace. Golaud explicitly asks Pelléas not to fool with Mélisande; she is about to become a mother, and the slightest excitement might harm her.

An extraordinary scene ensues, the first to vindicate one conductor's claim that the opera is not so much veiled symbolist drama as theatre of cruelty. Golaud uses his little son to spy on his half-brother and his wife. He lifts Yniold on to his shoulders and the child, looking into Mélisande's room, tells him that she and Pelléas are looking silently at the light. His father's jealous questioning terrifies Yniold, who begs to be let down.

ACTS FOUR & FIVE

Pelléas must leave the castle now that his father's health has improved, but he arranges first to meet Mélisande that evening in the park. The confidence of Arkel – who is symbolically blind to events around him – in a happy outcome for Mélisande is demolished by Golaud's savage treatment of her as he pulls her round the room by her hair in a fit of jealousy worthy of Othello.

In the park, Yniold is trying to lift a heavy stone when a shepherd leads his sheep across the back of the stage; they are silent, he explains, because 'this is not the way to the stable'. The image of lambs to the slaughter makes an ominous preface to the last meeting of Pelléas and Mélisande and is often overlooked when producers cut this enigmatic scene. Pelléas waits anxiously for Mélisande, and when she arrives they declare their love for the first and only time; Debussy avoids operatic convention by setting their expressions of 'I love you' unaccompanied.

They realize that Golaud is watching them again and embrace in desperation before he steps forward to strike Pelléas down. Mélisande flees in terror.

Time has passed when Act Five begins. Mélisande has given birth to a daughter and may be dying. The tranquillity is again broken by Golaud, who hounds her to her grave, brutally demanding to know the truth about her relationship with Pelléas. Mélisande passes away without another word. Arkel remarks that she died as mysteriously as she lived and comments, to music of infinite sadness, that her newborn child must now take her place.

The wintry atmosphere of Arkel's kingdom suggested by Jean-Pierre Ponnelle's stark designs in his production for Bavarian State Opera in 1973.

A rare staging of Berlioz's 'dramatic cantata', The Damnation of Faust, with suitably fantastical designs by Ernest Klausz (1932).

its influence on French composers was limited to Gustave Charpentier and his turn-of-the-century hymn to free love in Paris, *Louise* (1900). Exoticism remained the order of the day immediately after *Carmen*. *Samson and Delilah*, the only one of Saint-Saëns' twelve operas to retain a place in the repertoire, is a bold but unfortunately chaste attempt at biblical eroticism; Delilah's famous aria *'Mon cœur s'ouvre à ta voix'* ('My heart melts at the sound of your voice') is un-characteristically sensuous. There is real charm, though, in the Anglo-Indian conflict of Delibes' *Lakmé* (1883); this time the three love-duets and several of the en-sembles are as memorable and tuneful as the best-known number, the 'Bell Song' for coloratura soprano. Delibes was beaten in the Indian stakes by Jules Massenet, who scored his first major success with a five-act spectacular, *Le Roi de Lahore* (*The King of Lahore*) in 1877 at the Paris Opéra.

This performance marked the starting-point of Massenet's ascen-dancy. He was a prolific composer of operas, but although his choice of subjects ranged widely – from the noble chivalry of *Le Cid* to a one-act experiment in the art of *verismo*, *La Navarraise* (*The Girl from Navarre*) – he invariably plied what his fellow-composer Vincent d'Indy described as a 'dis-creet and semi-religious eroticism'.

It is overtly religious, perhaps, in *Thaïs*, the tale of a courtesan seeking God, and *Hérodiade*, a pre-Straussian, pre-Oscar Wildean foray into the story of Salomé and John the Baptist. This element is there, too, in *Manon*, Massenet's often passionate setting of the Abbé Prévost's novel, but is lacking (at least until a very late stage) in the only other of Massenet's operas to be staged regularly – *Werther*.

Werther is hardly the best of Massenet, but his delicate humour shines in a magically extended treatment of the Cinderella story, *Cendrillon* – a gently romantic contrast to the enlightened realism of Rossini's *La Cenerentola* – and, to a lesser degree, in *Chérubin* (1905), which follows up the libidinous adventures of Mozart's (as opposed to Beaumarchais') Cherubino. His richest, most fascinating and at the same time most pretentious work is *Esclarmonde* (1889), a dazzling farrago of medieval romance and supernatural extravaganza, which blends thundering imitations of Wagner with elements of Berlioz and late Verdi. *Esclarmonde* is stocked with those supple, flexible and typically French tunes in which Massenet and Delibes excelled, and which went, justifiably, by the generic term of '*mélodie éternelle*'.

The Wagnerization of which Bizet had stood accused in 1877 was now a reality. Some composers, such as Chabrier in *Le Roi malgré lui* (*King in spite of himself*, 1887), incorporated echoes of *Tristan and Isolde* effortlessly into a light-hearted context; others, like Massenet in *Esclarmonde* and Chausson in *King Arthur*, were perceived as having sold themselves down the road to Bayreuth.

In 1889 a young composer and pupil of Massenet, Claude Debussy, undertook the pilgrimage to Bayreuth and was deeply impressed by what he heard. Nonetheless, he conceived 'a different dramatic form in which music begins at the point where speech is powerless in expression; music is made for the inexpressible,' as he told his professor at the Paris Conservatoire, Ernest Guiraud. Debussy's ideal poet for an operatic subject was 'one who, saying things by halves, would allow me to graft my dream on to his; who could conceive characters whose story and background belonged to no time or place, who would not despotically impose on me the scene to be painted, and who would leave me free, here and there, to have more art than him and complete his work.'

Three years later, he discovered that ideal poet when he read the play *Pelléas et Mélisande* by Maurice Maeterlinck, a Belgian symbolist writer; yet it was not until 1902 that the opera based on the play finally reached the stage.

However revolutionary Debussy's setting of the text, in which the characters were to 'try to sing like natural persons and not in an arbitrary language based on antiquated traditions', he had not been able to escape the influence of Wagner in his use of mysterious orchestral leading-motives for the principal characters.

The première of *Pelléas*, which was another epoch-making event for the Opéra Comique, established it as a popular hit: by all accounts, it was not presented in the fey, bloodless style that some productions affect today and the role of Mélisande had two robust interpreters in Mary Garden and her successor Maggie Teyte. Young composers came to see the opera night after night, among them Maurice Ravel, who put Debussy's principles of natural declamation to good use in his song-cycle *Shéhérazade* (1903). One immediate sequel or 'pre-quel', since it touches on Mélisande's earlier history as a tormented wife of Bluebeard, was Dukas' *Ariadne and Bluebeard* (1907), but it is a less subtle work and *Pelléas* proved inimitable. After the First World War it was left to Ravel in his surprisingly profound one-act opera about a naughty child, *L'Enfant et les Sortilèges* (1925) and to Roussel in one of the last flourishings of exoticism, *Padmavati*, to plead the uses of enchantment.

Act Two of Siegfried *in the famous English-language production of Wagner's Ring cycle at the London Coliseum: the scheming Nibelung brothers Alberich (Derek Hammond Stroud) and Mime (Gregory Dempsey) in the forest.*

*N*ORTHERN EUROPEAN TRADITION

The dawn of romanticism in Germany gave rise to the supernatural horrors of
Weber's Der Freischütz *and the fervent hymn to freedom of Beethoven's* Fidelio.
The natural successors were Wagner, with his manifesto of opera as
music drama, and Richard Strauss, who followed savage turn-of-the-century
tragedy with comedies of manners. In Russia Glinka blazed a trail with
a patriotic kind of romanticism.

The operatic fairy-tale extravagance of Wagner's patron, King Ludwig II of Bavaria: view of Hohenschwangau Castle, with the even more fantastical Neuschwanstein Castle in the distance. Picture postcard, produced c.1910.

CHAPTER 7

German Romantic Opera

The most powerful German opera of the early 19th century, Beethoven's *Fidelio*, was an international hybrid of the enlightened nobility of Mozart on the one hand and the French operas of Cherubini, with their tales of wrongful imprisonment and dramatic rescue, on the other. It was not until Weber's *Der Freischütz* (*The Freeshooter*) that the concept of a specifically German work came into being. It is the first nationalist opera, and Weber's simple melodies achieved the status of folk-songs. He was also an archetypally romantic composer in his love of the supernatural: whereas *Fidelio* is an Age-of-Enlightenment hymn to liberty, the 'Wolf's Glen' scene of *Der Freischütz* makes the flesh creep in true romantic fashion.

Mozart and Beethoven appear to us as geniuses from different centuries – which, in a sense, they are: Mozart composed his masterpieces in the decade before his untimely death in 1791, whereas the turning-point for Beethoven was the first performance of his Symphony No. 1 on 2 April 1800. Within a couple of years he was to change the shape and scope of compositional ambition, paving the way for Wagner with the huge structures of the *Eroica* Symphony and the 17-minute long overture to *Leonore*, the first version of the opera we know as *Fidelio*. (The overture exists in two versions, following a shorter prototype which was discarded before the première but is still sometimes played in the concert-hall today.)

Yet Mozart and Beethoven did coincide, personally as well as musically. When the 17-year-old Beethoven travelled from Bonn to Vienna in 1787, he played for Mozart during his visit. The master was reputedly unimpressed until he heard Beethoven's talent for improvisation and is supposed to have remarked: 'Keep an eye on him; some day he will give the world something to talk about.' If the remark is not absolutely true, it is a pleasing attribution.

As a viola player in Bonn's Court Theatre, the young Beethoven became familiar with several Mozart operas – *Die Entführung*, *The Marriage of Figaro* and *Don Giovanni*; later he came to love *The Magic Flute* best – perhaps because the idealism of the young Tamino and Pamina was a theme which he, a man brought up in a seriously enlightened age, could heartily applaud – but considered the light-hearted plot of *Figaro* ill-matched to such superb music.

It was, however, the man who saw himself as Mozart's rival, Anton Salieri, who guided Beethoven in the art of vocal writing and prompted his first operatic exercise in 1796, the dramatic scena of a love betrayed: '*Ah! Perfido*'. It is as glorious a concert aria as any of Mozart's, in which Beethoven's musical ambitions already seem to be bursting romantically at the seams – especially in the long-protracted appeal for pity which breaks across the lively final section. Nevertheless, he observes the classical structure demanded by the occasion. The aria's first performance was given in Prague by Josepha Dusek – a further link with Mozart, who had enjoyed the hospitality of the Duseks' Prague villa at the time of *Don Giovanni*, and had written a concert aria for Madame Dusek by way of thanks. This redoubtable lady, who limited herself to concert appearances only, was still in good vocal health when she sang '*Ah! Perfido*' in place of the singer for whom Beethoven had originally intended it.

Another of Mozart's artistic colleagues, the actor-impresario Emanuel Schikaneder (librettist of *The Magic Flute* and the first Papageno) commissioned what would have been Beethoven's first opera, had he found the inspiration for it. But the Roman subject, *Vesta's Fire*, meant nothing to him, and he was relieved of his contract when Schikaneder left his theatre.

FIDELIO

It was the new craze for operas that dealt with subjects of heroic rescue which captivated Beethoven's imagination. The finest of these to have survived – apart from Beethoven's own response to the theme – is Cherubini's opera *Lodoiska*, a triumph in revolutionary Paris during the 1790s and one of several imports from Paris which Beethoven would have seen in Vienna. (*Lodoiska* has recently been revived at La Scala, Milan.) It was to a French text that Beethoven now turned – *Léonore ou l'Amour conjugal* (*Leonora or Married Love*) by the prolific dramatist Jean Nicolas Bouilly.

The succinct tale of the courageous Leonora who, disguised as a man, saves her wrongfully imprisoned husband from the clutches of a tyrant took on a special meaning at the time of *Leonore*'s first performance on 20 November 1805. Napoleon, the

Continued on page 104

A romantic portrait of Beethoven by Ferdinand Schimon. The composer's passionate support of libertarian ideals is reflected in his only opera, Fidelio.

A great Florestan and Leonora reunited in Act Two: Jon Vickers and Helga Dernesch, 1971.

ƒIDELIO

WHO'S WHO

FLORESTAN (*Tenor*)
A Spanish Nobleman, Wrongfully Imprisoned

LEONORA (*Soprano*)
His Wife, Disguised as Fidelio

DON PIZARRO (*Baritone*)
Governor of the Prison

ROCCO (*Bass*)
A Gaoler

MARCELLINA (*Soprano*)
His Daughter

JAQUINO (*Bass*)
Rocco's Assistant

DON FERNANDO (*Bass*)
King's Minister

PRISONERS, SOLDIERS & PEOPLE

The two concise and powerful acts of *Fidelio* comprise a substantial reworking of the three-act opera *Leonore*, which was given an unsuccessful première in Vienna on 20 November 1805. The first performance of *Fidelio*, on 23 May 1814, also took place in Vienna. Leonora was sung by Anna Milder, who had created the role in 1805 at the age of 20.

The 1814 overture to *Fidelio*, which is considerably shorter than the miniature tone-poems that preceded it in 1805 and 1806 (see page 100), is dominated by the vigorous rhythm which launches it.

ACT ONE

The light-hearted mood in which the opera begins gives no hint of the heroics that are to follow later and looks back to the world of Mozart and *Singspiel* (sung play), which, with its combination of set numbers and spoken dialogue, *Fidelio* outwardly adopts. In the courtyard of a state prison near Seville, Jaquino pleads with Marcellina to marry him, but she avoids the issue: in a rapturous moment while Jaquino goes to the wicket to receive a parcel, she reveals that she is in love with Fidelio, her father's new assistant.

Marcellina, alone, expands on this in a short, sweet aria. 'Fidelio' arrives with newly-forged chains and letters. Different reactions are expressed in a quartet: Marcellina still ecstatic ('*Mir ist so wunderbar*'), Leonora horrified that Marcellina has fallen for her disguise, Rocco delighted at the prospect of this love-match and Jaquino despondent. Since the quartet is in the form of a canon, in which each of the voices enters with the same melody, there is no room for conflicting expressions; but at the same time Beethoven fashions one of the most radiant numbers in the whole of opera.

Rocco reminds the young people that love cannot function without money and Leonora reveals her attitude in the ensuing dialogue by arguing that 'the union of two hearts that beat as one is the source of true conjugal happiness'. She asks Rocco to let her accompany him on one of his visits to the underground dungeons and we learn of the political prisoner who has languished there for the past two years. In a trio Rocco agrees and Marcellina radiates her customary happiness while Leonora's music sets her apart in her hopes and fears. A surprisingly amiable march introduces the governor Pizarro, whose vengeance aria is in a 'storm and stress' tradition earlier observed by Mozart (in the Queen of the Night's second aria

from *The Magic Flute*). Pizarro learns that the King's Minister, suspecting that the prison might contain 'victims of arbitrary force', is on his way to inspect it. Pizarro decides that he will have to murder Florestan before the Minister's arrival. In a duet full of dark, furtive touches he asks Rocco to do the deed and, when the gaoler refuses, seeks his assistance in digging a grave while he himself will strike the fatal blow.

Leonora becomes aware of Pizarro's plot. Her magnificent set piece maintains the tension and

The prisoners emerge bewildered into the light in the 1990 Salzburg Festival production.

uses the old form of the grand aria favoured by Mozart – recitative, slow cantabile passage, and fast, dramatic final section – to express her fears, hope and courage, with three horns as a crucial component of the orchestral support. Hoping perhaps to catch a glimpse of her husband, she asks Rocco to allow the prisoners to take a walk in the garden of the fortress; the gaoler agrees and the cells are unlocked.

The prisoners emerge into the light, filled with painful joy, and sing a deeply moving four-part male chorus. Leonora learns that she is to be allowed to accompany Rocco to the depths of the prison; perhaps it is her husband's grave that she will be helping to dig. Pizarro learns of the prisoners' moment of grace and rails against Rocco, who invokes 'the king's name-day' as an excuse.

The prisoners return to their cells and the characters so far encountered voice their different reactions; Leonora has the last, outraged word (just) and the orchestra commands a quiet curtain as 'Fidelio' and Jaquino turn the keys to the cells.

ACT TWO

In the depths of the fortress Florestan in chains sings of his appalling surroundings, the consolation of a clear conscience and a vision of his wife; his large-scale aria is the perfect counterpart to Leonora's big number in Act One. Leonora, entering with Rocco, is prepared to rescue the prisoner, whoever he is. Their whispered dialogue takes place against a suitably dark orchestral accompaniment – the combination of spoken word and music known as melo-drama. She thinks she hears her husband's voice and Rocco, giving the prisoner some wine, allows her to offer bread; Leonora's recognition of Florestan, his gratitude for an act of human kindness and Rocco's fears combine in a suitably momentous trio.

Pizarro enters and prepares to commit murder. 'First kill his wife!' cries Leonora, throwing herself between Pizarro and Florestan; then she draws a pistol on the governor just as the trumpet he has commanded to warn him of the Minister's arrival sounds from the tower. Jaquino enters to tell the governor that the Minister has demanded a list of the prisoners; Pizarro has no choice but to receive him. Leonora and Florestan are rapturously reunited in a brief but blazing duet.

The scene changes to the outdoor parade ground of the castle, where people and prisoners salute their long-desired delivery from tyranny. The King's Minister, Don Fernando, announces the King's command to 'uncover the night of crime' and is amazed to find that Florestan, the friend who fought for the cause of truth, is still alive. Pizarro is arrested and Leonora is commanded to liberate her husband from his chains. It is she whom the assembled company salutes in the triumphant final ensemble and chorus, 'saviour of her husband's life'.

hero who in Beethoven's eyes turned villain when he proclaimed himself emperor – the composer angrily crossed out the dedication to Bonaparte forthwith – had by now marched his troops into Vienna, and the opera was performed to a sparse audience largely made up of Napoleonic soldiers. History repeats itself, and many have testified to the thrill that ran through audiences in the occupied countries during the 1940s when the word 'freedom' was sung.

Leonore was not a success, either at its première or in the drastically revised form (reduced from three acts to two) which was presented in the spring of 1806. The hugely ambitious overture survives in the concert hall as *Leonore No. 3*, a kind of tone-poem before its time with its dramatic summary of the forthcoming action and its offstage trumpet call; but it is the thoroughly transformed version of the opera that Beethoven made eight years later in 1814 which is seen on most opera stages today. Beethoven took on a new librettist, Georg Friedrich Treitschke, and gave the opera the name that Leonora assumes in her purposeful male disguise, Fidelio. There is loss in terms of some of Beethoven's earlier inspirations, but gain in the way in which, after a leisurely and sometimes Mozartian beginning, the drama moves forcefully towards its crisis and glorious resolu-

tion. In between *Leonore* and *Fidelio*, Beethoven searched desperately for new operatic subjects, but did not find one that suited him, although the incidental music to Goethe's *Egmont* – another hymn to the fight against tyranny – comes close to opera at times.

WEBER

Fidelio is very much an operatic product of the Age of Enlightenment, reflecting the revolution and reforms of the times in which Beethoven came to maturity. By way of contrast, Carl Maria von Weber's *Der Freischütz* (*The Freeshooter*), first performed in 1821, is the first German romantic opera to survive in the repertoire. Romantic art is not an easy term to categorize: if, in one crucial aspect, it is supposed to deal with the extremes of passion, awe-inspiring pain and courage, then Mozart's *Don Giovanni* is a romantic opera as well as Beethoven's *Fidelio*. If its brief is to encompass a feeling for nature and the supernatural in a typical early nineteenth-century manner, then *Der Freischütz* is the first true masterpiece of its kind (although *Don Giovanni* qualifies briefly too, by virtue of the stone guest and the protagonist's tumble into hell).

Weber was no pioneer; he simply built on a new tradition, the earliest specimen of which was *Undine* (1816). *Undine's*

Jon Vickers

THE GREATEST HEROIC TENOR (*HELDENTENOR*) OF RECENT YEARS, VICKERS' IMMENSE VOCAL STAMINA HAS STOOD HIM IN GOOD STEAD FOR THE TAXING DEMANDS OF SUCH ROLES AS FLORESTAN IN BEETHOVEN'S *FIDELIO* AND VERDI'S OTELLO. MOST POWERFUL OF ALL IS HIS PORTRAYAL, AS CAPTURED IN RECORDING, OF WAGNER'S TRISTAN; NO TENOR HAS REVEALED GREATER STRENGTH OR ARTISTRY IN TRISTAN'S THIRD-ACT MONOLOGUES. IN LATER YEARS, THE CANADIAN PUT HIS ACTING ABILITIES TO GOOD USE AS BRITTEN'S TORMENTED FISHERMAN IN *PETER GRIMES* AT COVENT GARDEN. UNTIL THEN, THE ROLE HAD ALWAYS SEEMED TO BE THE SPECIAL TERRITORY OF THE LIGHTER-VOICED PETER PEARS; VICKERS BROUGHT OUT THE HEROIC ASPECT OF BRITTEN'S OUTSIDER.

composer, E. T. A. Hoffmann, became the hero of Offenbach's last-ditch attempt at true opera and his tales inspired Delibes' and Tchaikovsky's ballets *Coppélia* and *The Nutcracker*. One of the first operas to dispense with simple set pieces by providing a wider frame of reference with themes that appear and re-appear in slightly altered forms, *Undine* was praised by Weber as being 'a self-contained work of art in which all elements, contributed by the arts in co-operation, disappear and re-emerge to create a new world.'

No-one put it better than Hoffmann himself, whose words provide a touchstone not only for Weber but also for Wagner's early achievements: 'The opera should be … treated not merely as a succession of musical numbers … [or] musical drama, but as having the value of poetry … [in which] speech is raised to the power of music, events are raised to that of the marvellous, men to the heights of gods; and this highest order of opera, the romantic, must be a poetry in which all that is holiest and most mysterious is incarnated in shapes of the utmost sensuous richness … in which these glorious creations of the mind pass before the eye of the delighted spectator in all the charm of a setting in which pictorial and architectural beauties combine with miming and the dance.'

This was a time when Germany was rediscovering its folklore. The Brothers Grimm brought out their first volume of tales four years before *Undine* and their complete edition two years before the première of *Der Freischütz*. Weber wanted 'nothing modern', but like German dramatists of the time who took heed of the Grimms' magic world, he also required a hint of realism: as in *Undine*, the supernatural is all the more powerfully offset by a precisely-imagined everyday world. *Der Freischütz* is set, in Weber's words, 'after the Thirty Years War, deep in the wooded mountains of Bohemia'. Like Beethoven, Weber was indebted to French forms – in this instance the light and graceful *opéra comique* – and also like Beethoven (but in quite a different fashion) ended up by serving a political purpose. Forests, 'the people' (*Das Volk*) and supernatural happenings soon became the stock ingredients of a specifically German, national work of art (and remained so even up until the Second World War, when Hitler used them as part of the National Socialists' propaganda machine). Weber served the fatherland in patriotic vocal pieces, but his only overt intention in *Der Freischütz* was to combat Italian influence. With the première skilfully engineered by the manager of the Prussian Court Theatre in Berlin

to take place on the sixth anniversary of the Battle of Waterloo, and the easy simplicity of the opera's melodies taken up as a continuation of Germany's folk heritage, *Der Freischütz* took on a significance that Weber could not have anticipated. It became the first nationalist opera of the 19th century, to be followed by Glinka's *A Life for the Tsar* and Smetana's *The Bartered Bride*. Its immense popularity in Paris prompted French composers to turn towards German romantic subjects for their operas (see Chapter Six).

FANTASY & MAGIC

Der Freischütz was also a hit in Vienna, where it prompted the Italian impresario Barbaia to commission from Weber a supernatural grand opera, *Euryanthe*, and in London, where taste was less sophisticated and ran to pantomime-like spectacles with dialogue and set pieces. Here, in 1826, Weber wrote his last opera, *Oberon* to a libretto by James Robinson Planché, the man who had translated *Der Freischütz* for the London stage (as well as, amongst others, *Figaro*, *The Magic Flute* and *Norma*). The librettist's unstylish attempts at a hotchpotch of fairy-story and fantasy have been mercilessly lampooned by the writer Anthony Burgess, who tried to give the music of *Oberon* a

libretto to which modern audiences could respond. The fantasy and imagination of Weber's writing in *Oberon* do indeed reveal a third step forward after *Der Freischütz* and *Euryanthe*. Unfortunately, the composer's untimely death at the age of 39 in the year of *Oberon*'s première prevented him from further experimentation with magical subjects and from turning *Oberon* into the kind of German opera he wanted it to be; perhaps the best attempt was made at the end of the 19th century by Gustav Mahler in his performing edition.

A vital link in the history of German romantic opera before Wagner appears on the scene is Heinrich Marschner. His first success, *Der Vampyr* (*The Vampire*, 1828), is a viable box-office choice now that the blood-sucking anti-hero of romantic legend is back in fashion, but it is also a fascinating precursor of Wagner's *The Flying Dutchman*. The mezzo-soprano's lugubrious ballad was to influence Wagner in the scene he described as the core narrative of *The Flying Dutchman*, Senta's ballad. Marschner's reputation as a true German nationalist was properly established five years after *Der Vampyr* with *Hans Heiling*, He wrote 14 operas; yet he is considered at present to be little more than an interesting precursor to the greatest German composer of the 19th century.

Homage to the German romantic painter Caspar David Friedrich in London's Royal Opera production of Der Freischütz *(1977).*

DER *f*REISCHÜTZ

WHO'S WHO

MAX *(Tenor) A Huntsman*

CASPAR *(Bass) A Huntsman*

OTTOKAR *(Baritone)*
Prince of Bohemia

CUNO *(Bass)*
The Prince's Head Ranger

AGATHE *(Soprano)*
His Daughter

ÄNNCHEN *(Soprano)*
Her Cousin

KILIAN *(Tenor)*
A Young Peasant

SAMIEL *(Spoken)*
The Demon Black Hunter

A HERMIT *(Bass)*

PEASANTS, HUNTSMEN,
BRIDESMAIDS & COURTIERS

Weber's first great success, *Der Freischütz*, was produced in 22 German theatres during the year that followed its première in Berlin on 18 June 1821. It proved no less popular in other European cities and led to further commissions – *Euryanthe* (for Vienna in 1823) and *Oberon* (for London, premièred in 1826, the year of Weber's death).

The overture is typical of Weber's concern to bind together themes from his operas in a dramatic orchestral introduction; it follows horn-laden romantic atmosphere with optimistic assertion that all will be well.

ACT ONE

In a forest clearing in Bohemia Max has been defeated by the young peasant Kilian in a prize-shooting. Cuno, the head ranger, warns him that if his present bad form continues and he fails at tomorrow's shoot, which is to be held before Prince Ottakar, he will be refused not only the hand of Cuno's daughter Agathe but also the succession to the title of head ranger that goes with it.

Downcast, Max sings an aria of great beauty – *'Durch die Wälder, durch die Auen'* ('Through the forest and the meadows') – the serenity of which is clouded by his musings on the possible causes of his bad luck; the watchful demon Samiel hovers in the background. Max's cheerless fellow-huntsman Caspar hands him a rifle and tells him to fire at an eagle circling high in the sky overhead. Max succeeds in his aim, and Caspar tells him that the rifle was loaded with a magic bullet (the real meaning of the hard-to-translate *Freischütz* is 'one who shoots with magic bullets'). Caspar suggests that they meet in the Wolf's Glen at midnight in order to cast a further supply of magic bullets for use during the following day's shooting competition. Caspar's malevolent romantic character is summed up in the aria which he sings, alone, at the end of the act.

ACT TWO

Agathe is entertained in her room by her lively, soubrettish cousin Ännchen. The heroine is less confident: she fears for Max's well-being and muses on the fact that the hermit deep in the forest gave her some roses – for what purpose? She sings of her love in the famous *'Leise, leise'*, a gentle melody capped by a more dynamic theme which we recognize as the triumphant outcome of the overture – a gift for the leading soprano. Max finally enters, to learn that Agathe was hit by the falling picture of Cuno's ancestor at the very time he shot the eagle with the magic bullet, but this does not deter him from leaving for the Wolf's Glen against the girls' advice.

Weber conjured up the most supernatural effects that the musical world had ever heard in 1821 for the romantic terrors of the Wolf's Glen. Midnight sounds and Caspar invokes Samiel, to whom he has sold his soul. They strike a bargain: Caspar will make sure that Max takes his place as Samiel's victim, while he for his part will provide seven magic bullets for Max, the last of which will strike whatever target Samiel wishes. Max arrives, terrified, and helps Caspar with the moulding of the bullets. Samiel appears on the casting of the seventh, to cap the supernatural horrors of the scene.

Der Freischütz.

C.M. v. WEBER.

Operntextverl. v. G.Mode, Berlin.

Kilian: „Schau der Herr mich an als König! Dünkt ihm meine Macht zu wenig?"

Caspar: „Kartenspiel und Würfellust, und ein Kind mit runder Brust führt zum ew'gen Leben!"

Aennchen: „Kommt ein schlanker Bursch gegangen, blond von Locken oder braun."

Agathe: „Wie nahte mir der Schlummer, bevor ich ihn gesehn Ja,Liebe pflegt mit Kummer stets Hand in Hand zu gehn!"

fürst Ottokar (zu Max): „So eile mein Gebiet zu meiden! Und kehre nimmer in dies Land."

Eremit: „Wer legt auf ihn so schweren Bann? Ein Fehltritt, ist er solcher Büßung werth?"

A late 19th-century German caricature of the stock romantic characters in Der Freischütz, *with appropriate quotations from the opera.*

ACT THREE

There could be no greater contrast to the musical terrors of the Wolf's Glen than Agathe's simple cavatina as she prepares for the wedding which will take place if Max is successful in the prize-shoot. It is matched by the Bridesmaids' Chorus, one of several melodies in the opera which were taken up as true German folksongs. But all is not well; Agathe's forebodings are confirmed by the present inside the box that Ännchen brings in – a funeral wreath. Agathe suggests that they counter this by weaving a bridal crown from the hermit's roses, which prove significant.

Huntsmen follow bridesmaids with another jolly, folk-like song. The big shooting-match is due to commence on the outskirts of the woods. One bullet is left in Max's rifle after the hunt – the seventh bullet controlled by Samiel. Prince Ottokar orders Max to shoot at a flying dove, and as Max raises his rifle, Agathe rushes in to prevent him, accompanied by the hermit. It is too late; he hits the dove and it is Agathe who falls – but only in fright. She has been protected by the garland of roses, and Caspar is the one to die. (It turns out that Samiel had no power over Max, who came to the Wolf's Glen under the sway of Caspar, and so Caspar has to be the victim).

Samiel appears for the last time in the opera to claim Caspar, who expires while cursing both heaven and the devil.

Striking a new and noble tone in the proceedings, the hermit intervenes to prevent the Prince's sentence of banishment on Max. The proclamation is commuted to a year's probation and the music from Agathe's Act-One aria (and the overture) ends the opera with a joyful hymn of thanksgiving.

Wotan (Donald McIntyre) leaves his daughter Brünnhilde asleep on the rock surrounded by flames in Patrice Chereau's electrifying Bayreuth centenary production of Wagner's Ring cycle.

CHAPTER 8

Wagner

The most astonishing genius in the history of music took time to develop his art, starting with operas in the Italian style and only gradually progressing to his concept of 'the total work of art' (*Gesamtkunstwerk*) in which poetry, music and set design would combine. Wagner evolved his art-form above all during the long course of work on his most ambitious project, *The Ring of the Nibelung*, which he interrupted in 1857 to compose *Tristan and Isolde* and *The Mastersingers of Nuremberg* and to which he returned with renewed confidence in 1869. The festival-house at Bayreuth was conceived as the ideal home for his *Ring* tetralogy. *Parsifal*, his last opera, was written as a kind of religious offering for the Bayreuth shrine.

Officially, Richard Wagner owed his musical education – an education that set him on the path to composing the richest and most ambitious operas of the 19th century – to the academic virtues of his home town of Leipzig. In fact, it was his intense capacity for responding to the operatic masterpieces popular in his youth which provided him with the most fertile soil for his own genius.

Wagner's father died only five months after his birth on 23 November, leaving it to his stepfather, Ludwig Geyer, to recognize the boy's musical potential on his own deathbed only eight years later: Wagner wrote in *Mein Leben* (his occasionally fanciful autobiography) that he was encouraged by his mother Johanna to play what he could on the piano, and Geyer asked, 'What if he has a talent for music?' The tune played by the eight-year old was the Bridesmaids' Chorus from Weber's *Der Freischütz* (*The Freeshooter*). The dying man's comment was linked in Richard's mind with future possibilities: 'I remember that for a long time after, I used to imagine that something would become of me.' Then, in 1829, he saw and heard the great soprano and actress Wilhelmine Schröder-Devrient as Leonora in *Fidelio*. He later wrote that her performance gave, 'as by lightning flash, a glimpse of the ideal and the real together', and

described it as the most powerful experience of his life.

THREE EARLY OPERAS

Each of Wagner's first three operas pays tribute to a genre. *Die Feen* (*The Fairies*) of 1833 is based on a fable by the Italian 18th-century playwright Gozzi (whose other tales were to furnish Puccini with the outline of the plot of *Turandot* and Prokofiev with the essence of *The Love for Three Oranges*), but the aesthetic is that of German romantic opera, with its clash of real life and the supernatural. The two most familiar examples, *Der Freischütz* and Marschner's *The Vampire*, were still popular with audiences at the time Wagner wrote *Die Feen*, and Marschner's *Hans Heiling* was given its première in the year of composition of *Die Feen*. Although he later came to dislike Italian opera, Wagner praised its power of song in 1834 and was to remain faithful to the need for *bel canto* in his later works. The immediate result was *Das Liebesverbot* (*The Ban on Love*), which transports the hypocritical Viennese censorship in Shakespeare's *Measure for Measure*, on which the opera is based, to the blazing Sicilian sunshine.

The première of *Das Liebesverbot* in Magdeburg on 29 March 1836 was a failure, mostly because the singers had not memorized

their roles and the leading tenor fell back on snatches of Auber's *Fra Diavolo* and Hérold's *Zampa*; on the following evening, there were only three people in the audience a quarter of an hour before curtain-up, and following a fight between the husband of the leading lady and the second tenor, which seems to have developed along the lines of the midsummer night's street brawl in *The Mastersingers*, the performance was cancelled. It failed elsewhere on account of the risqué nature of Wagner's (and Shakespeare's) subject matter; nor did it turn out to be a neglected masterpiece when, seven years after the composer's death, this self-styled 'sin of his youth' was rehearsed in Munich and deemed not fit for the public. According to the Wagnerian tenor Heinrich Vogl, 'the arias and other numbers were such ludicrous and undisguised imitations of Donizetti and other popular composers of that time that we all burst out laughing and kept up the merriment throughout the rehearsal.'

Rienzi (1838–40) has fared better, if only as a pompous celebration of French grand opera, Wagner's new passion by the late 1830s: the conductor Hans von Bülow summed it up rather neatly as 'Meyerbeer's best opera'. Wagner considered that it owed more to the earlier, Paris-based composer Spontini, but in any case

by 1860 he was anxious to dissociate himself from another 'sin of his youth', claiming that he lay on it 'no special emphasis, for in it there is not yet evident any important instance of the view of art which I later came to assert.' The subject is at least representative of his political sympathies: the portrait of the Roman tribune Rienzi as the leader of an oppressed populace in Henry Bulwer Lytton's novel (the opera's source of inspiration) tied in with Wagner's revolutionary ideals – though some have seen in the hero a fascist before his time. This view was given unfortunate support by the fact that the young Adolf Hitler saw the opera in 1906 and wrote of his Nazi movement, 'in that moment it began'.

THE FLYING DUTCHMAN

With *The Flying Dutchman* (1843) Wagner returned to the world of German romanticism and in the process laid down some dramatic guidelines for the works to come. He had read of the mythical Flying Dutchman, doomed by the devil to sail the oceans until Judgment Day and redeemable only by the love of a woman faithful until death, in the ironic retelling of the German poet Heine's *Memoirs of Herr von Schnabelewopski*. That was in 1838, during his brief, unhappy time as music director in Riga (now the capital of Latvia). Yet it was only when he was forced to flee the city – and his debtors – with his wife Minna the following year that the story came to life for him. Buffeted by storms off the coast of Norway, the ship taking them to London found harbour in the fjord of Sandwike (according to *Mein Leben*, although Sandwike is a village on an island). Wagner's colourful retelling of the incident is worth repeating: 'The enormous granite walls echoed with the calls of the crew as they cast anchor and furled the sails. The sharp rhythm of the call struck me as a mighty consoling omen, and soon shaped itself into the theme of the sailors' song in *The Flying Dutchman*... under the impressions I had experienced, it [the idea of the opera] acquired a distinct poetic and musical colour.'

So much for the elements that play such an exciting part in the opera. Working on the score in the relative comfort of a village outside Paris during May 1841, Wagner also developed the other 'germ' of *The Flying Dutchman*, Senta's ballad, which he described as 'the poetically condensed image of the whole drama'. The ballad's triumphant conclusion has to wait until the end of the opera, when Senta puts into practice her feelings about the 'pale man' and leaps into the sea. Wagner's original finale was uncomfortably abrupt, giving the cue to some producers to

present the legend as a figment of a neurotic Senta's imagination and end the opera with her suicide, but in 1860, with the experience of *Tristan* behind him, he softened the ferocious triumph of the first version and provided a radiant transfiguration of Senta's and the Dutchman's themes as they ascend heavenward, the curse lifted.

TANNHÄUSER

Although the framework of *The Flying Dutchman* is something elementally new in opera, more powerful even than the Wolf's Glen scene in *Der Freischütz*, traces still remain of plain Italianate writing along the lines of Bellini and Donizetti. They are a feature, too, of *Tannhäuser* (1845), though the roots of the tale are even more proudly Germanic than those of the *Dutchman* and mark the beginnings of Wagner's knowledgeable fascination with medieval romances. He chose the subject of the minstrel Tannhäuser, who is torn between the pure love of the maiden Elisabeth and the spectacular orgies he enjoys in the domain of Venus under the mountain (the Venusberg), because of his own disgust with 'the immediately recognizable sensuality in life' of the present day and his search for 'something pure, chaste, virginal and inaccessibly and unfathomably loving.' But he was

Continued on page 116

Caricature of Wagner the ear-splitter by Gill, 1869.

tHE rING OF THE nIBELUNG

THE RHINEGOLD

WHO'S WHO

WOTAN (Bass-Bar.)
Lord of the Gods

FRICKA (Mezzo) *His Wife*

FREIA (Soprano) *Her Sister & Goddess of Youth*

DONNER (Bass-Bar.) *Their Brother & God of Thunder*

FROH (Tenor) *God of Strength*

LOGE (Tenor)
God of Fire & Cunning

ERDA (Contralto) *Earth Mother*

FASOLT & FAFNER
(Bass-Bar./Bass) *Giants*

ALBERICH & MIME
(Bass-Bar./Ten.) *Nibelungs*

WOGLINDE, WELLGUNDE & FLOSSHILDE (Sopranos/Mezzo)
Rhinedaughters

Wagner described *The Rhinegold* as a 'preliminary evening', a fantastical and sometimes comic prelude to the forthcoming dramas. He set it to music in 1853, following a 'vision' of the wave-like Rhine-music; the Munich première was not until 1869.

In the depths of the river Rhine the Rhinedaughters are playfully guarding the gold; only one who is prepared to renounce love is able to forge the metal into a ring which will give him 'measureless might'. Alberich the Nibelung dwarf, driven to distraction by the teasing Rhinedaughters, leaps up to the high reef on which the gold is resting, snatches it and plunges into the darkness.

Black waves cover the scene, and in the grey light of dawn an open space on the mountains appears. In the distance is the stronghold which was constructed for Wotan and his fellow-gods by the giants, Fasolt and Fafner. Wotan, who like Alberich has made a sacrifice for power – in his case, an eye in return for his all-governing spear – has promised Freia as payment to the giants. Now that he refuses to hand her over, the giants abduct Freia. Without her golden apples of youth, the gods begin to grow old. Cunning, mercurial Loge

has a solution, revealing Alberich's theft: since the dwarf has already foresworn love, the gold is there for the taking. The giants will accept it in place of Freia.

Wotan and Loge descend to Nibelheim, where Loge employs his cunning to capture Alberich: when Loge feigns disbelief at the magical properties of the Tarnhelm – a helmet fashioned for Alberich by his unfortunate brother Mime, which gives the wearer the powers of both invisibility and transformation – the dwarf boastfully turns himself into a toad which Loge then seizes.

Dragged to the gods' stronghold, Alberich furiously yields the Rhine-treasure and, finally, the ring fashioned from it, but lashes out with a titanic curse on the ring's wearer. The giants return for the gold, requesting as much as will cover the bartered Freia. A chink remains: that ring on Wotan's finger will cover it. When Wotan refuses to give it to them, Erda appears from the depths of the earth to warn him of the end of the gods – he must yield up the ring. The giants fight over it, and Fafner kills Fasolt. The Nibelung's curse has claimed its first victim.

The gods vaingloriously cross the rainbow bridge to Valhalla, their newly-christened stronghold (here Wagner's music speaks of empty pomp), impervious to the pleas of the Rhinedaughters down in the depths to return the ring.

The giants prepare to take their ransom, Freia, in Chereau's centenary production at Bayreuth.

Beginning work on the score of *The Valkyrie* in March 1854, Wagner completed it exactly two years later. Munich again played host to the first performance, less than a year after *The Rhinegold*, on 26 June 1870.

Wotan has sought knowledge from Erda, and she has borne him a daughter, Brünnhilde, whose duty as a Valkyrie, along with her eight sisters, is to bring dead heroes to defend Valhalla. Wotan has learnt that the world can be saved only by a 'free man', and has fathered two more children (this time by a mortal woman) – Siegmund and Sieglinde, who have been separated since childhood. Wotan's third significant act has been to plant a sword, Nothung, in the tree which grows in the centre of the home of Sieglinde's husband Hunding. The sword can only be removed by a hero.

ACT ONE

A storm drives Siegmund to seek shelter in the home of Hunding. He is attracted to Sieglinde, who offers him drink and shelter. When Hunding arrives, he discovers that Siegmund is in flight from his own violent kinsmen and challenges him to fight the following day. Sieglinde drugs her husband. Rapturously,

Siegmund and Sieglinde sing of their feelings for one another and learn without shame that they are brother and sister. Siegmund draws the sword from the tree and they fall into each other's arms.

ACT TWO

Wotan is confident that Siegmund will be victorious over Hunding, and sends his favourite Valkyrie, Brünnhilde, to protect the hero. As guardian of marriage vows, Fricka is incensed at Wotan's support for the incestuous adulterers. Her intransigent attitude makes Wotan realize that his claims for Siegmund as a 'free' hero are false, since he has helped him too much. He reveals the trap in which he finds himself to Brünnhilde, and commands her to fight instead for Hunding and Fricka's cause. She is confused by his transfer of loyalty.

Brother and sister rush on to the scene and Sieglinde is torn between love and panic. Brünnhilde solemnly appears before Siegmund and announces to him that he is to die and become a guardian of Valhalla. He refuses to leave Sieglinde. Deeply moved, Brünnhilde decides to break her father's command and help Siegmund, but when the fight takes place Wotan intervenes and shatters Siegmund's sword with his spear, sending him to his death. Brünnhilde flees with Sieglinde.

Valkyries on the raised ring of John Gunter's design for Peter Hall's production of The Ring *at Bayreuth.*

THE *VALKYRIE*

ACT THREE

Brünnhilde breaks in on her sisters' triumphant exhilaration at the battlefield (the 'Ride of the Valkyries'). She announces that Sieglinde is to bear Siegmund's child, Siegfried, and gives her the pieces of the sword which her son will weld together again. Nothing can save Brünnhilde from Wotan's wrath. For daring to act as his conscience, choosing love against duty, she is to be stripped of her warrior status, put to sleep and left, unprotected, on a rock for the first man who comes along. With great emotion Wotan yields to his daughter's request to surround the rock with fire so that only a hero will brave the flames. He kisses her farewell, and leaves in profound sadness.

WHO'S WHO

THE GODS
WOTAN & FRICKA

THE VALKYRIES
BRÜNNHILDE *(Soprano) Wotan's Favourite Daughter by Erda*

GERHILDE, HELMWIGE, ORTLINDE, WALTRAUTE, ROSSWEISE, SIEGRUNE, GRIMGERDE & SCHWERTLEITE
Her Sisters

THE HUMANS
SIEGMUND *(Tenor) Wotan's Natural Son & a Member of the Volsung Tribe*

SIEGLINDE *(Soprano) His Sister*

HUNDING *(Bass) Her Husband*

The heroic tenor Jean de Reszké as Siegfried.

The first two acts of *Siegfried* were written between September 1856 and May 1857; Wagner did not take up the third act until 1869, having composed *Tristan and Isolde* and *The Mastersingers*. The first performance took place as part of the complete *Ring* cycle at Bayreuth on 16 August 1876.

Sieglinde has died in childbirth; Siegfried has been brought up by Mime. The dwarf hopes that the boy will repair the sword, kill the giant, Fafner – now, by means of the Tarnhelm, transformed into a dragon guarding the gold deep in the forest – and bring him the ring. Wotan has left Valhalla and is roaming the world disguised as the Wanderer, waiting for the end.

SIEGFRIED

WHO'S WHO

SIEGFRIED (*Tenor*)
Son of Siegmund & Sieglinde

MIME (*Tenor*)
A Nibelung, now his Guardian

ALBERICH (*Bass-Baritone*)
Mime's Brother

WOTAN (*Bass-Baritone*)
Now Disguised as the Wanderer

ERDA (*Contralto*)

A WOODBIRD (*Soprano*)

BRÜNNHILDE (*Soprano*)

ACT ONE

In Mime's forge at the edge of the forest the impetuous, burly youth Siegfried forces Mime to tell him about the shattered sword and his own origins. In a potentially deadly game of riddles with the Wanderer, Mime learns that only one who knows no fear can weld the fragments of the sword back together. Fearless Siegfried fits the bill, forges the sword and Nothung is ready for new adventures.

ACT TWO

In the depths of the forest Alberich is lurking outside Fafner's cave, waiting to win back the ring. Siegfried carries out part of Mime's plan by killing the dragon with his sword. The dragon's blood gives him the power to understand the song of a bird, on whose advice he takes the Tarnhelm and the ring, kills the treacherous Mime and rushes off to find the bride the woodbird describes as being asleep on a mountain surrounded by fire.

ACT THREE

Wotan is distressed that power may pass from the gods to the human breed of Siegfried and Brünnhilde and summons Erda from a deep sleep, but she is unable to help him. Tired yet noble, he renounces the godly rule of the world to a younger order, the order of human love. Siegfried, guided to the mountain by the bird, approaches and provokes the god to fresh anger; Wotan tries to bar his way with the spear, but this time it is the sword which shatters the spear. Siegfried makes his way through the flames, awakens the sleeping Brünnhilde and gradually wins her love in a long and ultimately passionate duet.

The text for Wagner's final *Ring* opera was the first to be written – as 'Siegfried's Death' in 1848 – but *Twilight of the Gods* (*Götterdämmerung*) was not completed until November 1874. The first performance followed *Siegfried* in the first complete cycle at Bayreuth, on 17 August 1876.

Alberich has fathered Hagen by a mortal woman. Wotan awaits news of the ring in Valhalla.

PROLOGUE & ACT ONE

The Norns predict the end of the gods and the rope of life snaps, confirming their pessimism. At daybreak Siegfried leaves Brünnhilde and sets out for more adventures along the Rhine, giving her the ring as a token of his fidelity.

In the hall of the Gibichungs, Hagen counsels his half-brother and sister to ends that will lead to possession of the ring: Gunther must marry Brünnhilde, but it is only the hero Siegfried who can brave the flames. Siegfried for his part must be matched to Gutrune. He arrives and Hagen gives him a magic potion which makes him forget Brünnhilde. Swearing blood-brotherhood, Siegfried goes to find Brünnhilde, using the Tarnhelm to disguise himself as Gunther.

On the mountain, Waltraute tells Brünnhilde of Wotan's despair, but she loves Siegfried too much to give up the ring. The flames rise and a stranger – Siegfried as Gunther – tears the ring from her finger and sleeps beside her, with Nothung separating them.

ACTS TWO & THREE

Alberich agitates for the recovery of the ring. Gunther presents his distraught bride to the Gibichung people, and a desire for revenge overwhelms Brünnhilde when she sees Siegfried with Gutrune. She tells Gunther and Hagen that Siegfried can be wounded in his back, the only part of his body that is unprotected by her magic charms.

Siegfried laughs off the Rhinedaughters' warnings about the power of the ring. Joined by the Gibichung hunting-party, he is given a potion of remembrance by Hagen, and as he relives his wooing of Brünnhilde, Hagen spears him in the back. Siegfried dies with the name of Brünnhilde on his lips. A massive funeral march sums up the thematic history of the Volsungs.

Gunther and Hagen fight over the ring and Gunther is killed. Brünnhilde reappears; she has learnt the wider significance of events from the Rhinedaughters and goes through the flames to join Siegfried's body on the funeral pyre. The Rhine rises up to reclaim its gold and the gods are seen in Valhalla, engulfed by fire. Is this the end, or a new beginning?

*t*WILIGHT OF THE *g*ODS

Brünnhilde (Gwyneth Jones) prepares for immolation in the Bayreuth centenary production.

SIEGFRIED & BRÜNNHILDE **WHO'S**
(Tenor & Soprano) **WHO**

GUNTHER *(Baritone)*
Chief of the Gibichungs

HAGEN *(Bass)*
His Half-brother, Alberich's Son

ALBERICH *(Bass-Baritone)*

GUTRUNE *(Sop.) Gunther's Sister*

WALTRAUTE *(Mezzo)*
Brünnhilde's Sister

THE THREE NORNS *(Mezzos/Sop.)*
Guardians of the Thread of Life

WOGLINDE, WELLGUNDE &
FLOSSHILDE *(Sopranos/Mezzo)*
Rhinedaughters

Kirsten Flagstad

THE NORWEGIAN SOPRANO KIRSTEN FLAGSTAD IS
BEST KNOWN AS A GREAT WAGNERIAN SINGER,
ALTHOUGH SHE HAD SUNG A WIDE REPERTOIRE IN
SCANDINAVIA BEFORE MAKING HER NAME AT BAY-
REUTH FOLLOWING HER FIRST SEASON THERE IN
1933. IT WAS A BAD TIME TO WORK AT BAYREUTH,
SINCE IT COINCIDED WITH THE ABUSE OF WAGNER'S
SHRINE AS AN ARTISTIC SHOWCASE FOR HITLER, BUT
THIS DID NOT PREVENT FLAGSTAD APPEARING AT THE
METROPOLITAN OPERA, NEW YORK, OR AT LONDON'S
COVENT GARDEN, WHERE HER ROLES INCLUDED
BRÜNNHILDE AND ISOLDE. HERS WAS NOT A SENSU-
OUS OR EVEN A VERY FLEXIBLE VOICE, BUT ITS SECU-
RITY AND STRENGTH MADE HER UNIQUE AMONG
WAGNERIAN SOPRANOS. SHE ALSO GAVE THE FIRST
PERFORMANCE OF STRAUSS' *FOUR LAST SONGS* IN
1950, A YEAR AFTER THE COMPOSER'S DEATH.

fooling no-one: despite the radiant utterances of Elisabeth, the pageant of the minstrels' competition and the famous Pilgrims' Chorus, the siren-song of Venus is as pleasurable and irresistible as the tempests of *The Flying Dutchman* – especially in the revision of 1861 for a Paris production, with its extra titillating Venusberg music to serve for the ubiquitous Parisian ballet.

Medieval virtue is decidedly more triumphant, musically speaking, in *Lohengrin* (1850), where the shining valour of the hero, a Knight of the Holy Grail, is blended more or less seamlessly with the ceremonials of grand opera and offset by the pagan machinations of Wagner's most imposing villains to date, Telramund and Ortrud. From the very first, ethereal bars of the prelude, *Lohengrin* marks a step forward in terms of sonorous, gleaming orchestration and was praised as such by Richard Strauss, when he came to revise Berlioz's treatise on the orchestra, and by Liszt, who in 1850 was persuaded by Wagner – in exile for his part in the Dresden revolution of 1848 – to make sure *Lohengrin* received its first performance that year.

It was also in 1850, in his longest essay, *Opera and Drama*, that Wagner first formulated some of the ideas which were to power his new-found art of music drama.

The long gap between the completion of *Lohengrin* in August 1847 and the beginnings of work on *The Rhinegold* in October 1853 turned out to be simply a gestation period before he embarked on the most ambitious project in the history of opera. Indeed, he had already begun work on the libretto of the work which would be the crowning glory of the *Ring* cycle in the autumn of 1848 – he called it 'Siegfried's Death' – and worked backwards to the text of *Siegfried* in 1851, followed by the words for *The Valkyrie* and, finally, those for *The Rhinegold*, the 'preliminary evening' which would provide a context for the three longer works that would follow.

THE RING

Wagner had long been his own poet, but the verse-forms he used for the text of *The Ring of the Nibelung* had a special significance, harking back to the old German style of using alliteration, known as *Stabreim*. (A simple example of this is Siegmund's command to Brünnhilde in Act Two of *The Valkyrie* – 'Schweig und schrecke/die Schlummernde nicht', where the sound as well as the sense is reproduced in Andrew Porter's translation: 'Still! You'll waken / My sister from sleep'). Wagner explains in *Opera and Drama* how this melody-friendly poetry and music unite – the melody will simply grow out of the verse. Even more importantly, he outlines how 'melodic moments' – fragments of music repeated or used as reminiscences as the drama evolves – will become 'feeling-signposts' (*Gefühlswegweiser*).

THE *LEITMOTIF*

Though he does not describe it as such, this 'signpost' is the notion of the *Leitmotif* or leading-motif, which, once established, can be used again – often by the orchestra alone – under varying circumstances, reminding us of its origin.

In fact, the *Leitmotif* is often far from a simple signpost, since it changes and develops according to the mood and psychological state of the character with whom it is connected; but the simplest and most rudimentary 'leading-motives' are easily recognizable, such as the heroic motives associated with 'sword' and 'hero', which even confirmed anti-Wagnerians come out of a performance singing.

Other motives are less well served by being labelled with a name, and their significance, as well as their orchestration and harmony, shifts from act to act and from scene to scene.

A TWELVE-YEAR GAP

Inevitably, this vast web of recognition and reminiscence would accumulate tremendous weight as the operas progressed, and it was vital that, musically if not texturally, Wagner should proceed in chronological order. He began with *The Rhinegold* as a kind of allegory on the political implications of power in the mid-19th century: it was not unreasonable, in the light of Wagner's socialist views in the late 1840s and early 1850s, that George Bernard Shaw should interpret *The Ring* in socio-political terms, with Wotan and Alberich being seen as capitalist tyrants of different sorts and Siegfried as the young anarchist who came to overthrow corrupt institutions.

Understandably, Shaw found it difficult to cope with Wagner's change of heart – his pessimism concerning the possibility of change, the way in which he eagerly embraced the philosopher Schopenhauer's call for the denial of the will and the search for extinction in a kind of Buddhist nirvana – in the years between his breaking-off work on *The Ring* with the second act of *Siegfried* in 1857 and his resumption of the third act in 1869.

Continued on page 120

Lauritz Melchior

LIKE MANY OF THE GREAT HEROIC TENORS, THE STALWART DANE LAURITZ MELCHIOR BEGAN HIS CAREER AS A BARITONE BEFORE ENCOMPASSING A HIGHER RANGE AND MAKING HIS SECOND DÉBUT IN 1919 AS WAGNER'S TANNHÄUSER. TRISTAN IN WAGNER'S *TRISTAN AND ISOLDE* WAS HIS MOST FAMOUS ROLE, AND HE SANG IT MORE THAN 200 TIMES. HIS SEVERAL RECORDINGS OF THE ROLE TESTIFY TO THE UNIQUE RESONANCE OF HIS TRULY HEROIC INSTRUMENT. HE WAS NOT, HOWEVER, INCAPABLE OF A LIGHTER DRAMATIC TOUCH, AS HE PROVED IN SEVERAL AMERICAN MOVIES (*LUXURY LINER* IN 1947 AND *THE STARS ARE SINGING* IN 1952). LIKE KIRSTEN FLAGSTAD, HIS EQUALLY CELEBRATED ISOLDE, HE MADE HIS NAME AT BAYREUTH, THOUGH UNLIKE FLAGSTAD HE DID NOT SING THERE DURING THE HITLER YEARS.

The great designer Alfred Roller's costume for Isolde in a 1903 Vienna State Opera production conducted by Gustav Mahler.

tRISTAN AND iSOLDE

WHO'S WHO

TRISTAN *(Tenor)*
A Cornish Knight

ISOLDE *(Soprano)*
An Irish Princess

BRANGÄNE *(Mezzo)*
Her Attendant

KURWENAL *(Baritone)*
Tristan's Servant

KING MARKE OF CORNWALL
(Bass)

MELOT *(Baritone) A Courtier*

A SAILOR, A SHEPHERD &
A HELMSMAN *(Tenors & Bar.)*

SAILORS & KNIGHTS

Work on *Tristan and Isolde,* conceived in 1854, proceeded alongside Wagner's relationship with the married Mathilde von Wesendonck; they cast themselves in the roles of a latter-day Tristan and Isolde. The first performance of the opera took place in Munich on 10 June 1865.

The prelude is harmonically the most revolutionary of all operatic openings and begins with the music of the lovers' yearning provoked by the love-potion in Act One. The movement then builds slowly (anything from ten to 14 minutes, depending on the conductor) towards a passionate climax before subsiding.

ACT ONE

In the silence that ensues, a Cornish sailor sings an unaccompanied song about a 'headstrong Irish maid'. Isolde, on board a ship bound for Cornwall, furiously takes the song to be a reference to herself. She has been entrusted to Tristan, nephew of King Marke of Cornwall, who is bringing her from Ireland to marry his uncle. There is no quelling the storm within Isolde; the music tells us that the cause is her love for Tristan. But when she sends her maid Brangäne to bid him come to her, he refuses and his servant Kurwenal mocks the women with a reminder of how Morolt, Isolde's betrothed, came to seek tribute from Cornwall and was instead executed by Tristan.

Isolde's increasing fury sets off a longer narrative of past history. She tells Brangäne how Tristan, wounded, came to her to be healed under the name of 'Tantris'. When she found a notch in his sword, into which fitted a splinter she had found in the dead Morolt's head, she was about to take revenge, but Tristan looked into her eyes and she let the sword fall. She healed him, but now regrets having done so. Brangäne's arguments in Tristan's favour are in vain. She brings a casket of magic potions prepared by Isolde's mother and offers her mistress a love-philtre; but it is a death-potion that Isolde chooses.

Face to face with Tristan in the tense focal scene of the act, she tells him how she nearly killed him in revenge for Morolt. He offers her his sword now, but she suggests that they drink to a reconciliation. Tristan realizes that the cup must be poisoned and welcomes it as a release from the hopelessness of the situation (he is honour bound to conceal his feelings for Isolde). They drink from the cup and the music of the prelude returns as, in the words of Wagner's stage direction, they 'look fixedly into each other's eyes, in which the expression of defiance of death soon gives way to the glow of love.' Brangäne has substituted the potions. As the ship reaches land, the lovers are disorientated by the cries of the sailors hailing King Marke.

ACT TWO

It is night in the garden of King Marke's Cornish castle. Brangäne and Isolde listen to the sound of a royal hunt in the distance; Brangäne warns Isolde to watch out for Melot, a man capable of treachery, who has arranged the hunt so that the lovers can meet. Isolde orders her to put out the torch, the signal to Tristan for their meeting. Brangäne is reluctant and, to an overwhelming burst of orchestral activity, Isolde extinguishes the beacon herself. The first part of Tristan and Isolde's love duet is a complicated discourse on the conflict between night and day, in which Wagner's reading of Schopenhauer's philosophy reveals itself at its most abstruse. But then the pulse of time dissolves, all agitation slips away and the *Liebesnacht* (night of love) truly begins with the voices overlapping each other against a luminous orchestral commentary. Twice Brangäne's voice rides the orchestra in a distant warning of impending daybreak, but the lovers take no notice.

The passionate vocal climax of their duet is interrupted by the sudden arrival of King Marke and his court, led by Melot. The King reproaches Tristan for his betrayal of loyalty in a sympathetic monologue. Tristan has no answer: he can only go off into the dark night

Isolde (Helga Dernesch) offers Tristan (Jon Vickers) the potion in a 1972 Salzburg Festival production.

and asks Isolde to follow him. When she agrees, he kisses her on the forehead and makes no attempt to defend himself against Melot, who wounds him with his sword.

ACT THREE

After a prelude of deepest gloom, the curtain rises on Tristan's ancestral home of Kareol in Brittany. A lone cor anglais voices the sad and yearning song of a shepherd, whom Kurwenal has requested to turn to happier strains if Isolde's ship should appear. The wounded Tristan is close to death and asleep on a couch in the shade of a lime-tree. If Act One belonged to Isolde,

this is Tristan's challenge: by sheer effort of will, he revives initially by thinking of Isolde – now in the light while he is in darkness – and then, when Kurwenal tells him that she is on her way to heal him, at the prospect of seeing her. His first, euphoric sighting is a false one; then the shepherd's tune changes to a joyful one, and tearing the bandage from his wound, Tristan rushes to meet Isolde, only to die as he looks up at her one last time.

The shepherd tells Kurwenal that another ship has landed: King Marke has arrived with his retinue. Kurwenal, wanting to avenge Tristan and thinking that Marke has come to claim Isolde, kills Melot,

and attacks King Marke's retinue, but is killed himself. Marke, grief-stricken again, explains that he has come to marry Isolde to Tristan. Brangäne tries to rally her lady, but Isolde, unaware of her surroundings, is lost to the world. She sings instead to the dead Tristan with increasing ecstasy in what has been described as the 'love-death' or *Liebestod* but is more accurately a 'transfiguration through love' (*Liebesverklärung*). Wagner's stage directions must have the last word: 'Isolde, as if transfigured, sinks in Brangäne's arms gently on to Tristan's body. Deep emotion and sense of exhilaration among those present. Marke blesses the bodies.'

The King's garden, at night: Marke reproaches Tristan in a 1983 production designed and staged by Jean-Pierre Ponnelle.

The rest of us find it equally difficult to accept a stridency in some of Wagner's opinions during those years – the cultivation, for example, of a fashionable 19th-century anti-semitism which he voiced in a virulent revision of his 1850 article *Jewishness in Music*. Nevertheless, his is the strange and extraordinary case of an artist whose many unsound ideas as expressed in print did not find their way into his stage works. A sinister, retrospective light may have been cast by the Nazis' adoption of *The Mastersingers* as a paean of insular virtues; and yet there could be nothing more wholesome, sane or humane than the opera itself, an extraordinary artistic balance to the withdrawn, hyper-sensuous world of the lovers in *Tristan and Isolde*. The contrast expresses itself in the nature of the music as well as the subject: while the 'modern', restless harmonies and the almost hallucinogenic quality of Tristan and Isolde's 'night of love' had more influence on the course of musical history than any other work written that century, *The Mastersingers* paid homage to a German musical heritage that embraced Bach and the 17th-century composer Heinrich Schütz. No genius was ever more capable of seeing both sides of the human condition – the dark and the light – than Wagner when he gave them an opera apiece with *Tristan and Isolde* and *The Mastersingers* in the twelve-year gap between Act Two and Act Three of *Siegfried*.

RETURN TO *THE RING*

Wagner returned to the challenge of *The Ring* with renewed confidence in his mastery in every department. By now he was lucky in love (long since estranged from

Minna, he had met and moved in with Cosima, daughter of Liszt and, at the time of their meeting in 1864, wife of Hans von Bülow) and secure in the royal patronage of Bavaria's King Ludwig II. The king's generosity allowed him to complete *The Ring* and to think again about arranging a special festival, along with a special festival theatre, for performances on four successive evenings of *The Ring*'s prelude and three dramas – much as the Greeks had staged dramas in ancient Athens. As early as 1850, while in exile, he had thought of 'a theatre constructed of boards' to be built for three free performances of 'Siegfried's Death' (the first part of the completed libretto, which became *Twilight of the Gods* or *Götterdämmerung*), but it was only with Ludwig's support in 1864 that he could begin to realize the plan. King Ludwig reneged on his promise of a new theatre in Munich, but it was there, following the première of *The Mastersingers* in 1868, that the first performances of *The Rhinegold* and *The Valkyrie* took place in 1869 and 1870, respectively.

BAYREUTH

Wagner was dissatisfied with the circumstances of the Munich premières and ordered the construction of a stark wooden theatre in the Bavarian town of Bayreuth. It was to be built like a gymnasium; no expense was to be spared on the stage machinery and the sets, but the singers and musicians would receive expenses only. The first season, which featured three *Ring* cycles, was launched on 13 August 1876, and the musical world came to see it. Wagner was not satisfied; all he witnessed was 'the birth of an ordinary child of the theatre', but the huge deficit did not permit a bigger, better *Ring* the following season. The theatre stood empty until the première of the 'stage consecration festival play' *Parsifal*, which presented the story of Lohengrin's father and his quest for the grail in quasi-religious form, on 6 July 1882. The rich ceremonials of the knights of the grail, with their supremely noble, sonorous orchestral colouring, could only have been conceived with the unique acoustics of Bayreuth in mind, where the orchestra is invisible in what Wagner called 'the mystical abyss' between audience and stage.

The cult aspect of *Parsifal* – and woe betide the spectator in a German opera house who claps too precipitately at the end of the Act One grail ceremony – was fostered by the Bayreuth Festival's 30-year embargo on the opera being performed anywhere else, following Wagner's death in Venice seven months after the première, on 13 February 1883. The ritual became positively unhealthy during the 1930s, when Bayreuth became the handmaid of Hitler owing to the wholehearted adoption of the ideals of the Nazi party by Winifred Wagner, the English wife of Wagner's son Siegfried.

Bayreuth has lived on to become a truly international festival, which offers ample rehearsal time and ultimately the most profoundly perceptive productions of these complex works. A million people watched the televised treatment of the 1977 Bayreuth centenary production of *The Ring*; with the spread of video and film, millions more are likely to be riveted by future sagas of gods, giants and courageous human beings. The fall of the Berlin wall, the collapse of communism – all are grist to the Wagner director's mill. Events in history can only enrich new productions of the world's most inexhaustible music dramas.

Hans Hotter

BAYREUTH'S GREATEST EXPONENT OF THE ROLE OF WOTAN IN WAGNER'S *RING* OPERAS DURING THE POST-WAR YEARS WAS HANS HOTTER. THE GERMAN BASS-BARITONE FIRST SET HIS MAGISTERIAL SEAL ON THIS ROLE IN 1931 AT THE TENDER AGE OF 22, WHEN HE SANG THE WANDERER IN *SIEGFRIED,* AND PROCEEDED TO THE OTHER OPERAS DURING HIS YEARS IN PRAGUE IN THE LATER 1930S. THE FORCE WITH WHICH HE WAS ABLE TO CONJURE UP WOTAN'S TITANIC WRATH ALSO MADE HIM A POWERFULLY DOOMED FLYING DUTCHMAN, THOUGH THIS MOST SENSITIVE OF SINGERS WAS ALSO A REFINED INTERPRETER OF *LIEDER,* SINGING SCHUBERT'S *WINTERREISE* (*WINTER JOURNEY*) SONG-CYCLE FOR THE LAST TIME AT THE AGE OF 80. EVEN AFTER 1989 HE STILL APPEARED IN SMALLER ROLES, SUCH AS THE SEEDY SCHIGOLCH IN BERG'S *LULU*. HE WAS ALSO A MEMORABLE COLLEAGUE OF RICHARD STRAUSS IN THE LAST YEARS OF THE COMPOSER'S LIFE, CREATING THE ROLES OF THE POET OLIVIER IN STRAUSS' *CAPRICCIO* AND JUPITER IN *DIE LIEBE DER DANAE* (*THE LOVE OF DANAE*).

The idea for the prelude to *The Mastersingers of Nuremberg* came to Wagner in November 1861, but he did not complete the full score until 1867. The first performance took place the following year at the Royal Court Theatre in Munich on 21 June, during midsummer week.

The prelude immediately establishes civic virtues and a bright summer atmosphere which contrast totally with the withdrawn world of the lovers in *Tristan and Isolde*, the opera's immediate predecessor. The subject of inspired genius brought to work within a tradition is ultimately illustrated by a skilful combination of themes – including snatches of Walther's

a few words with him after the service, and Magdalene explains to Walther that Eva's father, Pogner, will offer her hand to the winner of the following day's song-contest. Before she and Eva leave, Magdalene tells her lover, David, who is Sachs' apprentice, to instruct Walther in the many and complex rules of Mastersinging, so that Eva may marry the man she loves.

berg, who lived from 1494 to 1576) defends 'the knight's song and melody – I found them new, but not confused'. A merry ensemble of perplexity develops, the apprentices siding with Walther, and ends with the proud departure of the knight, followed by the Mastersingers. A solo oboe plays the most inspired snatch of the trial song as Hans Sachs looks thoughtfully at the singer's recently vacated chair before the curtain falls.

THE *M*ASTERSINGERS OF *N*UREMBERG

HANS SACHS *(Bass)*
Cobbler & Mastersinger

VEIT POGNER *(Bass)*
Goldsmith & Mastersinger

EVA *(Soprano) His Daughter*

WALTHER VON STOLZING *(Tenor)*
A Young Knight, in Love with Eva

SIXTUS BECKMESSER *(Bass)*
Town Clerk & Mastersinger

MAGDALENE *(Mezzo)*
Eva's Companion

DAVID *(Tenor)*
Sachs' Apprentice

'Prize Song' alongside the Mastersingers' pomp and circumstance. Wagner's good-humoured treatment never draws undue attention to his technical accomplishment.

ACT ONE

Tradition continues with a church chorale: the scene is set in the church of St Katherine's in mid-16th-century Nuremberg, on the eve of the feast of St John (Midsummer's Day). Between the verses, expressive orchestral interludes reflect Walther's state of rapture as he communicates silently with Eva. She manages to exchange

The Mastersingers arrive for a meeting, and Pogner explains that Eva will have the right to refuse the winner of the contest, but that she can only marry a Master. The man with the highest hopes in the company is Sixtus Beckmesser, town clerk and arch-critic (a caricature of the feared 19th-century music critic Eduard Hanslick). He gleefully agrees to act as 'marker' when Walther steps forward to present his trial song. Beckmesser scratches down all the technical faults in the young man's rhapsody, thus securing Walther's rejection. Hans Sachs (a real cobbler and poet in Nurem-

ACT TWO

The same evening, in a Nuremberg street with Sachs' shop on the left and Pogner's house on the right, David and the apprentices are putting up the shutters when Magdalene arrives and is dismayed to learn of Walther's failure. Eva and her father enter, tenderly discoursing against a balmy, summer-evening flow of orchestral melody. Magdalene tells Eva of earlier events and the advent of Beckmesser, who is coming to woo her. Beneath the lime tree, centre-stage, Sachs reflects on the outcome of the trial, toying with Walther's inspired theme and the sweet song of spring and youth it seemed to represent. The tender mood of the evening continues as Eva engages Sachs in conversation. He makes it clear, with the lightest of touches, that if Eva were to reject Beckmesser, she might well consider a

widower like himself; but when he discovers how she feels about Walther, he selflessly aims to help her. Eva arranges for Magdalene to take her place at the window during Beckmesser's serenade, but her plans to elope with Walther – to the sweetest of love-music – are overheard by Sachs, and he subtly prevents their immediate departure. He also thwarts Beckmesser's tuning-up by hollering a cobbler's song at his work-bench.

Now it is Sachs' turn to act as critical 'marker', striking the anvil at each of the manifold mistakes committed by Beckmesser. David is awoken by the noise and, seeing his Magdalene being serenaded, cudgels the would-be seducer. A vivid street brawl ensues; at its height, the lovers' music peals out as Sachs prevents the elopement and forces Walther into his shop. The Night Watchman crosses the now-empty stage a second time, sees nothing and exits to the last few bars of orchestral magic.

ACT THREE

A new note of solemnity sounds in the long and beautiful prelude. Its meaning is revealed inside Sachs' shop on midsummer morning, when Sachs sends the eager David away and reflects, to the same music, on human folly; how can he turn the previous evening's madness to useful purpose? Walther enters to tell him of a beautiful dream and is asked to turn the words into the song which Sachs believes can win the competition.

Two verses are left on the desk when Beckmesser enters, sore from his drubbing but delighted to find the prize song he believes is Sachs'. The cobbler returns and gives him as a present the two verses he has intended to steal, knowing he will make a fool of himself with them. Eva arrives at the shop with the excuse of tight shoes; when Walther sings her the final verse of the prize song, Sachs reveals his heart-break, and Eva salutes his generosity with emotion.

He tells them he has no intention of playing King Marke to this Tristan and Isolde (Wagner provides the appropriate musical quotation). Magdalene and David arrive, the apprentice is promoted to a journeyman, and a radiant quintet crowns this wonderful scene.

At an open space on the banks of the river Pegnitz the guildsmen and apprentices sing and dance. The Mastersingers arrive, with Pogner leading Eva by the hand, and the assembled company salutes Sachs. Contestant Beckmesser, of course, mangles the melody and the words, failing miserably, before Walther steps up to win the prize in the style that Sachs earlier commended. Walther refuses to join the Mastersingers who rejected him until Sachs reminds him that honourable art with all its traditions unites them. (The fact that it was 'holy German art' led the scene to be used as a rallying-cry for the Nazis; yet in spite of the undeniable element of 19th-century nationalism, this was something that Wagner could not have anticipated.)

Hans Sachs becomes the undisputed hero of the opera as Eva crowns him with Walther's wreath and everyone hails 'Nuremberg's dear Sachs' in an optimistic finale.

Walther's Prize Song at Sadler's Wells, London (later the English National Opera).

CHAPTER 9

Richard Strauss

Born into a comfortable, conservative and musical household in Munich, Richard Strauss moved steadily away from his father's idols, Mendelssohn and Schumann, and closer to the Wagnerian 'music of the future'. In the first decade of the 20th century, he shocked the world with his violent and progressive one-act operas *Salome* and *Elektra*. Then, it seemed, he turned his back on the spirit of an age that was spoiling for conflict by pleasing himself – along with his collaborator, Hugo von Hofmannsthal – with a 'second Figaro', *Der Rosenkavalier*. Throughout the rest of his life his two musical gods, Wagner and Mozart, struggled for ascendancy in his own sensuous style. In the end, warmth and wit gained the upper hand.

The Levée scene, based on Hogarth, in Strauss' Der Rosenkavalier. Sena Jurinac as the Marschallin at London's Covent Garden.

Richard Strauss came to be known as 'Richard the Third' – because after Wagner there could be no 'second' – and yet he was brought up in a Munich household where the name of Wagner was hardly welcome. His father, Franz, was the principal horn-player of the Munich Court Orchestra and, as such, was obliged to participate in the first performances of *Tristan and Isolde* – for which he must have been rehearsing at the time of Richard's birth in June 1864 – and *The Mastersingers*. Franz played marvellously, but his conservative tastes could not tolerate the forward-looking music of 'that drunkard Wagner'.

It was not until his early twenties that Richard Strauss was to discover the glories of Wagner for himself. He became a conductor, assisting at Bayreuth, supervised his own, uncut, performance of *Tristan and Isolde* as court conductor at Weimar and duly married his Isolde, the fine soprano Pauline de Ahna (better known to posterity – to some degree unfairly – as a real virago of a wife). Strauss' first opera, *Guntram*, is certainly an inexperienced tribute to Wagner in terms of its fusty, convoluted libretto (by the composer himself), and the title role is immensely taxing for the tenor. Nevertheless, much of the orchestral writing in the opera has a familiar Straussian richness – he had already composed the famous tone-poems *Don Juan* and *Death and Transfiguration* – and the epilogue is the first in a long series of serene and deeply moving operatic farewell scenes.

EARLY OPERAS

The end of *Guntram* also marked a new departure for Strauss: while on holiday in Egypt during December 1892, he decided on a final twist to the plot which was bound to shock the holy guardians of Bayreuth. The hero, Guntram, having murdered the cruel husband of his beloved Freihild, would disregard the prescriptions of the Wagnerian brotherhood which had so far guided him, and would decide his fate as he thought best. This was an autobiographical gesture for the young composer: Strauss' reading of the then-fashionable German philosopher Nietzsche led him to break free of his own mentors. The musical style hardly changed – the last act, as Strauss himself pointed out, remained 'hyper Tristanish' – but the move was vital for the composer's own philosophy. Looking back in 1945, he observed that his path was 'clear at last for uninhibitedly independent creation'.

The failure of *Guntram* at its Munich première on 16 November 1895 prompted a strange and typically humorous type of operatic revenge five years later. In collaboration with the satirist Ernst von Wolzogen, who like Strauss and Wagner before him had also suffered rejection at the Müncheners' hands when he tried to introduce an experimental cabaret, Strauss decided on an adaptation of an old Flemish legend. In it a jilted suitor seeks revenge on the girl who, by leaving him hanging in a basket half-way to her bedroom, has made him the town's laughing stock; he enlists the aid of a magician who extinguishes the town beacons – hence the tale's title, *The Extinguished Fires of Oudenarde* – and proclaims that they can only be re-lit by a flame from the girl's backside. The ending of this strange story was modified in the opera, *Feuersnot* (*Fire Famine*), in which the girl's sacrifice of her virginity proves sufficient to restore light and love. Turning the tale into a satire on Munich conservatism, Strauss indulged his Bavarian wit in a string of folk-like waltzes and crowned the opera with an ecstatic orchestral depiction of the (offstage) love-scene. Both elements were to come in useful for *Der Rosenkavalier* (*The Knight of the Rose*), his first successful comedy, 11 years and three operas later.

Although tone poems as diverse as the Nietzsche-inspired *Also sprach Zarathustra* (*Thus Spake Zarathustra*) and the comic *Till Eulenspiegel* had long established Strauss as a master of the orchestra, he had yet to make his operatic reputation. He did so by keeping his finger on the decadent turn-of-the-century spirit with an adaptation of Oscar Wilde's *Salomé*, which he first saw as a stage play in Berlin in 1902.

SALOME

Strauss found music in the constant refrains and repetitions of Wilde's poetic prose, and he made his own careful selection of key lines and scenes ready to set to music. Strauss' father, who died at the end of May 1905, six months before the opera *Salome*'s première, had not been wrong when he exclaimed at a play-through, 'Oh God, what nervous music! It is exactly as if one had one's trousers full of maybugs'. In this short, shocking but compelling tale of the teenage princess whose thwarted lust for the prophet John the Baptist turns to rage and the command for his execution, nervous movement combines with an iridescent orchestral palette to conjure the violent beauty of the middle-eastern night – which the composer had already observed for himself in Egypt. This strange mixture of gruesomeness and sensuous beauty continues through to the final scene of Salome's monologue, delivered to the severed head of John the Baptist, in which Strauss conveys a

powerful sense of nostalgia for what might have been: in a good interpretation Salome moves and repels us simultaneously.

This one-act shocker was an immediate sensation. Following the Dresden première, with its 38 curtain calls, *Salome* ran into censorship difficulties in Berlin, where the Kaiser demanded a last-minute appearance of the Star of Bethlehem to suggest that all would be well; and in London the Lord Chancellor at first demanded that Salome address her final thoughts to an empty platter. This only helped to spread *Salome*'s reputation. Strauss turned to another, even more violent subject for his next opera – not out of a desire to repeat box-office success, but because he had found the operatic collaborator of his dreams in the Viennese poet and playwright Hugo von Hofmannsthal, whose version of Sophocles' stark tragedy *Electra* impressed him as deeply as the Berlin production of *Salomé*.

ELEKTRA

Hofmannsthal, a precocious artist whose major poetry was written in his teenage years, grappled with the problem of matching the artist's vision with the harsh contemporary world around him in a series of allegorical dramas. His adaptation of Sophocles' *Electra* veered away from this theme in a frightening vision of family values gone awry: with the recent interest in Freud and his *Interpretation of Dreams*, Freudian explanations could be given for Elektra's hatred of her murderous mother and her mourning for her dead father. It was a fascinating reworking of Greek tragedy, and though Strauss and Hofmannsthal discussed many other possible subjects together, Elektra was the theme they finally chose. Strauss, who was doubtful of following *Salome* with something similar and anxious to proceed to a comedy, was finally persuaded by the poet's argument that whereas

Continued on page 130

Richard Strauss in the 1930s, at work on the score of his comic opera, Die Schweigsame Frau (The Silent Woman).

Strauss' first collaboration with the Viennese poet and playwright Hugo von Hofmannsthal was an operatic adaptation of Hofmannsthal's play, itself based on the Greek tragedian Sophocles' version of the Electra myth. The first performance was in Dresden on 25 January 1909.

℮LEKTRA

Long before the action of the opera begins, Agamemnon, the commander of the Greek forces against Troy, was murdered on his return to Mycenae by his wife Klytemnestra and her lover Aegisthus (their reason – not cited by Hofmannsthal – was Agamemnon's sacrifice of his daughter Iphigenia to appease the goddess Artemis and allow the becalmed Greek fleet to sail on to Troy). Years later, the couple's other children have grown up, with the potential (and, in earlier treatments of the myth, the obligation) to extract vengeance on their murderous mother.

The three-note theme associated with Agamemnon, a brooding presence throughout the opera, is blasted out by the full orchestra as the curtain rises instantly on maidservants bickering in the courtyard of the Mycenean palace. They discuss Elektra's cat-like behaviour, spitting and howling for her dead father. Only the fourth and fifth maids deplore her harsh treatment at the hands of Klytemnestra and commend her regal bearing; the fifth maid is sent inside the palace to be flogged for her pains. Elektra appears on the empty stage. Launching one of the most taxing roles in the repertoire, Strauss and Hofmannsthal give her a powerful monologue in which she narrates her father's cruel fate and looks forward to the time when his death can be avenged. Between the grim conjuring up of Agamemnon's murder in his bath and the wild cavortings of Elektra as she anticipates revenge, a deeply nostalgic melody suggests the tenderness of the family ties that once existed.

Chrysothemis, a weaker creature who is frustrated in her desire for love and affection, arrives to warn her sister that their mother and Aegisthus are plotting to lock Elektra in a dark tower; Elektra is scornful of the idea, scoffing at Aegisthus' effeminacy.

Noises within the palace indicate the approach of Klytemnestra, terrified by a bad dream about Orestes' return from the exile into which Elektra had delivered him for safe-keeping. The queen stands at the window, looking fearfully down at her daughter. Hofmannsthal's description is memorable: 'in the dazzling torchlight her wan and bloated face seems more pale against her scarlet robes... The queen is completely covered in precious stones and charms. Her arms are covered in bracelets, her fingers with rings. Her eyelids are exceptionally large and it seems to cause her considerable effort to keep them open.' Elektra flatters her mother in order to detach her

Blood sacrifice at Klytemnestra's command in the Welsh National Opera production, 1992.

from her snake-like confidante and train-bearer, and Klytemnestra descends for the central confrontation of the opera. She tells Elektra of her sleepless nights; the orchestral illustration of the 'nameless something' that hangs over her is the most shockingly progressive passage in a score that is Strauss' most adventurous. Elektra sings with ambiguity of the sacrificial victim which must be slaughtered; then she rounds on her mother. At the height of her ghastly triumph, the confidante returns to whisper something in Klytemnestra's ear. She rushes out full of wild joy.

The reason for her change of mood becomes clear when Chrysothemis returns with the news that Orestes has died in a chariot race. Elektra comes to a sudden, wild decision: she and her sister must do the deed alone. Chrysothemis refuses to help her. As Elektra digs for the buried axe with which her father was killed, a man appears in the gateway. He has come, he sings to solemn music, as messenger of Orestes' death; but when he learns that the creature before him is Elektra, the time is right to reveal himself: her brother, still alive. In a great release from all the tensions that have until now accumulated relentlessly, Elektra serenades her brother in a heart-rendingly beautiful song. His tutor tells them that there is no time to lose: the murders must be carried out at once.

The men go into the house and Elektra, in despair, realizes that she has forgotten to hand the axe to Orestes. Two screams from within signal Klytemnestra's end. Then Aegisthus returns to the palace, unaware of the turn in events. To a weird and glutinous Viennese waltz, Elektra feigns subservience as she lights his way to meet his fate inside the palace. He soon appears at a window, screaming for help before the avengers strike him down: does nobody hear him? 'Agamemnon hears you,' is Elektra's response. The action is now entirely of Hofmannsthal's devising, going beyond any Greek version of the myth. Offstage voices acclaim Orestes, but Elektra is oblivious to events around her: in a wild, liberating but dangerous finale, she 'steps down from the threshold, her head thrown back like a Maenad'. The librettist's stage directions continue: 'she jerks her knees up, flings her arms around in some unknown dance.' Chrysothemis and other people from the palace watch her as 'she does a few more triumphant steps with the utmost effort' before falling down dead from exhaustion. Chrysothemis batters against the palace door, crying out her brother's name, but the only answer comes from the orchestra, which mercilessly repeats the Agamemnon theme: revenge has been achieved, but at what cost?

Amy Shuard as Elektra, caressing her weaker sister Chrysothemis (Maureen Guy), Covent Garden, 1965.

Birgit Nilsson

FEW SOPRANOS HAVE PROVED MORE EQUAL TO THE
DEMANDS OF STRAUSS' ELEKTRA AND SALOME, AS
WELL AS THE MAJOR WAGNERIAN ROLES, THAN
BIRGIT NILSSON. HER HUGE STAMINA WAS EQUALLED
BY A CAPACITY FOR SUBTLETY AND WARM, BRIGHT
TONE RARE IN A HEROIC SOPRANO; THE TENDENCY
HAS BEEN TO COMPARE HER WITH HER LESS FLEX-
IBLE, IF SOMETIMES MORE IMPOSING, FELLOW-
SCANDINAVIAN KIRSTEN FLAGSTAD. SHE MADE HER
DÉBUT IN HER NATIVE SWEDEN IN 1946, SINGING
THE ROLE OF AGATHE IN WEBER'S DER FREISCHÜTZ,
(THE FREESHOOTER) AND PROGRESSED IN THE 1950S
TO MORE TAXING ROLES. SHE WAS BAYREUTH'S
LEADING SOPRANO IN THE 1960S AND RETIRED, WITH
HONOURS, ONLY AT THE BEGINNING OF THE 1980S.
SHE NOW GIVES REGULAR MASTERCLASSES.

in the 'purple and violet' *Salome*, 'the atmosphere' was 'torrid', in *Elektra*, it was 'a mixture of night and light, of black and bright'.

Strauss was, however, determined to have his way with a subject that was more congenial to his own un-neurotic and good-natured character in his next collaboration with Hofmannsthal. This time he wanted something that was reminiscent of a Mozart comedy but with 20th-century overtones.

DER ROSENKAVALIER

Hofmannsthal finally hit upon with the right idea in discussion with his friend Count Harry Kessler in February 1909: a pantomime-like entertainment set in 'the old Vienna under the Empress Maria Theresa'. As the project took shape, plot-lines from Molière and another French writer, Louvret de Couvray, were combined with detail from Hogarth's engravings and the historical precedent of a papal custom whereby a golden rose was presented to daughters of the nobility. This was transformed into a wedding ceremony with a silver rose and became the pivotal action of *Der Rosenkavalier*. As work on the opera progressed, it was the *grande-dame* figure of the Marschallin, rather than the rose-cavalier Octavian or Baron Ochs, a boorishly comic Viennese Falstaff, who became in Hofmannsthal's

words, 'the central figure for the public', the one 'to touch...the more sublime chords of tenderness'. Deliberately anachronistic Viennese waltzes proliferated at Hofmannsthal's suggestion, and it was Strauss who shaped the second act and demanded more lines for the lyrical climax of the opera – the final trio and duet. Given the equal wealth of human and incidental detail in both the music and the action, it was hardly surprising that *Der Rosenkavalier* should set the seal on one of the greatest partnerships in the history of opera. What makes our understanding of the creative collaboration so much richer is the remarkable correspondence between Strauss and Hofmannsthal, which has fortunately been preserved for posterity along with the end results.

ARIADNE AUF NAXOS

In many ways the realistically detailed plot of *Der Rosenkavalier* was a departure for Hofmannsthal. From now on his working relationship with Strauss would be less easy-going. In *Ariadne auf Naxos* (*Ariadne on Naxos*, 1912) the lofty characters of 'serious' opera battle for prominence with a troupe of *commedia dell'arte* players. The framework was an odd one – a lengthy evening's entertainment which consisted of two-thirds play (Hofmannsthal's adaptation of one

Jessye Norman

BEST SEEN ON STAGE IN RESPLENDENT ISOLATION AS ARIADNE ON STRAUSS AND HOFMANNSTHAL'S DESERT ISLAND, THE AMERICAN SOPRANO APPEARS MORE FREQUENTLY ON CONCERT PLATFORMS THAN ON THE OPERATIC STAGE, THOUGH HER RANGE OF ROLES ON DISC IS WIDE AND RECENTLY INCLUDED THE SURPRISING CHOICE OF BIZET'S CARMEN. THE VOICE, UNIQUELY WARM AND OPULENT IN ITS MIDDLE RANGE, IS ESPECIALLY SUITABLE FOR STRAUSS AND WAGNER. SHE MADE HER DÉBUT IN 1969 AS ELISABETH IN *TANNHÄUSER* AND HIS SINCE PROVED A FINE SIEGLINDE IN *THE VALKYRIE*. AN INTELLIGENT AND SEARCHING INTERPRETER, SHE ENCOMPASSES IN HER REPERTOIRE NEGRO SPIRITUALS, SCHUBERT *LIEDER* AND SUCH 20TH-CENTURY CHALLENGES AS THE ROLE OF THE WOMAN IN SCHOENBERG'S FRIGHTENING 'MONODRAMA' *ERWARTUNG* (*EXPECTATION*).

of Molière's plays, *Le Bourgeois Gentilhomme*) and one-third opera – and, even with the combined expertise of the great producer Max Reinhardt's theatre troupe and a fine team of musicians, this 'pretty hybrid', as Strauss called it, did not succeed in its original form. The real problem, though, was that Hofmannsthal tried to insist upon an airy-fairy symbolism for his mythological characters, which Strauss rightly feared would turn them to stone, though there was a happy return to the old, humorous vein in the prologue which the two provided in 1916 to explain the back-stage confusions that lead to the hybrid opera; it is in this version – prologue and opera together – that *Ariadne auf Naxos* has stayed in the repertoire.

DIE FRAU OHNE SCHATTEN

By the time that they were writing the *Ariadne* prologue Strauss and Hofmannsthal were running into difficulties with their most ambitious joint project, the fairy-tale *Die Frau ohne Schatten* (*The Woman Without a Shadow*). The composer lavished his most supernatural inventions on the first two acts, in which a quest for children brings down-to-earth mortals into conflict with superior beings, but Hofmannsthal hung fire for the crucial resolution. When the text reached him towards the end of the First World War, Strauss was not in the mood for finishing this 'massive and artificial' tale and an extravagant première was not appropriate in 1919. Work on the finale was laborious and sounds it – a pity, since in the earlier stages of *Die Frau ohne Schatten* he had woven just about every operatic style he had so far cultivated into a bewitching and inspired tapestry of sound, a perfect musical representation of the contrasts between the spirit world and the human plane.

ARABELLA

The Strauss–Hofmannsthal partnership reached a low ebb during the mid-1920s. Strauss aspired to becoming 'the Offenbach of the 20th century' in the mythological spoof *The Egyptian Helen*, while Hofmannsthal became more than ever bogged down in matters of deeper significance. The first act has a delightful lightness of touch; the second is a ponderous and unstageable nightmare. Older and wiser, the pair returned to the tried and tested formula of misunderstandings in old Vienna with *Arabella*, a light romance about

Continued on page 134

Baron Ochs (Fred Teschler) fusses over his wound from the 'duel' with Octavian, as dubious henchmen and a perplexed Faninal (Gunter Leib) look on.

DER ROSENKAVALIER

THE MARSCHALLIN *(Soprano) Wife of Field-Marshal Prince Werdenberg, in Her Early Thirties*

BARON OCHS OF LERCHENAU *(Bass) Her Country 'Cousin'*

OCTAVIAN, *known as* **QUINQUIN** *(Mezzo) A Young Gentleman*

HERR VON FANINAL *(Baritone) A Rich Merchant*

SOPHIE *(Soprano) His Daughter*

MISTRESS MARIANNE *(Soprano) Sophie's Duenna*

VALZACCHI *(Tenor) An Intriguer*

ANNINA *(Contralto) His Accomplice*

A WHOLE HOST OF MINOR CHARACTERS

Following the triumphant first performance of the opera at Dresden on 26 January 1911, Strauss and Hofmannsthal's second collaboration proved so popular that special *Rosenkavalier* trains had to be laid on between Berlin and Dresden. With Puccini's later works and Britten's *Peter Grimes*, it remains the most popular opera of the 20th century.

ACT ONE

After a night of love-making (graphically depicted in Strauss' prelude), the 17-year-old Count Octavian is lying in bed with the Marschallin, rejoicing at the absence of the Field-Marshal. Two interruptions suggest that the husband has returned from the hunt and send Octavian into hiding: the first is only the Marschallin's page-boy, Mohammed, bringing breakfast, and the second is the rude intrusion of Baron Ochs, a kind of Austrian Falstaff. Ochs' request is for an envoy to present a silver rose to his bride-to-be, Sophie von Faninal, but he is side-tracked by the charms of the Marschallin's maid 'Mariandel' – none other than Octavian, who has rapidly donned disguise. The Marschallin shows Ochs a portrait of Octavian, her candidate for the 'cavalier of the rose'. He is too busy cataloguing his rustic conquests to be surprised for long by the resemblance to 'Mariandel'.

At a levée full of colourful, Hogarthian characters, the Baron argues with a notary over the terms of his marriage-settlement and is approached by Valzacchi and Annina. The Marschallin is left alone and, in a delicately scored monologue, she is led by the situation to consider the cruelty of passing time and the right way in which to face it. When Octavian returns, he cannot understand her change of mood and leaves, wounded by her calm assurances that 'today or tomorrow' he will leave her for a younger woman. The Marschallin sends Mohammed after him with the silver rose and sits pensively as a solo violin rounds off what Strauss called the 'very Viennese sentimentality' of the closing scene.

ACT TWO

At Faninal's Sophie waits nervously for the arrival of the rose-cavalier. Octavian enters, dressed splendidly in silver. It is a case of confused love at first sight and the famous 'silver-rose' chords, coloured by celesta and harp, heighten the sense of unreality. Ochs arrives, lecherous and insulting, and fondles Sophie to the strains of his favourite waltz (a deliberate anachronism). Octavian and Sophie declare their love in another duet, only to be seized by Valzacchi and Annina, who scream for Ochs. He is merely amused, but his manner infuriates Octavian who draws his sword and, in a mockery of a duel, wounds Ochs slightly in the arm. Pandemonium ensues, with Faninal as well as Ochs screaming blue murder, but the Baron's good humour is soon restored by a glass of wine. In the famous waltz scene Annina brings him a note of assignation from

'Mariandel' and Ochs – neglecting to tip the bearer of good news – dances round the room in libidinous anticipation.

ACT THREE

At a Viennese inn of doubtful reputation Valzacchi and Annina have switched their allegiance and are now working with Octavian on a plan to discomfort the Baron. Ochs settles down to supper with his wench, but 'Mariandel' soon waxes maudlin and disturbs him by her resemblance to the young blade who wounded him. Ochs is further terrorized by Valzacchi's team of 'ghosts' and by Annina, who, disguised, is claiming to be his abandoned wife. He calls for the police but finds himself caught in a compromising situation which becomes still more farcical when the Faninals arrive. Only the Marschallin, called to the scene, can resolve the confusion. Both Ochs and Sophie quickly jump to the conclusion that Octavian must be her lover, but the Marschallin magisterially suggests that the Baron should act the gentleman and take his leave, which he does with flamboyance.

We are left with the ultimate triangle. Octavian, now confused, wavers between his two loves, but the older woman takes charge once again, true to her word, by letting go of her lover and guiding him towards Sophie. Strauss promised Hofmannsthal his 'best and supreme effects' at the end; the great trio and the young lovers' duet are the result. Finally, composer and poet remind us that this is after all a 'comedy for music' by having Mohammed trip across the empty stage to retrieve the handkerchief dropped by Sophie – a light-hearted symbol of the Marschallin's renunciation.

The Presentation of the Rose in John Schlesinger's Covent Garden production, with Barbara Bonney as Sophie and Anne Howells as Octavian.

the quest for the perfect suitor with surprisingly dark, Freudian undertones. The formula of *Der Rosenkavalier* was adapted rather than repeated – after all, *Arabella* begins in a shabby hotel room *circa* 1860 instead of a palace in the 1740s – though similarly abundant waltzes and equally affecting curtains to the first and third acts certainly help to account for *Arabella*'s popularity.

Hofmannsthal died, brokenhearted at his elder son's suicide, while working on the libretto of *Arabella* in 1929, and completion of the opera was a painful process for the composer. All the same, *Arabella* has become one of the few later operas by Strauss to reach a wider public.

AFTER HOFMANNSTHAL

At Glyndebourne in England, where close attention to detail does justice to the opera's finely-observed social comedy, *Arabella* has held equal honours with three other gems in Strauss' operatic output. These are *Intermezzo*, a fast-moving 1924 conversation piece in which the composer became his own librettist in a bid to fictionalize a tragicomic incident in his married life; *Die schweigsame Frau* (*The Silent Woman*), the first post-Hofmannsthal opera, for which he turned to the Jewish writer, Stefan Zweig, for an adaptation of Ben Jonson, just before the Nazis intervened; and *Capriccio* (1942), which is a lighthearted study of the relationship between words and music and the meaning of opera, and which was intended to be a connoisseur's piece but has since become so much more, perhaps by virtue of the gracious music that Strauss composed for the *prima donna*.

FINAL OPERAS

Capriccio is a fitting operatic farewell for a composer who had given his collaborating poets so much consideration, and yet it was almost an afterthought to a truly romantic swansong, *Die Liebe der Danae* (*The Love of Danae*). Although the verses hardly sprang to life in the hands of the librettist Josef Gregor, Strauss rose to great musical heights for the final scene where the god Jupiter takes his leave of the heroine Danae. At the dress rehearsal the composer pointed heavenward and said of

Kiri Te Kanawa

KIRI TE KANAWA'S ASSURED STAGE PRESENCE AND RICH, LUMINOUS SOPRANO HAVE MADE HER AN OUTSTANDING MARSCHALLIN – A NATURAL STEP FORWARD FROM HER MEMORABLE CHARACTERIZATIONS OF MOZART'S SOPRANO LEADS IN THE 1970S. THE ADOPTED DAUGHTER OF AN ENGLISH MOTHER AND A MAORI FATHER, SHE TRAINED IN HER NATIVE NEW ZEALAND (AS A MEZZO-SOPRANO) AND CAME TO STUDY AT THE LONDON OPERA CENTRE IN 1966. LIKE DAME JOAN SUTHERLAND, SHE SERVED HER APPRENTICE TERM AT COVENT GARDEN, THOUGH HER COUNTESS IN *THE MARRIAGE OF FIGARO* SOON LAUNCHED AN INTERNATIONAL CAREER. SHE IS AWARE OF THE LIMITS TO HER STRENGTH AND DOES NOT PUSH BEYOND THE LESS STRENUOUS ROLES OF VERDI AND PUCCINI, ASSURING HER LONG-TERM VOCAL HEALTH. AT HER BEST SHE COMES ACROSS AS AN INTELLIGENT AND VIVID COMMUNICATOR.

what he called this 'Grecian *Götter-dämmerung*', 'When I make my way up there, I hope I'll be forgiven if I bring this along too.' Present-day audiences have all too few chances to assess this opera's merits; the same can be said of the pastoral *Daphne* and the somewhat more ponderous work *Friedenstag* (*Day of Peace*), which first shared a double-bill in 1938. A celebration of the calm, placid nature-worship of the Greeks by way of a striking contrast to the hell of *Elektra*, *Daphne* reveals a new translucency in Strauss' marvellous orchestration – not least in the final scene where the eponymous nymph, on whom the god Apollo has taken pity, is transformed into a laurel tree and her wordless voice is heard from within the bark in the glow of the late-afternoon sunshine.

Daphne, *Die Liebe der Danae* and *Capriccio* are all astonishingly tranquil works in the light of the Nazi menace under which they were written; but then Strauss always did possess a surprising ability to turn his back on an ugly world. The end-products are always so profoundly touching, such genuine last embers of an earlier age and of a civilization which already lay in ruins, that we have no right to criticize his romantic retreat. Born a romantic composer, Richard Strauss died true to himself, making 'gentle, happy music' until the end.

Josephine Barstow as Salome, performing the famous Dance of the Seven Veils for Herod.

CHAPTER 10

Russian and Czech Opera

The story of true Russian opera begins in 1836, when Glinka's *A Life for the Tsar* was first performed. Glinka was soon dubbed the 'father of Russian music', while his near-contemporary, Alexander Pushkin, became known as the 'father of Russian literature'. Nearly all of the great 19th-century Russian operas, including Mussorgsky's *Boris Godunov* and Tchaikovsky's *Eugene Onegin* and *The Queen of Spades*, were based on Pushkin's works. The best-loved Czech opera, Smetana's *The Bartered Bride*, is typically Bohemian in its smooth and cheerful folk style. It was followed by the blunter and more uncompromising language of Janáček's *Jenůfa*, in which the composer demonstrated his conviction that there was song in every sentence of human speech; he took this idea of 'speech-melody' to new heights in the 1920s.

Mussorgsky's Boris Godunov in the Bolshoi production, Moscow. The crowd awaits its newly crowned Tsar outside the Cathedral of the Assumption.

*The founding
father of Russian
literature and
inspiration for
countless Russian
operas, Alexander
Pushkin, as
romantically
imagined by a
later generation of
artists. Portrait by
Ivanovsky and
Repin, 1888.*

Starting-points for new trends in opera are often hard to find; this was not so, however, in the case of the Russian school. St Petersburg, Peter the Great's window on the west, favoured foreign influence in the city's music as well as in its architecture; throughout the years of the late 18th century, Italian, German and French companies performed operas by their compatriots, while the few composers who wrote fresh works on Russian themes were foreigners.

This was still the situation in the early 1800s, when the Venetian composer Caterino Cavos grafted his Italian style on to Russian folk music, using legends like the tale of the Firebird or episodes from Russian history, such as the glorification of the 17th-century Russian peasant Ivan Susanin, who gave his life for the Tsar Mikhail Romanov. It was not, however, until 1836 that a Russian, Mikhail Glinka, set the same subject in his opera *A Life for the Tsar* and made history. His aim was, in his own words, 'to compose music in which my beloved fellow-countrymen would feel quite at home, and not to strut about in borrowed plumes'. He achieved this either by using the rich tradition of Russian folksong, with its abundance of free-flowing tunes in flexible metres, or by moulding the contours of his own melodies according to Russian folk formulas. As a result, *A Life for* the Tsar's first performance, given in December of that year, marked the true beginning of Russian national opera.

ALEXANDER PUSHKIN

If Glinka was revered by later Russian composers as 'the father of Russian music', there was also no doubt as to who laid the foundation-stone in the literary sphere. Alexander Pushkin (1799–1837) died romantically young, fighting the same kind of senseless duel over a matter of honour which he had described in his best-known work, the novel in verse, *Eugene Onegin*. He left behind an impressive body of work which furnished the sources for many of the great Russian operas over the next 75 years; no poet, not even Shakespeare, ever had such influence on his own countrymen. Pushkin's first major poem, *Ruslan and Ludmilla*, published in 1820, was the subject of Glinka's second opera, composed six years after *A Life for the Tsar* and harmonically more experimental (and influential). Glinka certainly went further in terms of dramatic devices, especially in the fantastical music of the fairy-story's villain, the wicked dwarf Chernomor who abducts the fair Ludmilla and from whose clutches she is eventually rescued by the gallant Ruslan. The cumbersome plot-lines of Glinka's

works prohibit regular stagings in the west; the dashing overture is all that we hear of *Ruslan and Ludmilla*. Both operas were nonetheless part of every 19th-century Russian composer's upbringing; the teenage Rimsky-Korsakov discovered the meaning of harmony by playing through excerpts from *Ruslan* on the piano, while Tchaikovsky, who later described himself as 'the progeny of Glinka', was taken as a ten-year-old to see *A Life for the Tsar* and remembered it for the rest of his life.

THE 'FREE SCHOOL'

Apart from the rather academic creations of Serov and Dargomyzhsky, whose opera based on Pushkin's tribute to the Don Juan legend, *The Stone Guest*, was a misguided attempt to make opera realistic through the constant use of dramatic recitative, there were no major Russian operas after Pushkin until the late 1860s and 1870s. The writing of large-scale works did not come easily to the 'free school' of Russian composers gathered round Mily Balakirev, who were campaigners against what they saw as the dry-as-dust rigours of the St Petersburg Conservatoire. Balakirev had strong ideas and natural talent, but not the technical knowledge to pass on to the four other gifted composers in his circle – and since Modest

Mussorgsky was a retired imperial guard, Borodin a full-time professor of chemistry, César Cui an engineering officer and the teenage Rimsky-Korsakov a naval cadet, none of them boasting a full-time musical education, technical knowledge was what they needed.

MUSSORGSKY

Mussorgsky never acquired that knowledge, and a drink problem eventually contributed to his early death in 1881 at the age of 42; but his was a rare case of instinctive genius. Unorthodox in both orchestration and harmony, his music was later subject to 'correction' from a well-meaning Rimsky-Korsakov – in whose performing version *Boris Godunov* is often given (though increasingly less so as respect for Mussorgsky's intentions increases). *Boris*, another operatic setting of a work by Pushkin (this time a historical play along Shakespearean lines) is the only opera that Mussorgsky completed. There are two versions: the seven-scene original rejected by the Imperial Theatres in 1870 and the expanded revision given at the Maryinsky Theatre in 1874. *Khovanshchina*, a complex historical drama based on the clash of reactionary princes and Russian-Orthodox Old Believers at the time of Peter the Great's coming to power in the late 17th century, was

left unfinished and – with the exception of a few folk-song verses sung by the mezzo-soprano Martha – unscored; Rimsky-Korsakov laboured on the orchestration for an 1886 première, though the 20th-century performing version by Shostakovich is often preferred as being truer to the stark, extreme orchestral colours that Mussorgsky might have used, and there is some debate over the ending (Stravinsky and Ravel made a joint completion for Diaghilev in 1913). Both *Khovanshchina* and other, shorter operatic fragments are worth reviving, if only because they tell us even more than *Boris Godunov* does about Mussorgsky's extraordinarily faithful method of setting Russian speech as naturally as possible. Contemporaries like Tchaikovsky may have shunned Mussorgsky's 'barbaric' methods, but he left the 20th century a great deal to think about.

Alexander Borodin was better regulated than Mussorgsky in his private life, even if he did have to deal with a household full of cats and endless visits from shabby, ailing relatives whom this kindest of men could never turn away. His real problem was in reconciling the demands of his successful full-time career – he was a much-respected pioneer in the field of chemistry – with his promise as a composer. He began an opera based on the 12th-century Russian poem *The Song of*

Continued on page 142

The great Bulgarian bass Boris Christoff at London's Covent Garden in 1965, with Elisabeth Robson as the Tsar's daughter, Xenia.

boris godunov

WHO'S WHO

Boris Godunov *(Bass) Tsar*

Fyodor & Xenia *(Mezzo & Soprano) His Children*

Xenia's Nurse *(Contralto)*

Prince Shuisky *(Ten.) Courtier*

Shchelkalov *(Baritone) Boyar*

Pimen *(Bass) Monk & Chronicler*

Grigory Otrepiev *(Tenor) Monk*

Marina *(Sop.) Polish Princess*

Rangoni *(Baritone) A Jesuit*

Varlaam & Missail *(Bass & Tenor) Vagabonds*

The Simpleton *(Tenor)*

Producers have four versions of *Boris Godunov* to choose from: Mussorgsky's first thoughts of 1868–69, the much-expanded form which was accepted for production by St Petersburg's Maryinsky Theatre in 1874, and two adaptations by Rimsky-Korsakov (1896 and 1906–08).

Dmitry, son of Ivan the Terrible, has died in mysterious circumstances in 1591 – murdered, the composer assumes, at the command of Boris Godunov (brother-in-law of Tsar Fyodor, Dmitry's weak-witted half-brother), who has governed until the Tsar's death. Now Boris has gone into retreat at Moscow's Novodevichy Monastery, where the action begins in 1598.

PROLOGUE & ACT ONE

A bewildered Russian people is compelled by police coercion to beg Boris to be Tsar. Shchelkalov emerges from the monastery to announce that Boris has refused; cry more loudly! A group of blind pilgrims joins in the exhortation, though individuals in the crowd remain puzzled – what are they shouting for? The scene ends with an abruptness that is typical of Mussorgsky's work.

Boris has accepted. Russian bells thrillingly resound. In the square of the Kremlin, before the Cathedral of the Assumption, Prince Shuisky urges the crowd to further acclaim, which they give in a traditional song of praise, 'Like the sun in the skies'. In the first of his troubled monologues Boris reveals that a secret sorrow haunts him. He prays for guidance before the procession resumes.

Five years later (1603) in the Chudov monastery Pimen resumes his chronicle of Russia. He tells the novice Grigory of his wild youth as a soldier on Ivan's campaigns in Kazan and Lithuania, praising the piety of Ivan and Fyodor before contrasting them with the murderous Tsar who now sits on the throne. Grigory also learns that Dmitry, had he lived, would now be his own age. As Pimen leaves, Grigory reflects on Boris' crime.

At an inn on the Lithuanian border, Grigory – now posing as the pretender Dmitry – becomes involved with two vagabond monks, one of whom (Varlaam, a characterful cameo for bass, which Chaliapin sometimes sang in addition to Boris and Pimen) he uses as a scapegoat when guards arrive with a warrant for his arrest. Primed by the hostess of the inn as to the best route to Poland, he escapes.

ACTS TWO & THREE

The Tsar's rooms in the Kremlin. Delightful vignettes of Boris' children – Xenia, weeping for her dead lover, and the cheerful Fyodor – with their nurse are followed by a tender portrait of Boris the father. As Fyodor resumes his homework, the Tsar further reveals his guilty conscience and is racked by visions of the dying Dmitry. A boyar reveals that Shuisky has been involved in a conspiracy; Shuisky arrives to undermine Boris' confidence with news of the false Dmitry and the support the pretender has received from Polish authorities and the Pope himself. He drives Boris half insane with a description of the dead but uncorrupted Dmitry, and the tormented Tsar prays to God to take pity on him as the curtain falls.

Mussorgsky composed the 'Polish act' to provide conventional love interest for the 1874 Maryinsky production; it is not in his original score. A love-affair between Grigory ('Dmitry') and the Polish princess Marina is complicated by the machinations of the Jesuit priest Rangoni, who persuades Marina to work for the conversion of Muscovy from Orthodoxy to Roman Catholicism when she comes to share the Russian throne with 'Dmitry'.

ACT FOUR

Mussorgsky's original plan in 1869 was for a scene outside St Basil's Cathedral. It marks the first appearance of the Simpleton, moved in 1874 to the final, Kromy forest scene; here, this 'Holy Fool', symbol of truth, actually confronts the conscience-stricken ruler with the knowledge of his own guilt.

In an emergency session of the Council of Boyars in April 1605, a decree is drawn up against the pretender. Boris appears, tormented by the apparition of Dmitry; his distress only increases when Pimen enters to tell the Tsar how the sight of a blind shepherd was restored at the tomb of the dead Tsarevich. Boris collapses. Realizing he is dying, he gives his son Fyodor advice on good government. A bell tolls and, still begging mercy for his sins, Boris dies.

Mussorgsky composed what in most productions is the final scene for the 1874 production. In a forest near Kromy the crowd threatens the anarchy that Boris' reign was meant to have averted, attacking a boyar and two Polish Jesuits before dragging them away to be hanged. Grigory/Dmitry appears in triumph on his way to Moscow, but the last word belongs to the Simpleton, whose lament rings true today: 'Weep, weep, Russian folk, poor starving folk'.

Starving crowds beg their Tsar (Nikolai Okhotnikov) for bread in St Petersburg's Kirov Opera production (1987).

Igor's Campaign in 1869; it remained less than one-third completed on his death 18 years later.

The composers of Balakirev's circle had been used to helping each other with matters of scoring and even with straightforward composition, so that the completion of *Prince Igor* by Rimsky-Korsakov and the phenomenally talented young composer Alexander Glazunov was well within an honourable tradition. Glazunov filled in Act Three (sometimes cut in stagings of this very long opera) and reconstructed the overture from his memory of having heard Borodin play it on the piano. The outcome was a striking epic, masterful in the consistently inspired second act (set in the camp of the pagan Polovtsians, opponents of Prince Igor and the Russians) and typical of the grander Russian operas, including *Boris Godunov*, in the way that characters disappear for whole scenes and sometimes whole acts in the interests of a wider historical canvas.

RIMSKY-KORSAKOV

It was only by virtue of a chance appointment that Nikolai Rimsky-Korsakov escaped the fate of his musically half-educated colleagues. In 1871 he was invited to join the staff of the St Petersburg Conservatoire as Professor of Practical Composition and Instrumentation.

In his wonderfully candid autobiography, *My Musical Life*, Rimsky-Korsakov explains how ill-equipped he was to face the task – a young, self-confident dilettante, who had composed the successful tone-poem *Sadko*, the Antar Symphony and one opera, *The Maid of Pskov*. He therefore schooled himself secretly, always keeping one step ahead of his pupils, and immersed himself in a cult of musical technique before emerging into the light again – mostly by virtue of his editing of Glinka's operas. 'It was an unexpected schooling for me,' he wrote. 'There were no bounds to my enthusiasm for and worship of this man of genius. How subtle everything is with him, and yet how simple and natural at the same time! And what a knowledge of voices and instruments! With avidity I imbibed his methods.'

Glinka's example led Rimsky-Korsakov to become the most imaginative and accomplished of all Russian orchestrators. His luminous colourings and feeling for natural effects can be heard in two magical adaptations of the great satirist Gogol's Ukrainian tales, *May Night* and *Christmas Eve*, and above all in the enchanting *Snow Maiden* (1880–81), which he composed under the happy influence of the Russian spring and the folk-melodies of the village where he was staying. The first Russian production of Wagner's *Ring of the Nibelung* in the 1888–89 season inevitably made a profound impression on Rimsky-Korsakov, and he introduced Wagnerian colours and effects into his orchestration that are conspicuous in the pagan ritual of *Mlada* (1889–90) – part opera, part ballet – and in the sounds of nature in *Sadko* (1894–96), incorporating themes from the early tone-poem of the same name in which a minstrel enchants the Sea-King in his underwater palace.

The scenarios of *Mlada* and *Sadko* provide plenty of opportunities for spectacular effect but little in the way of a profound message; they were, however, exactly the kind of pageants which audiences in tsarist St Petersburg had come to expect. Rimsky-Korsakov did offer some kind of political comment in his last two operas, *The Tale of the Invisible City of Kitezh* and *The Golden Cockerel*, in which the satirical portrait of a doddery and incompetent ruler led to severe government censorship. He also lost his post at the Conservatoire as a result of his support for students during the 1905 revolution. Fantasy, however, is the essence of all Rimsky-Korsakov's operatic work. Glittering orchestral effects combine with stirring folk-style ballads in a bright and cheerful spectacle full of childlike charm. Such genuine naivety is at last being valued again in the post-modernist era.

TCHAIKOVSKY

Pyotr Ilyich Tchaikovsky, on the other hand, is a composer we tend to associate with a morbid kind of romanticism. It is an unfair generalization because in his third opera – the first worthy of serious consideration – he wrote a comedy as vibrant and life-enhancing as any of Rimsky-Korsakov's fairy-tales. Rimsky apparently didn't agree, describing the music and libretto of *Vakula the Smith* as poor when he referred to his own treatment of the Gogol tale in 1894, a year after Tchaikovsky's death. But *Vakula*, which was composed in 1874 when the 34-year-old Tchaikovsky was still under the nationalist spell of Balakirev's circle, is stocked with exuberant ideas: merry gopaks, or Russian dances, for Solokha, the witch, and her suitor the Devil; ardent love-music for the hapless hero, Vakula; and a brilliant scene at the Russian imperial court. The opera was revised as *The Slippers* in 1885, when the composer was at the height of his fame, but the original version is the more charming and perfect.

Art and life are curiously intermingled in Tchaikovsky's next and best-loved opera (or, as he carefully called it, 'lyrical scenes') after Pushkin's *Eugene Onegin*. In 1877 he found himself in the same position as Pushkin's caddish hero in relation to a young woman,

Fyodor Chaliapin

THE MOST LEGENDARY BASS OF ALL TIME, FYODOR CHALIAPIN HAS TWO HOUSE-MUSEUMS DEVOTED TO HIS MEMORY – ONE IN MOSCOW AND ONE IN ST PETERSBURG – AND COUNTLESS BIOGRAPHIES HAVE BEEN WRITTEN ABOUT THIS FASCINATING FIGURE (INCLUDING A SOMEWHAT PARTIAL STUDY BY HIS FRIEND, THE REVOLUTIONARY WRITER MAXIM GORKY). OF PEASANT STOCK, HE CAME TO OPERA LATE, BUT WAS QUICK TO ESTABLISH HIMSELF IN THE 1890S. HIS HISTRIONIC GESTURES AND LARGER-THAN-LIFE CHARACTERIZATIONS DID NOT ENDEAR HIM TO ALL AUDIENCES, BUT HE WAS WITHOUT DOUBT THE FINEST INTERPRETER OF MUSSORGSKY'S BORIS GODUNOV THAT THE OPERATIC WORLD HAS EVER SEEN, AND HE MADE HIS LAST APPEARANCE IN THAT ROLE AT MONTE CARLO IN 1937.

Antonina Milyukova, who had written to him declaring her love, just as the romantic, impressionable Tatyana in the verse-novel writes to Onegin. Determined not to follow Onegin's example of rejecting such advances and anxious, too, to quash rumours about his homosexuality, he agreed to meet and marry Antonina, but made it clear to her that he could hardly love her in the conventional sense. After only two weeks of marriage Tchaikovsky had attempted suicide and left his wife, though Antonina, who was already unstable, was to have an unpleasant habit of turning up throughout the remainder of the composer's life. This crisis meant that work on the opera could not be resumed until 1878, a year before its first performance by students at the Moscow Conservatoire. Tchaikovsky was at first doubtful whether *Eugene Onegin*'s special character as an 'untheatrical' work peopled with real human beings (rather than the 'puppets' of grand opera, as he put it) would make the opera suitable for public consumption, but productions by royal command during the 1880s proved his doubts unfounded and did much to establish Tchaikovsky as a national hero.

Inconsistent in his own views on the type of opera he should be writing, Tchaikovsky surrendered to popular conceptions of full-blooded, spectacular theatre in his next three operas – *The Maid of Orléans*, a romanticized view of his childhood heroine, Joan of Arc, *Mazeppa* and *The Enchantress*. It was with another adaptation of Pushkin – *The Queen of Spades* – in 1890 that a subject truly took possession of him. Pushkin's eerie tale of Hermann, the outsider who is obsessed by the secret of three cards held by an old Countess, is brief and ironic; the opera, to a libretto by the composer's brother Modest, expands it by including an abundance of opulent diversions, including a ball scene crowned by the appearance of Catherine the Great, which certainly helps to slow the pace. Yet in the more supernatural moments, and particularly in the chilling scene where Hermann visits the old woman's bedchamber and frightens her to death without learning her secret, Tchaikovsky casts aside the set pieces of traditional opera and writes music that even now sounds remarkably modern in its tense illustration of the drama. 'Unless I am making a dreadful and unforgivable mistake,' he wrote to Modest whilst working on the opera in Florence, 'The Queen of Spades really will be my masterpiece. In some places, in Scene Four for instance [the scene mentioned above] which I have been arranging today, I experience such a sense of fear, dread and shock that the audience too is bound to

Continued on page 146

Sergei Leiferkus, a fine Onegin, at Covent Garden, 1987.

EUGENE ONEGIN

WHO'S WHO

EUGENE ONEGIN *(Baritone)*
A Young Dandy

LENSKY *(Tenor) A Poet*

TATYANA *(Soprano)*
In Love with Onegin

OLGA *(Contralto) Her Sister*

MADAME LARINA *(Mezzo)*
Their Mother

FILIPYEVNA *(Mezzo) The Nurse*

PRINCE GREMIN *(Bass)*
A Retired General

MONSIEUR TRIQUET *(Tenor)*

ZARETSKY *(Bass)*
Lensky's Second in the Duel

Knowing that his 'lyrical scenes' based on Pushkin's classic verse novel were not for the incompetent hands of the State Theatres in the 1870s, Tchaikovsky entrusted *Eugene Onegin* to the fresh talents of students at the première on 29 March 1879. Improved standards at St Petersburg's Maryinsky Theatre led to an overwhelmingly successful staging there five years later.

ACT ONE

A melancholy prelude based on a theme that is later associated with the heroine Tatyana's anticipation of her fate flows into an offstage duet for the two sisters, Tatyana and Olga. The fateful theme is also featured at the climax of the duet. Madame Larina and Tatyana's nurse, Filipyevna, sit in the garden of the Larin country estate on a late summer afternoon, listening to the nostalgic lyrics (Pushkin's original verses) of the duet which remind Madame Larina of her youth. Peasant reapers arrive to celebrate the harvest with a rustic chorus, and the girls come on to the balcony to listen to them. The chorus sends Tatyana off into the realms of romantic fantasy, while her worldly sister Olga only wants

to sing and dance, not to sigh and dream. Tatyana admits that she has been reading too much romantic fiction, and her mother kindly suggests that real life is quite a different matter.

The arrival of two gentlemen is announced – the young, ardent poet Lensky has brought along his wealthy friend Eugene Onegin. The latter is surprised at Lensky's choice of Olga; for him, Tatyana is the more interesting of the two sisters, and it is clear that Tatyana thinks she has found the dashing man of her dreams. They pair off for walks around the estate. While Lensky tells the unromantic Olga with obvious sincerity how much he loves her, Onegin coldly holds forth to Tatyana on the boredom

of country life. Filipyevna observes that her shy Tatyana may have fallen in love with the young Onegin as the scene ends quietly.

In Tatyana's room at night, the restless girl asks her nurse to entertain her with simple stories of her youth. Impulsively, she tells Filipyevna that she is in love and, dismissing her, spends the night writing a long, heartfelt love letter to Onegin (this, the famous 'Letter Scene', was the first part of the opera to be composed; Tchaikovsky clearly identified with the heroine's bittersweet yearnings). At sunrise, she persuades the nurse to ensure delivery of the letter.

Servant girls gather berries in the Larins' garden. Terrified and now regretful of having sent the

The St Petersburg ball, Act Three, in the Kirov Opera production.

letter, Tatyana comes face to face with Onegin. He tells her that he can love her only as a brother; the music is a good deal more compassionate than the clipped, correct words that Pushkin puts into the mouth of Onegin, as though Tchaikovsky were setting to music his own address to the woman he so foolishly married. All the same, our sympathies lie so much with the heroine that it is nonetheless a painful scene, though it brings the act to an inconclusive end.

ACT TWO

A country ball is being held in Madame Larina's house in celebration of Tatyana's name-day. In Pushkin's poem the guests stamp so hard that their feet go through the floorboards (so much for the elegance of Tchaikovsky's waltz). Onegin waltzes with Tatyana. The old women speculate rudely on Onegin's unpromising credentials, and he, overhearing them, decides to cause trouble. As Lensky is the one who made him come here, he will take his revenge by flirting casually with Olga. Following a diversion provided by the elderly French tutor, Monsieur Triquet, who sings a few verses in Tatyana's honour, the growing conflict between Onegin and Lensky finally comes to a head, when Lensky, out of control, challenges his former friend to a duel.

The two men meet by a watermill the following day. The central figure of Act Two is Lensky (as Tatyana was of Act One and Onegin will be of Act Three) and, to one of Tchaikovsky's most plangent melodies, he sings a tragic aria in which he seems to be reconciled to his fate. The absurdity of the practice of duelling – by which Pushkin himself was to meet his end, so young and so senselessly – is expressed in the identical private thoughts of Onegin and Lensky as they prepare to face each other: how is it that they are willing to kill in cold blood? It is Lensky who falls dead in the fatal shooting.

ACT THREE

After several years of restless wandering, described at length in Pushkin's verses, Eugene Onegin finds himself in the midst of a grand Polonaise at an elegant ball in a St Petersburg mansion. With astonishment he recognizes the beautiful woman on the arm of the elderly Prince Gremin as Tatyana. In a sympathetic aria Gremin sings of the light that Tatyana has brought into his life since their marriage two years ago. It is now Onegin's turn to fall in love, and the realization dawns on him to the same music as that sung by

Tatyana in Act One, when she made her passionate decision to write the letter.

The crucial meeting between Onegin and Tatyana takes place in a reception room of Gremin's house. She reminds Onegin of how the situation has been reversed, but has to confess her own sadness as they sing together of the happiness that was once so nearly theirs. She admits that she loves him, but asks him to act honourably and leave her. She is the one finally to summon up the courage to leave, and Eugene Onegin is left alone on the stage – the third victim of an all-powerful fate.

Tatyana (Larissa Shevchenko) contemplates the dawn after having written the fatal letter to Onegin. Kirov Opera, 1987.

as he may have been for some of his orchestral ideas, Janáček's real innovation was to go a good deal further than Mussorgsky in the musical setting of human speech.

JANÁČEK

It was in *Jenůfa* that Janáček pioneered the idea of 'speech melody' – the detection of music in every intonation, every rise and fall of the human voice. In an article written 15 years after the composition of *Jenůfa* he describes his joy at the beauty of the speech melodies he heard in everyday life, rejoicing 'at their aptness, at the ampleness of their expression...I knew that I could cope with the motif of any word, no matter how general or how solemn – that I could cope, too, with the banality of life and its deep tragedy – that I could cope even with the prose of *Jenůfa*. And I composed it to prose.' His source was as remarkable as the way in which he set it to music – a realistic play about Moravian folk life by a remarkable woman, Gabriela Preissová, that is unflinching in its portrayal of the cruelty of life. The theme of Preissová's play, *Her Foster Daughter*, is also extraordinary from a feminist point of view: there is understanding rather than condemnation of the rash actions of the two principal female characters in the opera.

Katyá returns from church, followed by her husband and observed by her merciless mother-in-law in Joachim Herz's 1971 Berlin Komische Oper production of Janáček's Katyá Kabanová.

feel the same, at least in some degree.' He wrote only one more opera before his untimely death in 1893, the fastidiously-crafted, one-act *Iolanta*, but if *Eugene Onegin* is Tchaikovsky's finest all-round operatic achievement, *The Queen of Spades* contains his most experimental and haunting passages.

The dramatic intensity of *The Queen of Spades* did not pass unnoticed by the Czech composer Leoš Janáček, who reviewed the first performance given in his home town of Brno in 1896. He praised Tchaikovsky's 'music of horror' and duly paid tribute to it in the second act of *Jenůfa*, the opera on which he was working at the time, but which he would not complete until seven years later. A Moravian who was more prone to look east

than his neighbours in Bohemia, Janáček willingly absorbed what Russian influence he could and remained a Slavophile for the rest of his life. Even the folk-music of Moravia, which he collected avidly in the late 1880s and used in his second opera, *The Beginning of a Romance*, was closer to traditional Russian melody than the warm, middle-European character of Bohemian folksong.

SMETANA & DVOŘÁK

Even so, the light-hearted folk style of *The Beginning of a Romance* owed its charms to the example of Bedřich Smetana's *The Bartered Bride* (1866). Smetana and his romantic heir, Antonin Dvořák, seem most at home when

sounding the native strains of Bohemia's woods and fields; yet Smetana managed the heroic touch in *Dalibor* and solemn pageant in *Libuse*, both of which are still core repertoire pieces in Prague's National Theatre, while Dvořák dabbled in loftily romantic historical dramas before achieving operatic fame with the sweet, sad tale of a water-sprite, *Rusalka* (1901). It is the only one of his operas to be popular outside his native land, yet the rumbustious *Devil and Kate* deserves to be heard more often – if only as a Czech comic alternative to the ubiquitous *Bartered Bride*.

Nothing in either Smetana or Dvořák – or indeed in the work of early Janáček – prepares us for the white-heat shock of the new in *Jenůfa*. Indebted to Tchaikovsky

THE 'KAMILA OPERAS'

Janáček's infatuation with a much younger woman, Kamila Stösslová, later in his life gave rise to another series of unusual female portraits. First there was Katya, the reluctantly adulterous heroine of *The Storm*, a play by the Russian Ostrovsky, with a central figure similar in character to Tolstoy's Anna Karenina; the composer described Katya to Kamila as 'a woman, so gentle by nature... a breeze would carry her away, let alone the storm that breaks over her'. The result, *Kátya Kabanová* (1921), is an unusual work for Janáček in that its ending is unequivocally – and operatically – bleak. Janáček's other late operas put human lives and tragedies in a wider perspective.

The heroine of *The Cunning Little Vixen* (1924) is a sensual and humorous animal with human traits. Yet her death at the hands of a poacher does not end the opera; nature's rebirth and the glory of the natural cycle triumph over individual concerns in a glorious epilogue.

The central character of *The Makropulos Case* (1926) is a 337-year-old woman who has renewed herself by the use of a magic potion, but comes to realize that life is empty when the soul has died and exultantly refuses to pass on the formula as she expires.

Before and after the three 'Kamila operas', Janáček ranged even more widely in search of unusual subjects. The libretto of *Osud* (*Fate*) has been casually dismissed as 'unsatisfactory', but it is a cinematic script before its time, enigmatically revealing different angles of an artist's life before piecing them together and making sense of them in typically Janáčekian style. *The Adventures of Mr. Brouček* takes a bourgeois, beer-swilling Prague citizen to the moon (to meet the artistic and intellectual avant-garde) and back in time to 15th-century Prague, where he is confronted by stirring patriotism and the most resplendent of Janáček's choruses. In his last opera Janáček turned again to his beloved Russia and championed the cause of an author whose work none of the great Russian composers had dared to set to music – Dostoyevsky. The choice of subject was even more extraordinary – Dostoyevsky's literary memoirs of his time as a political prisoner in a Siberian labour camp, *From the House of the Dead*. The cast, with two minor exceptions, is all male, and the format nothing more than a sequence of often harrowing prisoners' monologues. Nevertheless, thanks to the blazing, forward-thrusting intensity of Janáček's music, the stark originality of his orchestration (until recently considered unplayable and often given in 'simplified' editions by score editors) and the unquenchable humanity of the theme, *From the House of the Dead* is one of the most powerful works in the repertoire. Its composer grew up a romantic and never really left his romanticism behind, but developed (late) as the most original and uncompromising figure in 20th-century opera.

Elisabeth Söderström

AT HOME IN SEVERAL LANGUAGES, THE SWEDISH SOPRANO ELISABETH SÖDERSTRÖM WILL PERHAPS BE BEST REMEMBERED FOR HER MASTERY OF CZECH IN HER REMARKABLE PORTRAYALS OF THREE JANÁČEK HEROINES – JENŮFA, KATYÁ KABANOVÁ AND EMILIA MARTY. SHE HAS BEEN STRONGLY ASSOCIATED WITH STRAUSS ROLES AT GLYNDEBOURNE IN ENGLAND, MAKING HER DÉBUT THERE IN 1957 AS THE COMPOSER IN *ARIADNE AUF NAXOS*. SHE WAS ALSO AT LEAST PARTLY RESPONSIBLE FOR THE REVIVAL OF INTEREST IN TWO LATER STRAUSS OPERAS – *INTERMEZZO*, IN WHICH SHE TOOK ON THE TRUE-TO-LIFE PORTRAIT OF STRAUSS' WIFE WITH APLOMB, AND *CAPRICCIO*, IN AN ELEGANT PRODUCTION WHICH WAS SET (CONTROVERSIALLY) IN THE 1920S. THE SOPRANO'S DRAMATIC TEMPERAMENT IS OFFSET BY A RARE HUMILITY AND CHARM WHICH SHE REVEALS IN THE SPOKEN PRESENTATION OF HER SONG RECITALS.

JENŮFA

WHO'S WHO

JENŮFA *(Soprano) A Village Girl*

KOSTELNIČKA BURYJOVKA (THE KOSTELNIČKA) *(Soprano)*
Her Stepmother

LACA KLEMEN *(Tenor)*
In Love with Jenůfa

ŠTEVA BURYJA *(Tenor)*
His Half-brother

GRANDMOTHER BURYJOVKA *(Contralto)*
The Men's Grandmother

JANO *(Soprano) A Shepherd Boy*

FOREMAN OF THE MILL *(Baritone)*

VILLAGE MAYOR & HIS WIFE
(Bass & Mezzo)

KAROLKA *(Sop.) Their Daughter*

VILLAGE FOLK & MUSICIANS

Janáček's struggle for acceptance in Prague is reflected in *Jenůfa*'s performing history. Premièred in the regional city of Brno on 21 January 1904 (in a small theatre with an orchestra of 29 players which dropped to 18 by the end of the season), it did not reach the Czech capital until twelve years later.

The complexities of the family relationships are not central to the plot, but it is helpful to know a little of the background history. Laca Klemen was disinherited of the family mill when his mother married a second time (to the elder son of Grandmother Buryjovka) and the mill passed to the son of that second marriage, Števa. To complicate matters further, Buryjovka's second son also made two marriages – first with Jenůfa's mother, then with the Kostelnička.

ACT ONE

Jenůfa waits hopefully for the return of Števa, whose child she is secretly expecting and whom she cannot marry if he is conscripted. The restless outsider Laca observes her concern with jealousy. Jano thanks Jenůfa for teaching him to read. She has a man's brain, says Grandmother Buryjovka, like her

Offerings at the grave of Jenůfa's dead child: the movement group in Lyubimov's production for Covent Garden, 1986.

foster-mother. Jenůfa replies in a deeply moving phrase that all her intelligence has gone to waste.

Števa has escaped joining the army. He drunkenly flaunts his popularity with the girls in front of Jenůfa and his fellow-recruits. Communal singing and dancing are dramatically interrupted by the Kostelnička, who – unaware of Jenůfa's pregnancy – forbids her to marry Števa unless he can stay sober for a year. Her severity is partly explained by an important monologue, often cut, in which she confides that she does not want a repeat of her own unhappy marriage. Jenůfa pleads desperately with Števa to behave himself; she will commit suicide if he leaves her. He tells her not to worry – he loves her for her rosy-red cheeks. Laca overhears this remark and, in a swift final scene, loses control when rejected by Jenůfa and slashes her cheek with his knife.

ACT TWO

Concealed in the Kostelnička's home, a tormented Jenůfa reveals that the baby has been born, but still Števa shows no interest. The Kostelnička violently tells Jenůfa that she should pray to God to let the baby die, and, alone, reveals that she hates the boy as much as she hates his father. Still, she will have to consent to the marriage of Jenůfa and Števa. She prepares for

the humiliation of having to offer Jenůfa's hand to Števa, but when he arrives he says that he has stopped loving the girl since she has become disfigured and that her severity, like her stepmother's, frightens him. He is now engaged to the Mayor's daughter.

Laca arrives, wanting to find out whether Števa has asked for Jenůfa's hand in marriage. He offers to marry Jenůfa in his place, but when the Kostelnička reveals

the birth of the child, he hesitates. She makes the dreadful decision to tell Laca that the baby has died. There is no turning back: in the third, and most powerful, of her three monologues in the act, she convinces herself that taking the child's life is the only way of redeeming Jenůfa's existence, although if the village finds out, the persecution will be terrible. She rushes out to drown the baby.

Jenůfa, still drowsy from the drug that her stepmother has given her, looks in vain for her son and sings a poignant 'Ave Maria' for his protection. When the Kostelnička returns, she tells Jenůfa that she has been delirious for two days and that the baby has died. To understated music of the deepest tragedy, Jenůfa laments (as does Janáček, who later wrote that he 'would bind Jenůfa with the black ribbon of the long illness, the pain, and the sighing' of his son, who died in infancy, and his daughter, whose death at the age of 21 left the Janáčeks childless).

Blankly, Jenůfa consents to marry Laca. The Kostelnička gives her blessing to the couple, but is terrified by visions of retribution.

ACT THREE

Two months later, in the spring, cheerful wedding preparations are under way. Jenůfa is still understandably subdued – though she

forgives Laca the wrong he did her, and he is clearly sincere in his claim that he will 'never hurt her as long as I live'. Deft social observations abound: the Mayor comments on the Kostelnička's ravaged appearance and the Mayoress wonders why Jenůfa should wear such a sober dress to her wedding. Števa and the pert Karolka also pay a visit. There is embarrassment at first, but Jenůfa takes the initiative, making the two men shake hands and telling Števa without rancour that he has the looks while Laca has the kinder heart.

Agitated voices are heard outside: a baby has been found frozen to death under the ice. The village folk take Jenůfa's shocked reaction as a sign of guilt and threaten to stone her, but the Kostelnička reveals the truth – it is she who must face a trial. Jenůfa, in an extraordinary gesture of generosity which the music powerfully reinforces, forgives her foster-mother. The Kostelnička now sees that she loved herself more than she loved Jenůfa, and she goes out, supported by the mayor.

Only Jenůfa and Laca remain. She tells him that he will have to leave her. Laca replies that he can face anything with her if they have each other to comfort. And so an opera which has seen its share of violent and terrifying actions ends in a heart-stopping and hard-won blaze of optimism.

*Abattoir madness and red-guard tyranny in David Pountney's brilliant production
of Shostakovich's* Lady Macbeth of Mtsensk *for English National Opera, 1991.*

20TH CENTURY AND BEYOND

The 1920s were the time when sympathy for society's outcasts truly established itself as a fit theme for opera. Disturbing works, such as Berg's Wozzeck, *were eventually succeeded, in England by the operas of Britten, in which the 'outsider' figure plays an important part, and in America by Gershwin's* Porgy and Bess *and Weill's* Street Scene, *with its exile's view on the immigrant community. Stravinsky brought into play three centuries of operatic tradition, characteristically making the styles of other composers his own, in* The Rake's Progress. *The way forward now belongs either to the musical theatre of Sondheim or to the more complex experiments of Reich and Adams.*

CHAPTER 11

Modern Music Theatre

The techniques of the cinema played their part in the dramatic shaping of experimental music-theatre works; the short, tense scenes of Berg's *Wozzeck* and Shostakovich's *Lady Macbeth of Mtsensk* are strikingly cinematic in style. Berlin during the period of the Great Inflation gave a new urgency and an innovative sense to all art-forms, especially opera, while Paris in the 1920s encouraged modish novelty. The Soviet Union in its early days welcomed innovation, until Stalin's state screw began to turn in the mid-1930s. Stravinsky, a multi-faceted genius, wrote works for the stage in several different genres before settling in America and providing (in 1951) one of the richest operatic fables of the 20th century, *The Rake's Progress*, with a virtuoso libretto by W. H. Auden and Chester Kallman.

Baba the Turk and her cabinet of curiosities up for sale in Act Three of Stravinsky's The Rake's Progress. The production at Glyndebourne, England, with designs by David Hockney.

The First World War changed the face of the arts in Europe for ever. Vienna tried hard to pretend that nothing had happened, although in straitened times the lavish production of a romantic epic such as Strauss' *Die Frau ohne Schatten* (*The Woman Without a Shadow*) could not hope for an enthusiastic reception. Viennese taste ran more to lighthearted escapism. The irresistible 19th-century operettas of the waltz king Johann Strauss the Younger (the best-loved being, of course, *Die Fledermaus* or *The Bat*) were succeeded by the stickier confections of Franz Lehár. His greatest success came in 1905 with *The Merry Widow*, but he repeated the formulas well into the 1930s, when his fame began to decline.

The Vienna State Opera did continue to champion 'serious' new works, especially between 1919 and 1925, when Richard Strauss was the opera's co-director. The late romantic nature of most of these operas did not preclude new ideas from being formulated, occasionally resulting in a work of individual genius; Alexander von Zemlinsky's *Der Zwerg* (*The Dwarf*, 1922), based on Oscar Wilde's cruel fairy-story *The Birthday of the Infanta*, is perhaps the most remarkable. The conflict between romanticism and a new, racier brand of music theatre became apparent in the battle for pre-eminence between two operas

in 1927 – *Das Wunder der Heliane* (*The Miracle of Heliane*) by Erich Wolfgang Korngold and *Jonny Strikes Up* by Ernst Křenek. (The precocious Korngold had already achieved success in Vienna with *Die tote Stadt* or *The Dead City* in 1920.) Just how differently the two works were perceived was nicely summed up by the cigarette firm which produced two new brands – one, the cheaper of two, given the name 'Jonny' and the other, gold-tipped and perfumed, 'Heliane'.

'DECADENT' OPERA

While *Das Wunder der Heliane* is obviously the ultimate late-romantic, symbolist tale, *Jonny* is more than the jazzy adventure of a negro musician from the New World who becomes entangled in a bizarre and noisy chase towards the end of the opera. It also sums up the crisis of the 1920s in the shape of Jonny's opposite number, the romantic composer Max, who finally breaks free of his neurotic inhibitions and finds salvation in the outside world. Whatever the differences, both operas were soon to suffer total censorship at the hands of the Nazis – *Jonny* because of its 'decadent', irreverent action and its use of jazz, *Heliane* because its composer was Jewish (Korngold later fled to America and put his romantic talent at the service of the Hollywood movie).

Even Vienna came to welcome such tokens of the age as *Jonny Strikes Up* before the Nazis intervened. Yet Berlin was the place for progressive artists in the 1920s. In the words of the pianist Claudio Arrau, who lived there at the time, 'the twenties in Berlin was one of the great blossomings of culture in history', and he was well aware of the link with the Great Inflation that hit the city: 'everything was so difficult that people sought a better

Fatty (Arley Reece) and Jenny (Pamela Hebert) in a Washington production of Brecht and Weill's The Rise and Fall of the City of Mahagonny, *1972.*

life in culture'. A leading light of the musical world in the early years of the Weimar Republic was the Italian composer and virtuoso pianist Ferruccio Busoni, whose *Doktor Faust* (1925) is one of the strangest and most lugubrious musical treatments of the Faust legend, and whose stark experimentation was carried one stage further by his pupil Kurt Weill in such early works as *The Protagonist* (1926). Kurt Weill teamed up with Berthold Brecht in the late 1920s. Their first major hit, *The Threepenny Opera* (1928), took the outline of *The Beggar's Opera*, John Gay's tale set in 18th-century low-life London, and brought it up to date with the modern equivalents of the original ballads – popular songs using jazz forms, such as the foxtrot and the tango.

In *The Threepenny Opera*, their best-known collaboration, Brecht's poetic socialism gains the upper hand, but *The Rise and Fall of the City of Mahagonny* (1930), a scathing vision of mankind's incurable capitalism, puts Weill first. A fully operatic expansion of their 25-minute boxing-ring *Mahagonny-Songspiel* (1927), it skilfully blends the lessons of Weill's forward-looking musical training and the popular elements of *The Threepenny Opera* used with an even more deliberate irony. Forced to flee the Nazis in the early 1930s, Brecht and Weill worked together in Paris on a 'sung ballet', *The Seven Deadly Sins*, an inverted morality tale in which the 'sins' are virtues which the heroine Anna needs to suppress on her money-making tour of America. The music is both bitter-sweet and ironic, warmer and sadder than the bare bones of Brecht's text suggest.

After *The Seven Deadly Sins* there was a parting of the ways; Weill travelled to America, where he found ways of dealing with the American musical on his own terms. The rest of his story is told in the final chapter.

WOZZECK

Social concerns were also uppermost, though not attached to an explicit political message, in the most shattering opera of the 1920s. *Woyzeck*, the portrait of a poor victim of society harried by his superiors and finding no outlet for his supercharged imagination, had been written nearly a hundred years earlier by the playwright Georg Büchner. It remained unperformed until November 1913, and six months later it reached Vienna, where it had a harrowing impact upon the young composer Alban Berg; his experiences in the army during the First World War only increased his determination to set it to music.

Wozzeck has been described as the first atonal opera, taking one step further the often rootless and drifting harmonies of Wagner's *Tristan and Isolde* and Debussy's *Pelléas and Mélisande*. More significantly, it contains a highly-strung late romanticism within the boundaries of some of the most rigorous musical procedures ever applied to an opera. The result is anything but academic, and none put it better than Berg himself when he wrote that 'no one in the audience, no matter how aware he may be of the musical forms contained in the framework of the opera, of the precision and logic with which it has been worked out ... no one gives heed to anything but the vast social implications of the work which by far transcend the personal destiny of Wozzeck. This, I believe, is my achievement.' And he was right.

Wozzeck's successor *Lulu*, based on Frank Wedekind's bleak plays about a *femme fatale*, is what

Continued on page 158

Geraint Evans as the tormented soldier Wozzeck at Covent Garden, London, in 1975.

WOZZECK

WHO'S WHO

WOZZECK (Baritone)
A Soldier

MARIE (Soprano)
His Mistress

ANDRES (Tenor)
Wozzeck's Friend

THE DRUM-MAJOR (Tenor)

THE DOCTOR (Bass)

THE CAPTAIN (Tenor)

MARGRET (Contralto)
Marie's Neighbour

AN IDIOT (Tenor)

MARIE'S SON (Treble)

SOLDIERS, WORKMEN & TAVERN folk

Berg's operatic adaptation of Büchner's disturbing play was championed by Erich Kleiber, a man of rare vision, who conducted the première at the Berlin State Opera on 14 December 1925. *Wozzeck* did not reach the London stage until 1952, again through Kleiber's hard work.

Berg controlled the expressionist angst of the subject-matter within a series of taut musical devices. In a testament to the composer's genius these structures (set in italics below), as well as the musical interludes between each scene, only heighten the drama.

ACT ONE (FIVE CHARACTER PIECES)

'The Captain': Suite – Prelude, Pavane, Gigue, Gavotte, Air and reprise Each day Wozzeck shaves the Captain, whose neurasthenic chatter contrasts markedly with the soldier's automatic replies. When the Captain chastises him for living in sin and having an unbaptized child, Wozzeck bursts out with a strange plea for 'we poor folk'.

'Andres': Rhapsody on three chords and the three-verse hunting song of Andres In the country at night Wozzeck and Andres are cutting sticks. Wozzeck has visions; Andres, seeing nothing, is alarmed.

'Marie': Military march and Lullaby Like his late-romantic predecessor Mahler, Berg introduces elements of popular music into his scores – here a march headed by the Drum-Major. Marie admires him from her room, slams the window on an insulting neighbour and sings her child to sleep. Wozzeck enters and distractedly ignores the child. He leaves and Marie becomes frightened.

'The Doctor': Passacaglia with 21 variations The reason for Wozzeck's odd behaviour now becomes clear: the Doctor is paying him threepence a day to perform experiments on him.

'The Drum-Major': Andante affetuoso (like a Rondo) The Drum-Major struts before Marie. She is impressed, but struggles when he seizes her threateningly. Exhausted, she yields and they go into the house.

ACT TWO (SYMPHONY IN FIVE MOVEMENTS)

Sonata-form movement: exposition, reprise, development and reprise Looking in a broken mirror, Marie admires the earrings that the Drum-Major has given

her. Wozzeck sees them, but does not bully her into confession. He touchingly hands over his wages.

Fantasia and Fugue on three themes The Doctor intimidates the Captain with psycho-babble. The two 'superiors' taunt Wozzeck as he passes about Marie and the Drum-Major. He is mortified.

Largo (slow movement) Wozzeck interrogates Marie, who lies to him. He goes to strike her. She defends herself, crying 'Rather a knife in my guts than a hand on me.' Wozzeck's grip on reality loosens as he repeats her words.

Scherzo with Ländler *(Austrian country dance), Song and Waltz* In a pub garden, amidst drunken revellers, Wozzeck sees Marie dancing with the Drum-Major. 'On and on!' he cries, mesmerized, as the couples whirl past him. The Idiot smells blood.

Rondo marziale with introduction An extraordinary wordless chorus depicts the soldiers sleeping in their barracks. Wozzeck is restless. The Drum-Major enters, drunk, picks a fight with him and leaves him bleeding on the ground while the other soldiers, including Andres, go back to sleep.

ACT THREE (SIX INVENTIONS)

Invention on a theme, with seven variations and a fugue Half singing, half speaking, in the strange form of operatic delivery known as *Sprechstimme*, Marie reads the Bible stories about the adulteress and Mary Magdalene. She is tormented by guilt, and frightens her child.

Invention on a single note (the note B) By a pond in the nearby wood Wozzeck sits on a bench with the nervous Marie. He observes that the moon rises 'like

blood-stained steel' before plunging a knife into her throat. She dies; Wozzeck gets up fearfully and hurries away.

Invention on a rhythm At an inn, couples are dancing a wild polka to an out-of-tune piano. Wozzeck tries to dance with Margret. She notices blood and the crowd turns on Wozzeck, who rushes out.

Invention on a six-note chord Back at the pond Wozzeck looks for the knife. He stumbles on the body of Marie, finds the knife and throws it into the pond. He wades in after it and drowns. The Captain and the Doctor, passing by, hear Wozzeck's groans.

Invention on a tonality (the key of D minor) In the last of the orchestral interludes many of the

opera's main character-themes flit past as the music builds in a firm, powerful lament. The pity and terror of the tragedy are expressed.

Invention on a quaver rhythm Children are playing outside Marie's house. One of them tells Marie's son that his mother is dead. He stays behind a moment, then rides off on his hobby-horse with the others to see the corpse.

One of the crowd scenes in David Pountney's production of Wozzeck at English National Opera.

many people believe *Wozzeck* to be: a twelve-tone opera, in which the twelve notes of the chromatic scale, rather than the eight of the conventional scale, give rise to a rigorously-worked system. Again, such procedures need not worry us in a good performance; and again, the insight with which Berg portrays more of society's outsiders is astounding. Berg had not finished *Lulu* when he died in 1935, and although he left enough sketches for its completion – vital for a sense of the rigid symmetry with which the composer follows the heroine's rise and fall – it was only after his widow died in 1976 that the scholar Friedrich Cerha was able to work on the scenes that showed Lulu's succumbing to blackmail and prostitution and thus to furnish opera houses with a complete *Lulu*. Berg's true heirs in German music theatre have turned out to be Hans-Werner Henze, who favours a similar density of orchestral texture, and Bernd Alois Zimmermann, who committed suicide in 1970, but whose opera *Die Soldaten* (*The Soldiers*, 1965), boldly mixing traditional opera with mime, electronics and film, seems likely to survive in the repertoire.

Like *Wozzeck*, *Lulu* is a passionate character-study written by a true romantic. The twelve-tone system used in the opera is the only thing that Berg has in common

with his Viennese contemporary, and pioneer of the system, Arnold Schoenberg, whose masterpiece in the mode, *Moses and Aaron*, deals with the distortion of a higher truth in the quest to make God's message comprehensible. In this instance, the opera's incompleteness was a result of Schoenberg's perfectionism in his treatment of a profoundly religious and difficult subject; his dialectics hardly seem to need the third act he never got round to writing.

RUSSIA

Contrary to popular belief, post-revolutionary Russia in the 1920s and even the early 1930s was a healthy place for the arts. The last flames of an 'anything goes' liberalism can be heard in the two extraordinary operas of Dmitri Shostakovich.

In 1930, at the age of 23, Shostakovich bewildered the Russian public with a faithful adaptation of the 19th-century writer Gogol's dazzlingly satirical short story, *The Nose*, in which that appendage leaves the face of an ordinary man and struts around in officer's garb. The score was notorious for such modernisms as a four-minute interlude for percussion only, suggestive of official persecution, and a number of bizarre gallops, but at heart *The Nose* is a serious work.

So, too, is *Lady Macbeth of Mtsensk*, based on a novella by Leskov, in which a bored bourgeois housewife takes a lover, poisons her father-in-law and assists in the murder of her husband. Like many of the great opera composers of the 20th century, Shostakovich shows a deep sympathy for the heroine's situation, and the final act, which culminates in her death *en route* to a Siberian labour camp, touches Mussorgskyan depths.

Even though such elements as the graphic music accompanying a lovemaking scene were dangerous territory in the Russia of the 1930s, *Lady Macbeth* ran successfully for two years following its première in January 1934. Then, in 1936, the blow fell: the newspaper *Pravda* published an article entitled 'Muddle instead of Music', which attacked the 'decadent' cacophony of the opera, and Shostakovich immediately became a *persona non grata*. He survived by virtue of carefully coded reflections on the true state of the Stalin era in his next symphonies, but never wrote another opera and never again spoke out with so much musical boldness.

It was at exactly this time (1936) that Sergei Prokofiev made the mistake of returning to the Russia whose native soil he needed so badly for his inspirations. Like Shostakovich, he was subject to an increasingly virulent state censor-

ship, which reached its peak in the notorious 1947 show-trials of 'formalism in music', a blanket term applied to any composition that did not embrace the party ideology in wholeheartedly optimistic terms. Amazingly, Prokofiev also adapted without losing his true voice. His most ambitious opera is *War and Peace*, a selective but loving adaptation of Leo Tolstoy's novel, in which the composer runs the gamut of his many familiar styles – a radiant lyricism for the touching but fallible heroine Natasha, grotesquerie for many of the minor characters, and a heartfelt Russian strain in which he manages to find melodies for the Motherland at the time of the Second World War which are anything but hackneyed or banal. He died in March 1953, on the same day as Stalin, without having seen his epic opera staged in its entirety, but his wishes have been magnificently realized by, amongst others, his friend Mstislav Rostropovich, cellist and conductor extraordinary.

For all their iconoclasm, the earlier operas of Prokofiev are rooted in Russian tradition. After depicting a bizarre, orchestrally colourful gallery of Dostoyevskyan characters in *The Gambler* (1919), he turned his attention to fantastic comedy with the aid of the pioneering theatre director Meyerhold in *The Love for Three Oranges*, though he did not complete the

Dietrich Fischer-Dieskau

NO BARITONE HAS EVER COVERED A WIDER RANGE OF OPERATIC STYLES THAN THE GREAT GERMAN SINGER DIETRICH FISCHER-DIESKAU. HIS STYLISH PHRASING HAS SUITED HIM TO A LYRIC REPERTOIRE THAT HAS TAKEN IN MOST OF THE VERDI ROLES (INCLUDING, SURPRISINGLY, A WELL-UPHOLSTERED FALSTAFF). HE HAS ALSO MASTERED COMPLEX SCORES OF THE 20TH-CENTURY: BUSONI'S *DOKTOR FAUST* (IN THE TITLE ROLE OF WHICH HE IS PICTURED ABOVE), BERG'S *WOZZECK*, HINDEMITH'S STUDY OF THE PAINTER GRÜNEWALD, *MATHIS DER MALER*, AND ARIBERT REIMANN'S *KING LEAR.* HE MADE HIS DÉBUT AS RODRIGO IN VERDI'S *DON CARLOS* AT THE BERLIN STATE OPERA IN 1948 AND DEVOTED HIMSELF IN LATER YEARS TO THE *LIEDER* INTERPRETATIONS FOR WHICH HE IS BEST KNOWN. HE RETIRED IN 1993.

work, or see it staged, until he arrived in the United States of America, a refugee from Soviet Russia. The experimental buzz of Paris in the 1920s prompted him to his most extraordinary opera, *The Fiery Angel,* a dense musical setting of the Russian symbolist Bryusov's tale of demonic possession. Partly because of the enormously complex orchestral writing and the taxing demands of the principal soprano role, *The Fiery Angel* remained unstaged during Prokofiev's lifetime; recent productions have revealed it to be a work of hair-raising intensity.

Igor Stravinsky fared better in the Paris of the 1920s than Prokofiev. He was already fêted as the composer of three great ballets for Diaghilev's Ballets Russes – *The Firebird, Petrushka* and *The Rite of Spring* – though nothing he had written referred so comprehensively to all types and ages of music as the 'opera-oratorio' *Œdipus Rex,* a 'present' for the 20th birthday of the Ballets Russes in 1927, given in Paris. Jean Cocteau's pared-down treatment of the Greek tragedy by Sophocles had been further stylized in a Latin translation, and the music can sometimes seem like a collection of tributes, at times ironic – Monteverdi, Bach, Handel and Verdi as passed through the hands of a master-magpie who set his own, acerbic seal on everything he touched. In spite of the austere presentation, pathos and humanity are here too, no doubt because Stravinsky adored his compositional models. (In the early 1920s he was accused of disrespect for the 18th-century Pergolesi, whose music he had arranged for the ballet *Pulcinella,* and his reply says it all: 'You respect, I love').

The same love shines out in Stravinsky's last (and only full-length) opera. Elements of effective showbusiness in the crowd scenes of *The Rake's Progress* can be accounted for by the fact that the composer, having relinquished his French citizenship for American in the late 1930s, hoped for a Broadway opening. The rest is far from being pastiche: like W. H. Auden and Chester Kallman, his elegant librettists, Igor Stravinsky knew his references from the inside and transformed them with his own spare but profound emotion; and so too does the artist David Hockney, whose designs after Hogarth have so graced the famous production at Glyndebourne in England that it is very difficult to see *The Rake's Progress* done in any other way. Of all 20th-century creative artists, it is perhaps Stravinsky, Auden and Hockney who assert the values of tradition most powerfully without looking backwards. In *The Rake's Progress* the past is summed up in a way that is fresh, astonishing and totally theatrical.

THE *r*AKE'S *p*ROGRESS

Stravinsky had originally hoped that New York might be the first venue for his stylish collaboration with two other exiles in America, W. H. Auden and his lover Chester Kallman. *The Rake's Progress* was in fact premièred at the Venice Festival on 11 September 1951.

The brilliant fanfares of the short prelude section hark back to Monteverdi's *Orfeo* and suggest the 18th-century London in which the greater part of the opera is set.

ACT ONE

In Trulove's garden Anne and her sweetheart, the impecunious Tom Rakewell, serenade each other with pastoral idylls. Anne's father has misgivings: his impression of Tom as a weak young man is confirmed when Tom refuses his offer of employment in the city. Tom relies instead on Fortune. 'I wish I had money', he adds, and Nick Shadow appears immediately at the garden gate with the news that an unknown uncle has died and left his fortune to Tom. Nick will serve him in London, with terms to be decided a year and a day from now. Tom bids a poignant, almost Tchaikovskyan farewell to Anne and her father.

The progress of a Rake begins, with a blaze of light and noise, in Mother Goose's brothel. Surrounded by whores and roaring boys, Tom recites his new, self-serving creed to Mother Goose. Memories of Anne, however, are quickly kindled, and Tom's conscience begins to trouble him as he sings the wistful solo 'Love, too frequently betrayed'. He drinks to banish sorrow and the ritual of the bawdy-house proceeds as Mother Goose claims him for her own.

The music melts into the reflective mood of the third scene, a highly expressive Mozartian solo for Anne. She sings that she has received 'no word from Tom' for months, and resolves to seek him out in London. The final, brilliantly determined section of the aria, 'I go, I go to him', ends on a high C.

WHO'S WHO

TOM RAKEWELL (*Tenor*)
The Young Man Whose Progress is Followed

NICK SHADOW (*Baritone*)
His Devilish Guide

ANNE TRULOVE (*Soprano*)
Tom's Sweetheart

TRULOVE (*Bass*)
Her Father

BABA THE TURK (*Mezzo*)
Bearded Lady in a Circus

MOTHER GOOSE (*Mezzo*)
Brothel-keeper

SELLEM (*Tenor*) *Auctioneer*

KEEPER OF THE MADHOUSE (*Bass*)

WHORES & ROARING BOYS, SERVANTS, CITIZENS & MADMEN

Robert Tear's Tom Rakewell lies prostrate at the feet of Mother Goose at London's Covent Garden in 1979.

Anne Trulove plays Venus to mad Tom's Adonis in David Hockney's stylized madhouse for Glyndebourne in 1975.

ACT TWO

Disconsolate in his London residence, Tom seeks happiness and Nick advises him to marry Baba the Turk, the bearded attraction of St Giles' fair; by doing so, he will be defying both appetite and duty, and he can only be happy when he is free of their tyranny. Tom laughingly agrees.

Anne arrives outside Tom's house on an autumn evening. Servants bearing strange objects into the house are followed by a sedan chair, escorted by Tom. He implores Anne to leave the corruption of London, and the reason for his agitation becomes obvious when the occupant of the sedan makes her presence felt: it is Baba. Anne leaves hurriedly and the assembled townsfolk hail Baba; she unveils her flowing beard and salutes the crowd 'with the practised manner of a great artist'.

The morning room of Tom's house is now cluttered with the curiosities Baba has collected on her travels. She chatters incessantly and rages against the indifferent Tom until he silences her by slapping his wig over her head. He takes refuge in sleep; Nick hastens his financial downfall by promoting a bogus machine for converting stones into bread. Tom hopes that the philanthropic deeds he may accomplish with it will make him worthy of Anne's love.

ACT THREE

The machine has brought to Tom and his investors 'ruin, disaster, shame'. Sellem, auctioning off the items in the morning-room, finally comes to a mysterious object. It is Baba who, uncovered at last, springs to life and defends her possessions. She turns out – with slightly implausible sentimentality – to have a heart of gold, too, and tells the ever-persistent Anne that her love may yet save Tom; for her part, Baba will return to the stage.

Disturbing music for solo strings introduces a churchyard at night: an open grave awaits Tom, whose soul Nick now has the right to claim. Desperate, Tom plays cards to save himself; memories of Anne lead him to choose the right card three times. Deprived of his victim, Shadow condemns Tom to insanity for the rest of his life.

Among the lunatics in Bedlam, Tom believes himself to be the Greek youth Adonis and waits for his Venus. She comes: it is Anne, who humours him in his illusion and sings him a lullaby. Realizing she can do nothing, she leaves with her father. Tom awakes and, finding that his Venus is gone, dies of a broken heart. The lunatics soberly mourn the death of 'Adonis'.

Before the curtain, the principals point the moral: 'for idle hands and hearts and minds, the Devil finds a work to do'.

CHAPTER 12

British Opera

Although the singular importance of the operettas of Gilbert and Sullivan should not be underestimated, there were no true masterpieces of serious opera in Britain between Henry Purcell, in the 17th century, and Benjamin Britten, whose *Peter Grimes* was a token of native genius at the end of the Second World War. He never crammed so many dazzling ideas into one opera again, but refined his style in the 'chamber operas' – *The Rape of Lucretia, Albert Herring* and *The Turn of the Screw* – and expressed himself at his deepest level in *Billy Budd*. The operas of Sir Michael Tippett were further proof that British opera was flourishing, and the tradition continues with the fresh challenges of Sir Harrison Birtwistle and Mark-Anthony Turnage.

1920s fashion rules in Jonathan Miller's production of The Mikado *for English National Opera.*

In between the achievements of Purcell in the 17th century and Britten in the 20th century, British opera in the truest sense lay fallow. The very English satire of *The Beggar's Opera* found its Victorian counterparts in the operettas of the witty versifier W. S. Gilbert and the composer Arthur Sullivan, whose string of so-called Savoy Operas (named after the theatre to which the impresario Richard D'Oyly Carte transferred them in 1881) ran from the short, one-act *Trial by Jury* in 1875 to *The Grand Duke* in 1896.

GILBERT & SULLIVAN

Gilbert's lyrics have tended to get the better deal – especially since they remain uniquely applicable to the absurdities of the class-system in Britain today – but Sullivan's music is now being taken more seriously and is even being espoused by 'serious' opera singers (for instance, in a recent recording of *The Yeoman of the Guard*, a comic opera with a tragic ending). His most tender-hearted melodies and finest ensembles (including several poignant quartets and quintets) belong to *Yeoman* and to an otherwise dated attack on what the misogynistic Gilbert saw as the pretensions of women's education, *Princess Ida* (1884). Sullivan parted company from Gilbert in an attempt at grand opera, *Ivanhoe*

(1891), and according to an old-fashioned film on the partnership, Queen Victoria is supposed to have disapproved and asked instead for *The Gondoliers*. In fact *Ivanhoe* ran for an unprecedented 160 nights, though it remains unperformed today. Sullivan returned to his old collaborator, but they failed to recapture the old spark in their last two works together. Even so, the range and settings of the triumphs of their heyday – *HMS Pinafore*, *The Pirates of Penzance*, *Patience*, *The Mikado* and *The Gondoliers* – are still remarkable, and beloved of all amateur operatic societies in Britain, which is not to say that they do not deserve to be treated with the utmost care and professionalism. The transformation of the D'Oyly Carte Company from a complacent troupe that had long since relied on routine productions delivered in a uniform fashion into an enterprise which had to find new ways of staging Gilbert and Sullivan has certainly helped to put fresh blood into these ever-topical operettas.

Other sensations in 19th- and early 20th-century British music belonged to different musical spheres. The oratorio, in which biblical scenes were given dramatic treatment, thrived in the regional cities and drew Mendelssohn to Birmingham, where he conducted the first performance of his *Elijah*. In 1901 and 1902 the most signi-

ficant – and, at times, the most Wagnerian – specimen of the form, Elgar's *The Dream of Gerontius*, was performed in Germany, thereby furthering the international reputation that his *Enigma Variations* had begun to establish in 1899. Elgar never wrote an opera, though there is a sensuous duet for soprano and tenor in his dramatic cantata *Caractacus*, and this was indeed a work which he later considered adapting for the stage. The other orchestral and symphonic masters of the early part of the 20th century, Gustav Holst and Ralph Vaughan Williams, never quite matched their concert-hall originality in their works for the stage, though Vaughan Williams' striking tribute to Bunyan, *The Pilgrim's Progress*, has the same undeniable spirituality that can be found in several of his nine symphonies. He also tried his hand at comedy with *Sir John in Love*, a cheerfully English treatment of *The Merry Wives of Windsor* which makes an interesting alternative to Verdi's *Falstaff*, and with *The Poisoned Kiss*, a lame experiment in whimsy which is interesting for its use of popular dances after the manner of Walton's *Façade*.

The same feeling that vocal lines have been superimposed on richly scored orchestral music almost as an afterthought applies to the operas of the Bradford-born Frederick Delius. A recent attempt

in London to stage his psychological and often moving *Fennimore and Gerda* (1908–10) failed in the producer's honourable endeavour to render interesting a series of static tableaux; yet his turn-of-the-century masterpiece *A Village Romeo and Juliet* would hardly be likely to suffer the same fate, were it to be revived. The score is luminously Wagnerian, ending – as the young lovers die together in a sinking barge – in the same transfigured key and manner as Isolde's so-called *Liebestod* ('love-death') at the end of *Tristan*.

BRITTEN

The true turning-point for British opera came on the single night of 7 June 1945, with the première of Benjamin Britten's first major opera, *Peter Grimes*. The war was over; the public sought for signs of artistic rebirth on its own shores, and found exactly that. Although the première was not an immediate success and caused wrangling among members of the Sadler's Wells company (which 30 years later was to become the English National Opera), the composer's words to Imogen Holst later that month are significant: 'I must confess that I am very pleased with the way that it seems to "come over the footlights", and also with the way the audience takes it, and what is perhaps more, returns night after night to take it again! I think the occasion is actually a greater one than either Sadler's Wells or me, I feel. Perhaps it is an omen for English opera in the future. Anyhow I hope that many composers will take the plunge, and I hope also that they'll find the waters not quite so icy as expected'.

Britten's first work for the stage was the operetta for schools *Paul Bunyan*, a bold choice of an apple-pie American subject, which had been composed in collaboration with the poet W. H. Auden during the composer's self-imposed exile in America during the early part of the Second World War. *Peter Grimes*, on the other hand, could hardly be more English. Whilst he was still in America, Britten's thoughts turned to home when he read an essay by E. M. Forster – a future collaborator – about the Suffolk poet George Crabbe and his poetical descriptions of life in the seaside town of Aldeburgh, where Britten had already bought a house. Yet there was a more important theme at stake – the nature of the central character. Crabbe saw the fisherman Grimes as the symbol of a cruel society, while Britten not only tried to show that society might have made him what he was but showed pity for him as an outsider – the first of many in his operas. In his depiction of the protagonist and of the individuals who persecute or try to help him, the composer ranged far beyond his native roots in a stunning assimilation of 20th-century musical languages. Even as a precocious teenager, he had managed to absorb other influences into his own style, but this huge work of a man still in his early thirties was something else. Mahler, Copland, Berg and Shostakovich are all present in a bewildering parade of character-sketches, hugely demanding choruses and atmospheric interludes that sometimes goes too far in its generosity of invention at the expense of tightly-knit drama, but never falters in terms of personal inspiration.

Britten consciously scaled his next two operas down in terms of length and size. In collaboration with the artist John Piper and the writer Eric Crozier, he formed the English Opera Group in 1946 for the encouragement of new operas (not just his own). The orchestral ensemble for which he was writing had, by the nature of the enterprise, to be much reduced; his next step was to make this twelve-piece ensemble 'sound' as well as a full

Continued page 168

Janet Baker

Peter Pears, the singer for whom Britten wrote all his main tenor roles, as Peter Grimes at Sadler's Wells, London, in 1967.

PETER GRIMES

WHO'S WHO

PETER GRIMES *(Ten.) A Fisherman*

ELLEN ORFORD *(Soprano) Widow & Schoolteacher*

CAPTAIN BALSTRODE *(Baritone)*

AUNTIE *(Contralto) Landlady*

HER TWO 'NIECES' *(Sopranos)*

BOB BOLES *(Tenor) A Fisherman & Methodist*

NED KEENE *(Bar.) Apothecary*

MRS SEDLEY *(Mezzo) A Widow*

SWALLOW *(Bass) A Lawyer*

THE REVD HORACE ADAMS *(Ten.)*

HOBSON *(Bass) Carrier*

Britten decided to adapt *The Borough*, by the early 19th-century Suffolk poet George Crabbe, after reading an essay on him by E. M. Forster while he was living in the United States of America. The first performance, a landmark in British music, took place at London's Sadler's Wells on 7 June 1945.

PROLOGUE & ACT ONE

In the Moot Hall of the Borough (in reality Aldeburgh, the home of both Crabbe and Britten) an inquest is being held into the death at sea of Grimes' latest apprentice. Swallow, the coroner, returns a matter-of-fact verdict of 'accidental circumstances'. Grimes objects to his advice not to take on another apprentice. Ellen Orford, the Borough's sympathetic schoolmistress, is left alone with Grimes and tries to banish his pessimism. Their moving unaccompanied duet is followed by the first of the atmospheric 'Sea Interludes'.

This sound of wind and waves continues to lap around the inhabitants of the Borough as they go about their morning business in Act One. Only Captain Balstrode and Ned Keene help Grimes to bring in his boat. The carter Hobson at first refuses to fetch Grimes' latest apprentice from the workhouse, but Ellen takes a firm stand against general prejudice with a strong solo, and he yields to her plea. A storm begins to brew; as the crowd disperses, Balstrode challenges Grimes' course of action, but the fisherman is determined to do better, get rich and marry Ellen. Alone, he fully reveals his yearning for happiness: 'What harbour shelters peace?'

During the second interlude, the storm breaks in Mahlerian fashion. Later that night, at 'The Boar', Mrs Sedley irritates Auntie by hanging around for Ned Keene, who has promised to bring her a fresh supply of the laudanum on which she is dependent. The shrieking 'nieces' are molested by Bob Boles, the preacher. As the storm reaches its height, Ned Keene bursts in with the news that the cliff by Grimes' hut has been washed away. Grimes comes in soon after, a wild apparition, and, while the action freezes, sings with an almost visionary intensity of the natural phenomena: 'Now the Great Bear and Pleiades'.

At the climax of a vigorous ensemble, 'Old Joe has gone fishing', Ellen arrives with the new apprentice and Grimes leads the boy off into the storm.

ACT TWO

On a fine Sunday morning several weeks later – the third interlude depicts the brighter mood – Ellen is sitting on a bench outside the church with John, the new apprentice. The ensuing action takes place against a background of hymns and *Te Deums*. Ellen encourages the silent boy to speak; then she

Jon Vickers, a heroic-tenor Grimes, and Heather Harper as Ellen Orford in the 1984 Covent Garden production.

notices a bruise on his neck. Peter Grimes arrives to take the boy fishing, and brushes aside Ellen's objections. 'We were mistaken to have dreamed,' she sadly murmurs. 'Peter! We've failed, we've failed!' In a fury, he strikes her and rushes off with the boy. A crowd gathers and mob violence against Grimes rises in a menacing crescendo. Ellen, the 'nieces' and Auntie are left alone to provide a beautiful quartet of calm before the catastrophe.

The fourth interlude, a *Passacaglia* – a musical form in which a set of variations is played out above a repeated figure in the bass – serves as the darkly expressive heart of the opera. At its terrifying height, the curtain rises on the inside of Grimes' hut. He treats the boy badly, imagines he sees the ghost of the last apprentice and raves of his dreams for the future. On hearing the distant voices of the vengeful crowd he hurries John out of the back door. The boy falls on his way down the cliff. When the Rector, Swallow and Keene enter, the hut is deserted; the act ends on a note of chilling quiet.

ACT THREE

The fifth interlude, conjuring a moonlit summer evening, is both calm and poignant. From inside the Moot Hall a band plays tunes for a dance (one of several signs

that Britten was well acquainted with Berg's *Wozzeck*). The 'nieces' dodge the amorous Swallow; Mrs Sedley detects 'murder most foul' in the disappearance of Grimes' latest apprentice. She sees Ellen showing Balstrode the apprentice's jersey, which she found down by the tide-mark and identified by the anchor she had embroidered on it. Ellen's 'embroidery aria' brings

with it a passionate realization of tragedy. Ellen and Balstrode go off to find Grimes, while Mrs Sedley goads the rest of the community to a man-hunt.

The sound of fog-horns and the crowd's vicious cry of 'Peter Grimes' are now heard in the distance as the fisherman enters, tormented by the baying of his name and distractedly longing for peace

in what is a modern equivalent of the operatic mad-scene. Ellen and Balstrode find him. Balstrode tells Grimes to sail the boat out to sea and sink her. As day breaks, the Borough again goes about its business to the grey dawn music of the first sea-interlude. Out at sea, a boat is sinking, but no-one cares; it is only another day in the life of the fishing community.

Grimes and his second apprentice in the fisherman's hut, an upturned boat in the 1984 production at Covent Garden, London.

The 1962 Royal Opera première of Tippett's King Priam *at London's Covent Garden.*

orchestra. He did this to dazzling effect in *The Rape of Lucretia*, a short, tense two-act opera that developed a favourite theme, the destruction of innocence. As a complete contrast, *Albert Herring* (1947) was a comedy in which a short story by Maupassant was transferred to the same part of the world – Suffolk – as the setting of *Peter Grimes*, though, again, it had its serious side in the portrait of the 'outsider' Albert, who ultimately breaks free of his tyrannical mother's apron strings. It was the second of the many great roles, following Grimes, which Britten composed with the inflections and vocal timbres of his lifelong companion and lover, the tenor Peter Pears, very much in mind.

BILLY BUDD

Reticent in public life, as he had at that time to be, of his homosexuality and his relationship with Pears, Britten nonetheless expressed the tensions and pressures of his sexual nature in his music, and never more so than in his next large-scale opera after *Grimes*, *Billy Budd* (composed in 1951).

The catalyst here was the libretto of the more or less 'out and proud' writer E. M. Forster. His brilliant adaptation of Hermann Melville's sometimes cryptic tale of drama on an 18th-century merchant ship made explicit the attrac-

tion felt for the 'handsome sailor' Billy by the repressed Claggart, whose 'sexual discharge' according to Forster had 'gone evil', and also by the 'good' but uptight Captain Vere. In the opera, Vere – another role for Peter Pears – becomes the central character. His hopes for Billy are dashed when the sailor, halted by his fatal stammer as he attempts to answer Claggart's false accusations, lashes out with his fist and strikes Claggart dead.

Vere's crisis, as he is caught between his repressive role as a minister of justice and his passionate 'love that dare not speak its name' – brilliantly underlined by a sequence of chords as he goes to speak to Billy for the last time – remains unresolved. 'I've sighted a sail in the storm, the far-shining sail, and I'm content', he sings in the epilogue, an old man looking back on the incidents of 1797. In the light of Billy's destruction, it is a somewhat unsatisfactory statement, but the music provides the sense of release which has been so desperately needed. As at the end of *The Rape of Lucretia*, where a Christian message is grafted on to a pagan story, Britten's inspiration makes sense of what might in a straightforward play seem like an unsatisfying conclusion.

Taken as a whole, *Billy Budd* is Britten's masterpiece. Inexorable in its second-act unwinding of the tragedy, it employs the all-male ensemble to build a breathtaking portrait of life at sea that is at once both harsh and tender.

Until recently, *Budd*'s successor, *Gloriana*, had been written off as second-rate Britten. It had attracted a great deal of extra-musical bad press for its 'warts-and-all' presentation of Queen Elizabeth I, which was seen as no fitting tribute to the coronation of the second Elizabeth. As a masterly study of the tensions between public duty and private wishes, however, it is a marvellous work, a worthy 20th-century counterpart to Verdi's studies of the ruler and his (or her) conscience. Britten's music for the Elizabethan dance scenes, too, is no mere pastiche: he was always himself, even when paying tribute to past ages.

GHOSTS & ENCHANTMENT

For *The Turn of the Screw* (1954), Britten turned once again to chamber opera and created his most haunting study of innocence undermined. Myfanwy Piper's treatment of the story by Henry James brought with it the problem of 'real' ghosts who sing and act (in the story, they could well be in the imagination of the central character, governess to two children in a country house). Even so, the clash of purity, especially in the music of the treble, Miles, and knowing seductiveness remains terrifying; this is music that successfully invades one's dreams.

Beguiling enchantment of a different sort, though not without sinister overtones, was conjured in 1960 with *A Midsummer Night's Dream*. Britten worked with Pears on a careful adaptation of Shakespeare – only one line in the opera is not the bard's – concentrating on the magic of night and sleep, which had long been a preoccupation for the composer. Even the love-scene of the fairy-queen Titania and the weaver Bottom, temporarily transformed into an ass, came in for tender, idyllic music, though there was also successful comic pastiche in the 'play-within-a-play' *Pyramus and Thisbe*, which Shakespeare's rude mechanicals present before the Athenian court: here Britten parodies the mad-scenes of Donizetti, Verdian melodrama, Gilbert and Sullivan and cabaret. In 1970 Britten turned to another ghost story by Henry James, *Owen Wingrave*, which raised the question of pacifism, an issue about which he had long felt strongly. Written for television, it makes a successful obsessive study in that medium, as repeat showings of the 1971 broadcast have proved.

For his last opera (his 16th if we include the very personal realization of *The Beggar's Opera*, the delightful works for children *Let's Make an Opera* and *Noyes Fludde*, and the three 'church parables' – of which the first, *Curlew River*, is by far the best) Britten turned to Thomas Mann's short story *Death in Venice*. In characterizing Mann's *alter ego*, the ageing writer von Aschenbach who pursues youthful beauty to fatal extremes in cholera-ridden Venice, Britten wrote once again for the poetic sensibility of Pears – a demanding role indeed for a man in his sixties. As in *Billy Budd*, this single-minded study dwells on tight-lipped torment before last-minute emancipation, suggesting that Britten's demons pursued him right up to his death in 1976. Without them, his music would hardly possess its extraordinary capacity to challenge and disturb.

TIPPETT

Parallel with Britten's output, if by no means as certain of a long-term hold upon the repertoire, are the operas of Sir Michael Tippett. The most popular, and arguably the most successful in its high-flown aims, is the first, *The Midsummer Marriage* (1955) – a kind of *Magic Flute* for our times. As in Mozart's opera it has parallel pairs of lovers: the quest of a 'higher' couple is offset by the romance between a car mechanic and a secretary (the equivalents of Papageno and Papagena). Tippett believes in the 'collective experience' of opera, but one of his fundamental rules for the art-form is that 'while the collective, mythological material is always traditional, the specific twentieth-century quality is the power to transmute such material into an immediate experience of our day', and this is demonstrated in the dancing, leaping ritual of *The Midsummer Marriage*.

The composer's shift to a harder, grittier language in *King Priam* (1962), reworking an aspect of the Trojan War myth to shed new light on 'the mysterious nature of human choice', inevitably seems like a self-conscious move, and he has not returned to the exuberant style of *The Midsummer Marriage*. His argument was that the restless 1950s needed music of lyrical optimism, while the more comfortable decades that followed should be met by a more combative, aggressive response. Tippett's occasional weakness as his own librettist has dated *The Knot Garden* (1970) and *The Ice Break* (1977), though their dramatic structures show a constant self-renewal, and the attempt to come to grips with contemporary issues is brave. This falls flat in his most recent work to date, *New Year*, a dotty mixture of tributes to television science-fiction and reflections of street life which seem coyly out of touch with reality, or even any stylized reflection of it; if we

look for the best of Sir Michael in his later work, we find it in the symbolic melting-pot of his 1980s oratorio, *The Mask of Time*.

BIRTWISTLE

After Tippett, the most recent British composer to be accepted by the establishment is Sir Harrison Birtwistle, whose themes are sometimes more approachable than his music. Unlike Tippett, Birtwistle seems more preoccupied with form than meaning, and his first major work for the stage in 1965, *Tragœdia*, was a pointer for the composer's future in that he professed himself 'concerned with the ritual and formal aspects of Greek tragedy rather than with the content of any specific play.' His obsession with what sets Greek tragedy apart from our own dramas, instead of with what emotionally connects that distant past with the present, is apparent in *The Mask of Orpheus*, a complex examination of the Orpheus myth from several angles. It followed an expressionist version of the children's puppet show *Punch and Judy* – definitely for adults only – and was in turn succeeded by the 'mechanical pastoral' *Yan Tan Tethera* (1983–84). Birtwistle's most haunting use of myth yet is *Gawain* (1991), which again revels in the ritual aspect of a gripping adventure-story (in this case the

medieval poem *Sir Gawain and the Green Knight*). *Gawain* is typical of Birtwistle's heady orchestral brew – thickly scored and sometimes violently confrontational – and the spiky, sometimes voice-wrecking operatic style demanded of his singers. Give the vocal parts to members of the orchestra, as Birtwistle has done in *Gawain's Journey*, his tone-poem based on the opera, and it becomes clear that he composes with instruments rather than voices in mind. All the same, he remains a composer of strong dramatic instinct and a titanic force in British music.

Birtwistle's choice of subject-matter has its counterparts in the striking works of some of his fellow-countrymen. The northern ballad recreated by the poet Tony Harrison in *Yan Tan Tethera* finds its Scots parallels in the luminous, hypnotic and often humorous treatment by Judith Weir of three west-Highland tales in *The Vanishing Bridegroom* (1990), definitely a miniature masterpiece. The Greek strain is also to be heard in Mark-Anthony Turnage's *Greek*, a rocking adaptation of Steven Berkoff's streetwise *Œdipus* play, which follows in the Britten tradition, and in John Buller's *Bakxai*, a treatment of Euripides' tragedy which is faithful to tradition and, for the most part, sets the original Greek and exploits the exciting rhythms of the chorus to striking effect.

NEW DIRECTIONS

Bakxai was one of the works that English National Opera commissioned or mounted (one opera each year) in an attempt to establish the major operas of the present day. Others included the ambitious but ultimately once-only *Clarissa* by the neo-romantic Robin Holloway and *The Inquest of Love* by Jonathan Harvey. As Peter Jonas, the director of English National Opera at the time, boldly declared, the company has not found a master-work yet, but that is no reason for not still trying. Surprisingly, in view of the current climate for the arts, schemes to provide forums for the operas of young composers abound in London, yet depressingly few of these works exercise any lasting hold over the imagination. The fact remains that hardly any – and Turnage is a bold exception – observe what Verdi, Janáček and Gershwin instinctively knew: how close writing for the voice is, or should be, to the natural music of human speech. In that respect, the Americans remain closer to the vital core of opera as a direct, shared experience, and it hardly matters whether the form is musical theatre (Stephen Sondheim), fully-fledged opera (John Adams) or mixed-media experimentation (Steve Reich). The healthy path to this flourishing state of affairs is the subject of the next chapter.

The dramatic appearance of the Green Knight in the Royal Opera première of Harrison Birtwistle's Gawain, 1991.

A recreation of George Seurat's pointillist painting La Grande Jatte *in the production of Sondheim's* Sunday in the Park with George *at the National Theatre, London, 1990.*

CHAPTER 13

American Opera

The social issues that had been raised in the first great American musical, Jerome Kern's *Showboat*, found an operatic context in George Gershwin's masterpiece *Porgy and Bess* and were subsequently taken up to striking effect in Kurt Weill's *Street Scene* – a melting-pot of operatic and music-theatre styles which has a right to the composer's classification of 'American opera' – and Marc Blitzstein's *Regina*. The musicals of Stephen Sondheim have proved a special case in the world of serious music theatre, and America is by no means without a bright new generation of opera composers: John Adams' exuberant *Nixon in China* and Steve Reich's mixed-media experimentation *The Cave* point a new way forward.

Political rallying in the 1984 Seattle Opera production of Douglas Moore's The Ballad of Baby Doe, *a 1956 folk opera.*

Consult any brief histories of opera written before the 1950s and you will invariably find no mention of America's contribution. The reason is partly that there seemed to be no tradition, but also that American musical theatre at that time was regarded as a breed apart. Yet the musical had its roots in European culture. Victor Herbert, the sweet and innocent founding father of the musical, played the cello in the Metropolitan Opera Orchestra and knew his repertoire; clearly the operas of Gounod were firm favourites, for he introduced the French waltz-song into many of his shows – a tradition which continued through to Rodgers and Hammerstein, and beyond them to Stephen Sondheim.

GERSHWIN

Social concerns were slow to appear in the musical. The pioneering work in this respect is Jerome Kern's *Showboat* (1927), a vast historical canvas which deals honestly and movingly with questions of miscegenation and black oppression on the Mississippi. Nor is Kern's lush, often quasi-operatic style best dealt with by 'show voices'; the range of his vocal lines is huge and blossoms in the care of such opera singers as Frederica von Stade and Teresa Stratas (both featured on a scrupulously complete recording of *Showboat*).

For a compassionate view of the working class that can truly call itself an opera, however, we have to move forward seven years on from *Showboat* to George Gershwin's *Porgy and Bess*. The Brooklyn-born son of Russian-Jewish parents, Gershwin learnt his trade on Tin Pan Alley in the second decade of the 20th century and flourished as Broadway's best and jazziest tunesmith throughout the 1920s. The secret of his countless wonderful songs from those days is the same as that of Mozart, Verdi and Schubert as songwriters – the absolute naturalness of the

melodies: if you hear a Gershwin song, the setting of the words has such a natural shape that you can usually sing it back immediately. The same is true of many of the numbers that go to make up the melting-pot of *Porgy and Bess*; but this time the end-product is more than the sum of its tuneful parts. Gershwin had wanted to write a serious American music drama from the start of his career, and here he accomplished it. The opera has been criticized for failing, as the work of a white 'outsider', to give the black community its own true voice (it was not, incidentally,

the first opera for a black cast: that distinction belongs to Virgil Thomson's *Four Saints in Three Acts* of 1933, to a text by Gertrude Stein). It is true that apart from the many heart-stopping choral spirituals in *Porgy*, the inflections are not always what one might expect of the Charleston tenement-dwellers. What matters is that the composer strikes at universal emotional truths when he sympathizes with these often fallible characters: the fact that Serena's lament in the second scene of Act One is the most Jewish-sounding number in the whole of Gershwin's output, or that Bess' phrases are almost Verdian when she sings 'I loves you, Porgy', only add to the warmblooded diversity of the opera's musical language.

WEILL IN AMERICA

Gershwin died tragically young, without accomplishing the opera 'of New York City itself, with its blend of native and immigrant strains' that he had mentioned in the early 1930s. That task fell, in the mid 1940s, to a refugee from Hitler's Germany. Kurt Weill had quickly, and without any cynicism, adapted to Broadway with a string of musicals on slightly offbeat subjects, the most notable being *Lady in the Dark* (1940), a lively if necessarily flippant look at psychoanalysis. It was, however, in *Street Scene* six years later that he was able to combine his Broadway experience with the compassionate musical portrait of the poor and oppressed that he had pioneered in Berlin – sometimes in spite of Brecht's hard, cold texts. His theme now was a far-reaching view of New York tenement life, bleaker than Gershwin's vision of Catfish Row, with a domestic tragedy based on a real-life murder as its central plot. Sassy 'show numbers' contrasted with a touch of the old Berlin acerbity and fully-fledged arias for the frustrated housewife Anna Maurrant (sung at the first

performance by the lyric soprano Polyna Stoska), for her daughter Rose, who in a powerful final scene without a hint of false sentiment walks away from the tragedy, and for Rose's Jewish friend, Sam Kaplan. Weill called it, with total justification, 'an American opera', although until very recently the public regarded its hybrid nature with suspicion. Thanks, however, to the pioneering work in Britain of the joint production by Scot-

tish Opera and English National Opera, the composer's prediction that 'seventy-five years from now, *Street Scene* will be remembered as my major work' is on its way to becoming a reality.

Weill's American contemporaries also took social issues seriously. *The Mother of Us All* (1947) was Virgil Thomson's second collaboration with Gertrude Stein and focuses on the American feminist Susan B. Anthony, a lifelong cam-

paigner for women's rights. The central figure of Marc Blitzstein's *Regina* (1949) is the first utterly ruthless anti-heroine in opera since Monteverdi's Poppea, and a typical representative of the newly-rich class that began to replace the old aristocracy in the Deep South at the turn of the century; her music is flamboyant and compelling, a complement to the characterization of Bette Davis in the film of the play by Lillian Hellman, *The Little Foxes*, on which the opera, too, is based. Blitzstein, a pupil of Nadia Boulanger and Schoenberg, turned his skill to the purposes of direct expression – much like Hindemith in Germany – though his political beliefs, communist in the broadest sense, brought him into conflict with the American government.

MENOTTI

Gian Carlo Menotti was the most successful American composer of the 1940s and '50s, but is hardly of comparable stature. He had an unerring nose for gripping subjects – *The Medium* is chilling *Grand Guignol* and *The Consul* deals with the crushing weight of inhuman bureaucracy in an unnamed state – but his style, however effective, plays safe with Puccinian formulas. With Menotti American opera reaches a safe, temporary cul-desac and hands over the palm of ingenuity to the so-called musicals
Continued page 178

Flora (Maureen Forrester) with Monica (Janis Orenstein) in Menotti's The Medium, *Ontario, Canada, 1974.*

Cynthia Haymon, a truthful Bess, and the Jamaican bass Willard White as Porgy in Trevor Nunn's 1992 production for Glyndebourne, England.

PORGY AND bESS

Porgy and Bess, with a libretto by Du Bose Heyward and the composer's brother Ira Gershwin, is the opera George Gershwin had so long wished to write. Less than two years after the Boston première on 30 September 1935, he died of a brain tumour at the age of 38.

ACT ONE

On a Saturday evening in the courtyard of Catfish Row, a negro tenement in Charleston, Carolina, couples dance to the blues of pianist Jasbo Brown and Clara sings the famous 'Summertime' as a lullaby to her baby. A crap (card) game is in progress. Porgy's defence of Bess' reputation is interrupted by her arrival on the arm of her man, Crown, who drunkenly joins in the crap game. Crown loses to Robbins and kills him with a cotton hook. As he hurriedly leaves, he gives Bess permission to take another lover in his absence, but on a temporary basis only. Accepting some dope ('happy dust') from Sporting Life but rejecting his offer of a new life in New York, she goes into Porgy's room.

Robbins' body lies on a table in the middle of Serena's room. The assembled mourners contribute money for the burial; Serena accepts Bess' offering when she explains it is from Porgy and not from Crown. A detective enters, orders that the body be buried on the following day and singles out gentle Peter the Honeyman, one of the inhabitants of Catfish Row, to be held under arrest until Crown is found. Serena's lament, 'My man's gone now', contrasts with the optimistic final spiritual of the scene.

ACT TWO

A month later, Jake and the fishermen prepare to set out for sea, though Clara warns them of fierce September storms. Porgy plays the banjo and sings happily of his life with Bess: 'plenty o' nuttin'' is quite enough for him. Two visitors come to see him: a black lawyer who tricks him into buying a 'divorce' to free Bess of Crown, even though she has never married him, and the 'good' white man Archdale, who tells Porgy he will put up bail for Porgy's friend Peter, who used to be part of Archdale's family. As he leaves, Porgy and the chorus encourage an ill-omened buzzard to 'keep on flyin''. Porgy drives the human buzzard Sporting Life away from Bess, who has kicked the 'happy dust' habit, and they sing of their contentment together in the wonderful duet 'Bess, you is my woman now'. Bess reluctantly joins the others for a picnic on Kittiwah Island, leaving Porgy once more singing 'I got plenty o' nuttin''.

Amid vigorous singing and dancing on the island, Sporting Life gives his own interpretation of biblical events ('It ain't necessarily so'). As Bess prepares to leave with the rest of the party, Crown comes out of hiding. She tries to resist his powerful sexuality, but weakens and they go off into the woods.

Back at Catfish Row a week later, Jake and the fishermen set sail in the face of a rising storm. Peter is back from jail and Bess has returned delirious from Kittiwah Island. She recovers and is passionate in her insistence that she wants to be with Porgy in spite of what has happened; 'I wants to stay here' (better known as 'I loves you Porgy') reveals the new depths of her love for him. The wind rises and the hurricane bell is heard.

On the following dawn everybody huddles in Serena's room; the storm still rages outside, and the crowd prays fervently for salvation. Crown appears and asks Bess to come with him, but she refuses; Porgy is her man now.

Clara, at the window, sees Jake's upturned boat and rushes out into the storm, handing her baby to Bess. Crown goes out after her, but vows to return for Bess.

ACT THREE

On the following evening, after the storm, the inhabitants of Catfish Row grieve for Jake and Clara. Bess poignantly reprises 'Summertime' as she sings to Clara's baby. When Crown stealthily comes into the courtyard and passes under Porgy's window, Porgy stabs him in the back and kills him in the ensuing scuffle. 'Bess, Bess, you got a man now, you got Porgy!' he shouts triumphantly.

The following afternoon, the detective and the coroner question Serena and friends to no avail over the murder of Crown. They take a protesting Porgy with them to the police station to identify the body. As soon as he is gone, Sporting Life plays on Bess' weakness, persuades her to take more 'happy dust' and tempts her with the prospect of 'a boat dat's leavin' soon for New York'.

A week later, Porgy returns in the patrol wagon, having spent a week in jail for contempt of court (refusing to look on Crown's face). He hands out presents bought with his winnings from jailhouse crap games, but stops short when he learns that Bess has gone away with Sporting Life.

Following an emotional trio, in which Serena and Maria join him, Porgy sings the ultimate uplifting spiritual of the opera, 'Oh Lawd, I'm on my way' as he leaves for New York in his goat-cart, determined to find Bess.

Spirituals at Robbins' funeral, Act One, Scene Two, in the Glyndebourne production.

Leontyne Price

LIKE THE CONTRALTO MARIAN ANDERSON BEFORE HER, LEONTYNE PRICE EXPERIENCED SOME DISCRIMINATION AS A BLACK SINGER, AND ALTHOUGH SHE WAS SINGING IN THE EARLY 1950S, SHE DID NOT MAKE HER METROPOLITAN OPERA DÉBUT UNTIL 1961 (AS LEONORA IN VERDI'S *IL TROVATORE – THE TROUBADOUR*); SHE HAD INITIALLY TO ESCAPE TYPE-CASTING AS GERSHWIN'S BESS, WHICH SHE SANG MANY TIMES EARLY IN HER CAREER, AND WITH WHICH SHE MADE HER FIRST LONDON APPEARANCE IN 1952. HER LUSTROUS SOPRANO TIMBRE AND SUPERB BREATH CONTROL HAVE MADE HER ONE OF THE FINEST AIDAS OF OUR TIME AND HER VERDI IS MUCH ADMIRED. SHE HAS DONE MUCH TO PROMOTE THE CAUSE OF AMERICAN MUSIC, ESPECIALLY THAT OF THE ROMANTIC COMPOSER SAMUEL BARBER.

of Stephen Sondheim – a brilliant lyricist as well as composer who, perhaps because he thinks of his sentences in musical terms, often shares the instinct of Verdi or Gershwin for a singable tune.

SONDHEIM

In the range of his subjects Sondheim stands beside Verdi and Strauss. Following his work as an ingenious lyricist for Jule Styne (*Gypsy*) and Bernstein (*West Side Story*), he found his way with *A Funny Thing Happened on the Way to the Forum* and the oddball 1960s cult-musical *Anyone Can Whistle*. He put his finger fairly and squarely on the pulse of contemporary life in the ensemble-pieces *Company* (1970) and *Follies* (1971). *A Little Night Music*, his most operatic musical yet, came next, an adaptation of Bergman's magical film *Smiles of a Summer Night* which is predominantly in waltz time. But nothing could have prepared audiences for the dark and unashamedly operatic treatment of Victorian melodrama in *Sweeney Todd*, a flop on its first London run. The blame is unfairly laid on the Drury Lane production, but the fact remains that – as with *Street Scene* – the musical-going public expected something lighter and the opera-going public generally stayed away. The recent scaling-down of Jonathan Tunick's

orchestrations (which had been so effectively spine-chilling, Britten-style, in the original version) and the reliance on actors who could sing rather than singers who could act in the minimal production of London's National Theatre tell only half the story; *Sweeney Todd* still awaits a production by a major British opera company.

'MINIMALISM'

Since *Sweeney Todd*, Sondheim's themes remain dazzlingly original, if less operatic; they include painting – and specifically the pointillist artist Seurat in *Sunday in the Park with George*, the meaning of fairy stories in *Into the Woods*, and killers, or would-be killers, of American presidents in *Assassins*. His is not, however, the only way forward for music theatre. So-called minimalism has emerged from the repetitive patterns and the static rituals of Philip Glass' trilogy on key figures in world history (Einstein, Gandhi and Akhnaten) to develop as something that is both richer and rarer in the operas of John Adams.

With *Nixon in China* (1987) Adams applies the Shakespeare–Verdi combination of private soliloquies versus public spectacle to an event in recent history, Nixon's meeting with Mao Tse-Tung in 1972. *The Death of Klinghoffer* (1991) is a stylized and startling examination of the hijacking and killing on board the Italian cruise-liner, *Achille Lauro*. In the case of both operas by Adams, the vision of an extraordinary young producer, Peter Sellars, played a vital part in the impact of the premières: these were stagings to challenge and exhilarate, giving one a sense of what it must have felt like to be sure of a masterpiece on the first night of a Berg or Britten opera. Presentation was an all-important factor, too, in the 'mixed-media' event of *The Cave*, a true partnership between a third so-called minimalist, Steve Reich, and his wife, the video artist Beryl Corot. Computers hammered out passages from the Bible in breath-taking rhythmic precision, complemented by a vocal group delivering the same lines, while on giant video screens Palestinians, Israelis and finally Americans explained in interview what the Biblical story of Abraham, Ishmael and Hagar meant to them. Reich followed Janáček's principle of the melodies inherent in human speech, and as a string quartet took up 'treated' portions of the interviewees' words, one sensed the inexhaustible richness of these 'speech-melodies'. The experience could hardly be called an opera in the strictest sense, and whether its methods point a new way forward remains to be seen, but to attend such a vibrant and thought-provoking 'happening' was to feel confidence for the future of opera. Adams and Reich prove that there is life in the old art-form yet.

Sally Burgess as Nefertiti and the counter-tenor Christopher Robson in the title role of Glass' Akhnaten in the English National Opera production.

Broadway stars David Cryer and Judy Kaye as Sweeney Todd and Mrs Lovett in the 1980 production by Michigan Opera Theatre.

SWEENEY todd

WHO'S WHO

SWEENEY TODD *(Baritone)*
Formerly Benjamin Barker, a Barber

MRS LOVETT *(Soprano)*
Owner of a Pie-shop

BEGGAR WOMAN *(Soprano)*

ANTHONY HOPE *(Tenor) A Sailor*

JUDGE TURPIN *(Baritone)*
A 'Pious Vulture of the Law'

JOHANNA *(Soprano) His Ward*

BEADLE BAMFORD *(Tenor)*
The Judge's Sidekick

PIRELLI *(Tenor) A Quack*

TOBIAS RAGG *(Tenor)*
His Sidekick

PEOPLE OF LONDON, BALLAD-SINGERS & LUNATICS

Sondheim's darkest work, rooted in Victorian melodrama, opened on Broadway on 1 March 1979; it has since been taken up by several American companies. Only one of the six British productions so far has been presented by an operatic cast (students of London's Royal Academy of Music).

PROLOGUE & ACT ONE

A grave is being dug to the accompaniment of funereal organ music. As the piercing scream of a factory whistle is heard, members of the ensemble step forward and narrate 'The Ballad of Sweeney Todd'. As the crowd cries 'Swing your razor wide, Sweeney!', the *Dies Irae* (the Latin chant for the dead) is introduced; then Sweeney rises from the grave to advertize the play.

The story begins. Todd and Anthony step off a boat and the young sailor praises London; he is interrupted by an old beggar-woman, whose plangent cries for alms turn to a coarse offer of sexual favours. Todd chases her away and answers Anthony's paean with a grimmer vision of a city where the 'privileged few' mock 'the vermin in the lower zoo'. The second of the many ballads in the opera which reveal past history is that of Todd, a deeply moving narration of a barber who lost his wife to 'a pious vulture of the law'.

In her pie-shop Mrs Lovett racily admits to 'The worst pies in London' and notes competition from Mrs Mooney, who does better by 'popping pussies into pies'. Todd asks about renting a room above the pie-shop, and in another ballad she tells him what happened there: how the Judge sent the barber Benjamin Barker into prison exile on a trumped-up charge and raped his vulnerable wife at a party (the accompanying minuet ought to give observant listeners a clue as to Lucy Barker's fate – it is a stylization of the beggar-woman's music). Todd's cry convinces Mrs Lovett that he is Benjamin Barker. She tells him that Lucy took poison and that the Judge has charge of his daughter, Johanna; then she fetches him the razors she has preserved. He addresses them suavely in the operatic 'My Friends'.

In the house of Judge Turpin Johanna contemplates her caged birds; Anthony, seeing her from the street below, falls instantly in love and, in a Puccinian love-song, determines to win her. The scene changes to St Dunstan's, where Toby, assistant to the mountebank Pirelli, announces a cure for baldness – 'Pirelli's miracle elixir'. Todd and Mrs Lovett recognize it as a mixture of 'piss with ink'. Todd challenges Pirelli, a preening Italianate tenor, to a contest to see who can give the quicker, faster shave. Todd wins and invites the Beadle, who is presiding as umpire, to his shop. There, where Mrs Lovett attempts to soothe him with the eerie, habanera-like 'Wait', Todd has an unexpected visitor: Pirelli has recognized him as an old rival barber and attempts blackmail. The demon barber commits his first murder.

The lustful Judge determines to marry Johanna, who plans her escape with Anthony. Their love-duet is counterpointed by the Judge and the Beadle, who jointly resolve that the groom ought to smarten himself up by a visit to Todd's. As the barber prepares to give Turpin his closest ever shave, in the hypnotic duet 'Pretty Woman', Anthony bursts in with news of his engagement to Johanna. Enraged, Turpin storms out and Todd snaps. In the awesome 'Epiphany', he turns his murderous anger on the whole of mankind. Mrs Lovett's appalling bright idea – that Sweeney should provide her with meat for her pies to beat Mrs Mooney's – turns high drama into vaudeville as the lethal pair imagine the characteristics of their human meat pies – for example, 'shepherd's pie peppered with actual shepherd on top'. Sweeney's new mania gives this comic curtain a devastating edge.

ACT TWO & EPILOGUE

The plan has been put into action: pie-shop and tonsorial parlour have gone up-market, and a racy ensemble illustrates this chaotic business. The threads combine as Anthony searches for Johanna, now missing, and Todd, thinking of his daughter, cuts the throats of his customers and sends them down the chute to Mrs Lovett's bakehouse; the mysterious beggar-woman, smelling blood, hangs around the premises.

In a smartened parlour Mrs Lovett tries to tempt the preoccupied Todd with the prospect of married life in a guest-house 'by the sea' ('Have a nice sunny suite for the guest to rest in / Now and then, you can do the guest in…'). Anthony finds Johanna at Fogg's

lunatic asylum. Todd, furthering his own ends, sends him there in the guise of wigmaker to extract her. He writes the Judge a letter luring him to collect Johanna at the shop that evening. Mrs Lovett, who has 'adopted' Toby following the death of Pirelli, diverts his suspicions by sending him into the bakehouse. The Beadle arrives and is quickly despatched down the chute, to Toby's horror. Todd and Mrs Lovett go in search of Toby.

The finale begins with chilling reprises of 'the Ballad of Sweeney

Todd'. Johanna and Anthony escape – along with the rest of Fogg's lunatics. Disguised as a sailor, Johanna enters Todd's room but a new arrival sends her into hiding. It is the beggar-woman, confronted by Todd who hastily cuts her throat as he hears the Judge climbing the stairs. This time the outcome of 'Pretty Women' is the revenge Sweeney has been waiting for. Down in the bakehouse, Todd recognizes the dead beggar-woman as his long-lost wife. Mrs Lovett desperately

explains how she lied about Lucy's fate because she loved him herself. He waltzes her round to the music of the Act-One finale and hurls her into the oven. Left alone with the body of Lucy, he sings a last, tragic verse of 'The Barber and his Wife' before Toby, his wits turned by the carnage, steps forward and cuts the demon barber's throat. A final, full-ensemble reprise of 'The Ballad of Sweeney Todd' points the moral: 'To seek revenge may lead to hell, but everyone does it, and seldom as well as Sweeney Todd'.

Dennis Quilley cuts a throat in the British première production, Drury Lane, 1980.

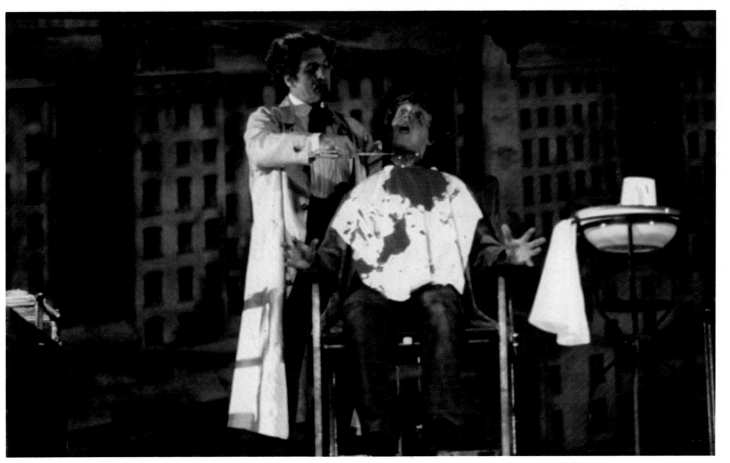

dISCOGRAPHY

For the following selection of operas on compact disc, great performances have been combined with a fair cross-section of the repertoire; if, however, a masterpiece has so far failed to receive its due public acclaim – as in the cases of Borodin's *Prince Igor* and Wagner's *Flying Dutchman,* to name but two – then it has not been listed for listing's sake. Recordings are listed alphabetically by composer, and in stereo unless indicated by (m) for mono.

ADAMS
NIXON IN CHINA
Sanford Sylvan, James Maddalena, Stephanie Friedman, Trudy Ellen Craney. Orchestra of St Luke's/Edo de Waart
Elektra Nonesuch 979 177-2 (3 CDs) R. 1987
Vibrant, incisive performance, with members of the original 1987 cast, of Adams' very human angle on the Nixon–Mao meetings in 1972. The label of minimalism can hardly be applied to so chameleonic and multi-faceted a score – one of the few late 20th-century operatic masterpieces.

BARTÓK
BLUEBEARD'S CASTLE
Christa Ludwig, Walter Berry. LSO/Istvan Kertész
Decca 414 167-2 (1 CD) R. 1966
Ludwig and Berry were the first married couple to record this deadly battle of wills (Fischer-Dieskau and his wife Julia Varady later followed suit). Hungarian conductor Kertész provides idiomatically flexible support.

BEETHOVEN
FIDELIO
Christa Ludwig, Jon Vickers, Walter Berry, Gottlob Frick, Ingeborg Hallstein, Gerhard Unger. Philharmonia/Otto Klemperer
EMI CMS7 69324-2 (2 CDs) R. 1962
The great Klemperer inspires powerful playing from the Philharmonia as the clouds gather. Mezzo Ludwig stands proud and firm in soprano territory, while Canadian *Heldentenor* Vickers gives us the most agonized Florestan of all.

BELLINI
NORMA
Maria Callas, Ebe Stignani, Mario Fillipeschi, Nicola Rossi-Lemeni. La Scala, Milan/Tullio Serafin
EMI CDS7 47304-2 (3 CDs) R. 1954 (m)
Callas' noble priestess just has the dramatic edge on the first and finest of Sutherland's two recordings. Serafin keeps the action moving.

I PURITANI
Joan Sutherland, Luciano Pavarotti, Piero Cappuccilli, Nicolai Ghiaurov. LSO/Richard Bonynge
Decca 417 588-2 (3 CDs) R. 1973
Bellini's inspiration may wane after a dramatic first act and the heroine's mad-scene – touching and dazzling in Sutherland's mature characterization – but it is worth waiting to hear Pavarotti manage his two top Ds in the third-act duet.

BERG
LULU
Teresa Stratas, Franz Mazura, Kenneth Riegel, Yvonne Minton, Robert Tear. Paris Opera/Pierre Boulez
DG 415 489-2 (3 CDs) R. 1986
Documenting the first production to use Friedrich Cerha's completion of Berg's unfinished opera, this already classic recording features the astonishingly accurate singing of Stratas and Boulez's crystal (at times clinically) clear orchestral balancing-act.

WOZZECK
Franz Grundheber, Hildegard Behrens, Walter Raffeiner, Heinz Zednik, Philip Langridge. VPO/Claudio Abbado
DG 423 587-2 (2 CDs) R.1989
Abbado's conducting captures all the frightening extremes as well as the terrible beauty of Berg's compassionate score.

BERLIOZ
BÉATRICE ET BÉNÉDICT
Janet Baker, Robert Tear, Christiane Eda-Pierre, Helen Watts, Thomas Allen, Jules Bastin. LSO/Colin Davis
Philips 416 952-2 (2 CDs) R. 1977
Berlioz's needle-point caprice is wisely cast and buoyantly conducted by the expert Davis.

LES TROYENS
Josephine Veasey, Jon Vickers, Berit Lindholm, Peter Glossop, Heather Begg.

Royal Opera/Colin Davis
Philips 416 955-2 (3 CDs) R. 1970
A labour of love from Davis and his excellent Covent Garden cast: every phrase of this masterly epic springs to life.

BIZET
CARMEN
Tatiana Troyanos, Placido Domingo, Kiri Te Kanawa, José van Dam. LPO/Georg Solti
Decca 414 489-2 (3 CDs) R. 1975
The late, great Troyanos is unforgettable as Bizet's gypsy. If the drama sometimes hangs fire in Solti's hands, the sound is vivid and the overall casting unbeatable, with all the minor roles perfectly taken.

BLITZSTEIN
REGINA
Katherine Ciesinski, Samuel Ramey, Angelina Réaux, Sheri Greenawald. Scottish Opera/John Mauceri
Decca 433 812-2 (2 CDs) R. 1991
Blitzstein's brittle style is not easy to accommodate to at first, but the Third Act rises to great heights, and this gripping studio realization does it proud.

BRITTEN
Six of the seven recordings listed here form part of the composer's huge recorded legacy as conductor and feature, in many instances, the singers for whom he originally wrote (though a new generation of recordings is now beginning to field some plausible rivals). Mackerras' razor-sharp *Gloriana* completes the Decca canon some 16 years after Britten's death, vindicating a neglected masterpiece.

ALBERT HERRING
Peter Pears, Sylvia Fisher, Johanna Peters, April Cantelo, Owen Brannigan, Joseph Ward, Catherine Wilson. ECO/Benjamin Britten
Decca 421 849-2 (2 CDs) R. 1964

BILLY BUDD
(C/W DONNE SONNETS, SONGS AND PROVERBS OF WILLIAM BLAKE)
Peter Glossop, Peter Pears, Michael Langdon, Owen Brannigan, Robert Tear. LSO/Benjamin Britten
Decca 417 428-2 (3 CDs) R. 1967

GLORIANA
Josephine Barstow, Philip Langridge, Della Jones, Yvonne Kenny, Jonathan Summers. Welsh National Opera/Charles Mackerras
Argo 440 213-2 (2 CDs) R. 1992

A MIDSUMMER NIGHT'S DREAM
Alfred Deller, Elizabeth Harwood, Peter Pears,

Thomas Hemsley, Josephine Veasey, Heather Harper, Owen Brannigan. LSO/Benjamin Britten
Decca 425 663-2 (2 CDs) R. 1966

PETER GRIMES
Peter Pears, Claire Watson, James Pease, David Kelly, Owen Brannigan. Royal Opera/Benjamin Britten
Decca 414 577-2 (3 CDs) R. 1958

THE RAPE OF LUCRETIA
(C/W PHAEDRA)
Janet Baker, Peter Pears, Heather Harper, Benjamin Luxon. ECO/Benjamin Britten
Decca 425 666-2 (2 CDs) R. 1970

THE TURN OF THE SCREW
Jennifer Vyvyan, Peter Pears, David Hemmings, Joan Cross. English Opera Group/Benjamin Britten
Decca 425 672-2 (2 CDs) R. 1955 (m)

CHERUBINI
LODOISKA
Mariella Devia, Bernard Lombardo, Thomas Moser, Alessandro Corbelli. La Scala, Milan/Riccardo Muti
Sony S2K 47290 (2 CDs) R. 1991
Cherubini's 'rescue-opera' – a prompt for Beethoven's Fidelio – live from La Scala and firmly and heroically guided by Riccardo Muti.

MEDEA
Maria Callas, Mirto Picchi, Renata Scotto. La Scala, Milan/Tullio Serafin
EMI CMS7 63625-2 (2 CDs) R. 1957
Another of Callas' great roles – searing drama matched to appropriately tempestuous music.

COPLAND
THE TENDER LAND
Elisabeth Comeaux, Janis Hardy, James Bohn, Dan Dressen, LeRoy Lehr. Plymouth Music Series Minnesota/Philip Brunelle
Virgin VCD 7 91113-2 (2 CDs) R. 1990
Surprising, Janáčekian passions lurk beneath the American pastoral surface of Copland's 'opera made easy', charmingly presented by this all-American cast.

DEBUSSY
PELLÉAS ET MÉLISANDE
(C/W DEBUSSY SONGS)
Irène Joachim, Jacques Jansen, Henri Etcheverry, Paul Cabanel. Orchestre Symphonique/Roger Desormière
EMI CHS 7 61038 2 (3 CDs) R. 1941 (m)
The classic Pelléas was recorded under conditions of wartime austerity; for the fresh-voiced Pelléas of Jansen, the wistful Mélisande of Joachim and Desormière's perfect pacing, it remains unrivalled.

DELIBES
LAKMÉ
Joan Sutherland, Alain Vanzo, Gabriel Bacquier, Jane Berbié. Monte-Carlo Opera/Richard Bonynge
Decca 425 485-2 (2 CDs) R. 1968
Treasurable not only for the dazzling coloratura of Sutherland's 'Bell Song' but also for the ardour of the supporting cast (especially Vanzo, the sweet-voiced French tenor to the life) in a string of memorable musical numbers.

DELIUS
A VILLAGE ROMEO AND JULIET
Helen Field, Arthur Davies, Thomas Hampson. ORF Symphony Orchestra/Charles Mackerras
Argo 430 275-2 (2 CDs) R.1990
An incandescent unfolding of Delius' post-Tristan romance from Mackerras. Hampson's dangerous Dark Fiddler is outstanding.

DONIZETTI
DON PASQUALE
Gabriel Bacquier, Barbara Hendricks, Luca Canonici, Gino Quilico. Lyon Opera/Gabriele Ferro
Erato 2292 45487-2 (2 CDs) R. 1990
The veteran Bacquier turns in a star *buffo* performance in the title role. Ferro provides comic pacing to match.

LA FILLE DU RÉGIMENT
Joan Sutherland, Luciano Pavarotti, Spiro Malas, Monica Sinclair. Royal Opera/Richard Bonynge
Decca 414 520-2 (2 CDs) R. 1967
Hard to choose between this and the Decca *L'Elisir d'amore* for spotlighting the comic talents of Sutherland and Pavarotti; pure champagne from start to finish.

LUCIA DI LAMMERMOOR
Joan Sutherland, Luciano Pavarotti, Sherrill Milnes, Nicolai Ghiaurov. Royal Opera/Richard Bonynge
Decca 410 193-2 (3 CDs) R. 1972
Sutherland's second Lucia brings added insights and a glamorous supporting cast; Callas may tear at the soul more effectively, but there is no denying the ultimate coloratura phenomenon in this mad-scene.

DVOŘÁK
RUSALKA
Gabriela Beňačková, Richard Novák, Vera Soukupová, Wieslaw Ochman. Czech PO/Vaclav Neumann
Supraphon C37-7201/3 (3 CDs) R. 1984
Beňačková's warm, rich soprano is perfect for the pathetic water-sprite. Neumann ensures that Bohemian romanticism shines at leisure.

JOHN GAY
THE BEGGAR'S OPERA
(BRITTEN PERFORMING VERSION)
Philip Langridge, Ann Murray, Yvonne Kenny, Robert Lloyd, Anne Collins. chamber ensemble/Steuart Bedford
Argo 436 850-2 (2 CDs) R. 1992
Britten's very personal arrangements of the traditional British airs fit seamlessly into the context of the dialogue in this feisty, strongly-cast realization of a popular hit.

GERSHWIN
PORGY AND BESS
Willard White, Cynthia Haymon, Damon Evans, Cynthia Clarey, Harolyn Blackwell. LPO/Simon Rattle
EMI CDS 7 49568 2 (3 CDs) R. 1988
It is the dramatic intensity of White, Haymon and Evans rather than the sometimes questionable speeds of Rattle that gives this set the edge over its Decca rival (brilliantly conducted by Lorin Maazel).

GLUCK
IPHIGÉNIE EN AULIDE
Lynne Dawson, Anne Sofie von Otter, José van Dam, John Aler. Lyon Opera/John Eliot Gardiner
Erato 2292-45003 (2 CDs) R. 1990

IPHIGÉNIE EN TAURIDE
Diana Montague, Thomas Allen, John Aler, René Massis. Lyon Opera/John Eliot Gardiner
Philips 416 148-2 (2 CDs) R. 1985
Gardiner realizes to perfection the lightning-flash intensity of the short, dramatic scenes in Gluck's two operas devoted to the events framing the Trojan Wars. The performances of von Otter and Montague are outstanding.

ORFEO ED EURIDICE
Kathleen Ferrier, Ann Ayars, Zoe Vlachopoulos. Southern Philharmonic Orchestra/Fritz Stiedry
Decca 433 468-2 (1 CD) R. 1947 (m)
Although it is abridged and stylistically a good deal less faithful than recent versions of the opera, this realization of *Orfeo* remains a classic nevertheless by virtue of Ferrier's singing – straight from the heart.

GOUNOD
FAUST
Nicolai Gedda, Victoria de los Angeles, Boris Christoff, Ernest Blanc. Paris Opera/André Cluytens
EMI CMS7 69983-2 (3 CDs) R. 1958
Cluytens' authentically French handling of the score provides a good basis for the strong characterizations of three great singers – Gedda, de los Angeles and Christoff.

HANDEL
JULIUS CAESAR
Janet Baker, Valerie Masterson, Sarah Walker, Della Jones, James Bowman. English National Opera/Charles Mackerras
EMI CMS7 69760-2 (3 CDs) R. 1985
A splendid record of the English National Opera production, courtesy of the Peter Moores Foundation's aim to record opera in English.

ORLANDO
James Bowman, Arleen Augér, Catherine Robbin, Emma Kirkby. The Academy of Ancient Music/Christopher Hogwood
L'Oiseau-Lyre 430 845-2DH3 (3 CDs) R. 1990
The leading counter-tenor of the present day in one his finest roles, backed up by a strong cast and Hogwood's lively authentic ensemble.

HAYDN
LA FEDELTÀ PREMIATA
Ileana Cotrubas, Frederica von Stade, Luigi Alva, Lucia Valentini Terrani, Tonny Landy. Lausanne Chamber Orchestra/Antal Dorati
Philips 432 430-2 (3 CDs) R. 1976
No Mozart when it came to comedy, Haydn nonetheless knew how to turn a pretty tune, and given such an excellent line-up of singers, this representative of Dorati's Haydn series is never less than delightful.

HINDEMITH
CARDILLAC; *MATHIS DER MALER (EXCERPTS)
Dietrich Fischer-Dieskau, Leonore Kirchstein, Donald Grobe, Pilar Lorengar, Cologne Radio Symphony Orchestra, Joseph Keilberth. *Berlin Radio SO/Leopold Ludwig
DG 431 741-2 (2 CDs) R. 1968, 1961
One-and-a-half of Fischer-Dieskau's greatest 20th-century roles, and a good way of becoming acquainted with Hindemith's distinctive sound.

HUMPERDINCK
HANSEL AND GRETEL
Edita Gruberova, Ann Murray, Christa Ludwig, Gwyneth Jones, Franz Grundheber, Barbara Bonney, Christiane Oelze. Staatskapelle Dresden/Colin Davis
Philips 438 013-2 (2 CDs) R. 1992
Humperdinck's fairy-tale opera has had more than its share of classic recordings, but this newcomer out-charms them all: it has the magic of a live performance.

JANÀCEK
Listeners may take issue with some of the casting in Mackerras' Janàcek series for Decca – Söderström's Jenůfa was recorded too late in her career, and Beňačková on Supraphon is certainly more apt – but it is unlikely to be surpassed for the white heat of the orchestral playing (Mackerras inspires the Vienna Philharmonic – there is no other way of putting it) and the vividness of the recorded sound.

THE CUNNING LITTLE VIXEN
Lucia Popp, Eva Randová, Dalibor Jedlička, Richard Novák, Vaclav Zítek. VPO/Charles Mackerras
Decca 417 129-2 (2 CDs) R. 1981

FROM THE HOUSE OF THE DEAD (C/W *MLADI, RIKADLA*)
Ivo Zídek, Jiri Zahradníček, Vaclav Zítek, Dalibor Jedlička. VPO/Charles Mackerras
Decca 430 375-2 (2 CDs) R. 1980

JENŮFA
(C/W OVERTURE, *JEALOUSY*)
Elisabeth Söderström, Eva Randová, Wieslaw Ochman, Petr Dvorský, Lucia Popp. VPO/Charles Mackerras
Decca 414 483-2 (2 CDs) R. 1983

KÁTYA KABANOVÁ
(C/W *CAPRICCIO, CONCERTINO*)
Elisabeth Söderström, Petr Dvorský, Nadežda Kniplová, Libuše Marová, Vladimir Krejčík. VPO/Charles Mackerras
Decca 421 852-2 (2 CDs) R. 1976

THE MAKROPOULOS CASE
(C/W LACHIAN DANCES)
Elisabeth Söderström, Petr Dvorský, Vaclav Zítek, Dalibor Jedlička, Vladimir Krejčík, Anna Czaková, Beno Blachut. VPO/Charles Mackerras
Decca 430 372-2 (2 CDs) R. 1978

KERN
SHOWBOAT
Frederica von Stade, Teresa Stratas, Jerry Hadley, Bruce Hubbard, Karla Burns. London Sinfonietta/John McGlinn
EMI CDS7 49108-2 (3 CDs) R. 1988
Heartfelt operatic delivery where appropriate, as well as the winning quality of the overall product, win this life-affirming recording a place here.

KORNGOLD
DIE TOTE STADT
Carol Neblett, René Kollo, Benjamin Luxon, Hermann Prey. Munich Radio Orchestra/Erich Leinsdorf
RCA GD87767 (2 CDs) R. 1975
Lavish casting for a gorgeous late-romantic extravaganza.

KŘENEK
JONNY SPIELT AUF
Heinz Kruse, Alessandra Marc, Krister St Hill, Michael Kraus, Marita Posselt. Leipzig Gewandhaus Orchestra/Lothar Zagrosek
Decca 436 631-2 (2 CDs) R. 1991

A jazzy, outrageous first issue in Decca's series featuring music branded as degenerate by the Nazis. Fine tenor Kruse and dramatic soprano Marc provide the very romantic love-interest.

LEHÁR
THE MERRY WIDOW
(C/W SUPPÉ OVERTURES)

Elizabeth Harwood, Teresa Stratas, Werner Hollweg, René Kollo. Berlin PO/Herbert von Karajan
DG 435 712-2 (2 CDs) R. 1973
The hyper-sensuous approach of Karajan and his Berliners works superbly well for Lehár; vocal charms are nearly on the same level.

LEONCAVALLO/*PUCCINI
PAGLIACCI/*IL TABARRO

Placido Domingo, Sherrill Milnes, Montserrat Caballé, Leontyne Price. LSO/Nello Santi, *New Philharmonia Orchestra/Erich Leinsdorf
RCA GD 60865 (2 CDs), R. 1971
Not the usual 'Cav 'n' Pag' double bill: Puccini's *verismo* one-acter is surely a worthier companion for Leoncavallo's fine craftsmanship. Starry casting, a touch short on passion at times.

MARTINŮ
THE GREEK PASSION

John Mitchinson, Helen Field, John Tomlinson, Rita Cullis. Brno State PO/Charles Mackerras
Supraphon 10 3611 (2 CDs) R. 1981
Deeply moving, true-ensemble approach to the Czech composer's late (1959) opera based on Nikos Kazantzakis' novel *Christ Recrucified*.

MASCAGNI
CAVALLERIA RUSTICANA

Renata Scotto, Placido Domingo, Pablo Elvira, Jean Kraft. National PO/James Levine
RCA RD 83091 (1 CD) R. 1978
Full-blooded, theatrical performances all round in this single-CD recording of Mascagni's Sicilian shocker – especially useful if you do not want Leoncavallo's *Pagliacci* too.

MASSENET
CENDRILLON

Frederica von Stade, Nicolai Gedda, Ruth Welting, Jules Bastin. Philharmonia/Julius Rudel
CBS CD79300 (2 CDs) R. 1979
Von Stade's Chérubin on another Massenet recording has been rightly praised, but this is one of her finest hours, too. Massenet wanted a mezzo prince for his Cinderella, but Gedda's tenor is so stylish that it hardly matters. Pure enchantment.

ESCLARMONDE

Joan Sutherland, Giacomo Aragall, Huguette

Tourangeau, Ryland Davies, Louis Quilico. National PO/Richard Bonynge
Decca 425 651-2 (3 CDs) R. 1976
Glorious excess on all fronts – vocal, orchestral and soundwise – for Massenet at his most Wagnerian. Sutherland is heard in her prime in one of the most taxing roles in the repertoire.

WERTHER

José Carreras, Frederica von Stade, Thomas Allen, Robert Lloyd. Royal Opera/Colin Davis
Philips 416 654-2 (2 CDs) R. 1980
Perfect casting for the lovers ill met by moonlight, with true magic from the Royal Opera orchestra under Davis.

MEYERBEER
LES HUGUENOTS

Joan Sutherland, Martina Arroyo, Nikola Ghiuselev, Gabriel Bacquier, Huguette Tourangeau. New PO/Richard Bonynge
Decca 430 549-2 (4 CDs) R. 1969
Sutherland takes only a brief centre stage in Meyerbeer's vast canvas, though the recording has come to serve as a memento of her last stage role. Elsewhere, there is appropriate vocal weightiness for the more sombre scenes.

MONTEVERDI
L'INCORONAZIONE DI POPPEA

Arleen Augér, Della Jones, Linda Hirst, James Bowman, Gregory Reinhart. City of London Baroque Sinfonia/Richard Hickox
Virgin VCT7 90775-2 (3 CDs) R. 1988
Restrained authentic treatment from Hickox's instrumental group and a lovely blending of voices from Augér and Jones in the final duet.

ORFEO

Anthony Rolfe Johnson, Julianne Baird, Lynne Dawson, Anne Sofie von Otter, John Tomlinson, Diana Montague, Willard White, Nigel Robson. English Baroque Soloists/John Eliot Gardiner
Archiv 419 250-2 (2 CDs) R. 1985
Rolfe Johnson, the supreme stylist in Monteverdi, is flanked by star casting in the cameo roles.

MOZART
LA CLEMENZA DI TITO

Stuart Burrows, Janet Baker, Yvonne Minton, Frederica von Stade, Lucia Popp. Royal Opera/Colin Davis
Philips 422 544-2 (2 CDs) R. 1976
A shining, heroic last-minute clemency from Burrows and Davis crowns a succession of finely sung set-pieces; Baker adds mezzo intensity to the (soprano) role of Vitellia.

COSÌ FAN TUTTE

Margaret Marshall, Agnes Baltsa, Kathleen Battle, Francisco Araiza, James Morris, José

van Dam. VPO/Riccardo Muti
EMI CMS7 69580-2 (3 CDs) R. 1982
A personal favourite on account of Muti's brio and Marshall's Mozartian style, though the usual preference is for the 1963 Böhm set (also on EMI) with the questionable Schwarzkopf.

DON GIOVANNI

Eberhard Wächter, Joan Sutherland, Elisabeth Schwarzkopf, Graziella Sciutti, Luigi Alva, Giuseppe Taddei, Piero Cappuccilli, Gottlob Frick. Philharmonia/Carlo Maria Giulini
EMI CDS7 47260-8 (3 CDs) R. 1959
Heavenly ensembles abound in this classic, which definitely comes down on the side of the innocent (the young Sutherland and the light tenor Luigi Alva, a wonderfully-cast noble pair).

IDOMENEO

Anthony Rolfe Johnson, Anne Sofie von Otter, Sylvia McNair, Hillevi Martinpelto. English Baroque Soloists/John Eliot Gardiner
Archiv 431 674-2 (3 CDs) R. 1990
Gardiner's authenticity electrifies Mozart's most dazzling experiment; the florid vocal demands are expressively met by Rolfe Johnson and the glorious von Otter.

THE MARRIAGE OF FIGARO

Jessye Norman, Mirella Freni, Ingvar Wixell, Wladimiro Ganzarolli, Yvonne Minton, Robert Tear. BBC SO/Colin Davis
Philips 426 195-2 (3 CDs) R. 1971
Sparkling recitatives power the action in this most durable of Figaros; some of the performances may be outshone elsewhere, but the overall feeling is of a true ensemble.

THE MAGIC FLUTE

Uwe Heilmann, Ruth Ziesak, Michael Kraus, Sumi Jo, Kurt Moll. VPO/Georg Solti
Decca 433 210-2 (2 CDs) R. 1990
The most successful of Solti's later recordings – his love for the score shines through. The cast sounds, for the most part, fresh and responsive.

MUSSORGSKY
BORIS GODUNOV

Anatoli Kotscherga, Liliana Nichiteanu, Valentina Valente, Sergei Larin, Samuel Ramey, Gleb Nikolsky, Philip Langridge. Berlin PO/Claudio Abbado
Sony S4K 58977 (4 CDs) R. 1993
Long overdue first-class treatment for Mussorgsky's original score (the only other recommendable versions employ Rimsky-Korsakov's colourful revision).

KHOVANSHCHINA
(ORCH. SHOSTAKOVICH)

Aage Haugland, Vladimir Atlantov, Vladimir Popov, Mariana Lipovsek, Anatoli Kotscherga,

Paata Burchuladze. Vienna State Opera/Claudio Abbado
DG 429 758-2 (3 CDs) R. 1990
Dark orchestral colours match the great line-up of basses in the first recording to make a plausibly fluent case for Mussorgsky's drama.

OFFENBACH
THE TALES OF HOFFMANN

Joan Sutherland, Placido Domingo, Gabriel Bacquier, Huguette Tourangeau. Suisse Romande Orchestra/Richard Bonynge
Decca 417 363 (2 CDs) R. 1972
Sutherland proves her versatility as all four of Hoffmann's loves. Bonynge's performing version is the most plausible and least piecemeal of the alternatives.

POULENC
DIALOGUES OF THE CARMELITES

Catherine Dubosc, Rita Gorr, Rachel Yakar, Martine Dupuy, José van Dam, Jean-Luc Viala. Lyon Opera/Kent Nagano
Virgin 7 59227 2 (2 CDs) R. 1992
A dedicated Lyon-based line-up for Poulenc's unbearably moving tale of religious persecution.

PROKOFIEV
THE FIERY ANGEL

Nadine Secunde, Siegfried Lorenz, Heinz Zednik, Petteri Salomaa, Kurt Moll. Gothenburg SO/Neeme Järvi
DG 431 669 (2 CDs) R. 1990
Sparks occasionally fly in this sensuous approach to Prokofiev's 1920s blood-curdler.

THE LOVE FOR THREE ORANGES

Gabriel Bacquier, Jean-Luc Viala, Vincent Le Texier, Didier Henry, Catherine Dubosc, Jules Bastin. Lyon Opera/Kent Nagano
Virgin VCD7 91084- 2 (2 CDs) R. 1989
The brilliant starting-point for Nagano's Lyon series; he paces the score as one long and glittering scherzo.

WAR AND PEACE

Lajos Miller, Galina Vishnevskaya, Wieslaw Ochman, Nicolai Gedda, Nikola Ghiuselev. French National Orchestra/Mstislav Rostropovich
Erato 2292-45331-2 (4 CDs) R. 1988
Rostropovich payed a debt to his friend Prokofiev with this labour of love – presenting the opera absolutely complete and cast from strength in the ensemble of 50 plus.

PUCCINI
LA BOHÈME

Victoria de los Angeles, Jussi Björling, Robert Merrill, Lucine Amara, Giorgio Tozzi. RCA Victor Orchestra/Thomas Beecham

EMI 7 47235 8 (2 CDs) R. 1956 (m)
Toscanini may have been more faithful to Puccini's every marking, but there is a special magic in Beecham's version, and a special charm about de los Angeles' smiling seamstress.

LA FANCIULLA DEL WEST
Birgit Nilsson, João Gibin, Andrea Mongelli. La Scala, Milan/Lovro von Matačić
EMI CMS 7 639702 (2 CDs) R. 1959
Nilsson thrills as the wild-west Valkyrie; Matačić proves a supple Puccini conductor, though there are the usual cuts.

MADAM BUTTERFLY
Renata Scotto, Carlo Bergonzi, Rolando Panerai, Anna di Stasio. Rome Opera/John Barbirolli
EMI CMS7 69654-2 (2 CDs) R. 1966
Most glowing of Barbirolli's opera recordings. Though Scotto went on later in her career to find even greater depths of expression, she never sounded lovelier than this.

TOSCA
Maria Callas, Giuseppe di Stefano, Tito Gobbi. La Scala, Milan/Victor de Sabata
EMI CDS7 47175-8 (2 CDs) R. 1953 (m)
A great diva and a great conductor meet in the classic *Tosca*, though some may find Gobbi's Scarpia too histrionic.

TURANDOT
Joan Sutherland, Luciano Pavarotti, Monserrat Caballé, Nicolai Ghiaurov, Peter Pears. LPO/Zubin Mehta
Decca 414 274 (2 CDs) R. 1975
Sutherland's most unexpected triumph, still selling well thanks to Pavarotti's hit 'Nessun dorma'. Caballé is perfectly cast, too, as Liù.

PURCELL
DIDO AND AENEAS
Janet Baker, Raimund Herincx, Monica Sinclair. ECO/Anthony Lewis
Decca 425 720 (1CD) R. 1961
Many mezzos have recorded Dido, but none has surpassed Baker's plangent, noble account of the great lament, 'When I am laid in earth'.

RAVEL
L'ENFANT ET LES SORTILÈGES
Françoise Ogéas, Jane Berbié, Michel Sénéchal. French National Radio Orchestra/Lorin Maazel
DG 423 718 (1CD) R. 1965
The time is surely right for new recordings of this enchanting masterpiece, but in the meantime Maazel's sharp-edged account fits the bill.

RIMSKY-KORSAKOV
THE TSAR'S BRIDE
Galina Vishnevskaya, Evgeny Nestorenko,
Vladimir Atlantov, Boris Morozov. Bolshoi Theatre/Fuat Mansourov
Le Chant du Monde LDC278 1035/6 (2 CDs) R. 1973
Few of the old-regime Melodiya recordings have resurfaced, leaving a dearth of Rimsky-Korsakov recordings, but here is one, at least, with a strong Bolshoi cast.

ROSSINI
THE BARBER OF SEVILLE
Thomas Allen, Agnes Baltsa, Franciso Araiza, Domenico Trimarchi, Robert Lloyd. Academy of St Martin-in-the-Fields/Neville Marriner
Philips 411 058 (3 CDs) R. 1984
Fiery comedy from the singers and nimble vivacity from the Academy under Marriner make this top of the Barbers.

LA CENERENTOLA
Cecilia Bartoli, Enzo Dara, William Matteuzzi, Alessandro Corbelli, Michele Pertusi. Teatro Communale, Bologna/Riccardo Chailly
Decca 436 902 (2 CDs) R. 1991
Bartoli captures perfectly both the pathos and the spirit of Rossini's Cinderella.

GUILLAUME TELL
Sherrill Milnes, Mirella Freni, Luciano Pavarotti, Nicolai Ghiaurov. National PO/Riccardo Chailly
Decca 417 154 (4 CDs) R. 1987
An Italianate angle on Rossini's grand opera for Paris, strongly cast and firmly conducted.

L'ITALIANA IN ALGERI
Agnes Baltsa, Frank Lopardo, Enzo Dara, Ruggero Raimondi. VPO/Claudio Abbado
DG 427 331 (2 CDs) R. 1989
Orchestral high spirits spread to the singers – notably the sparring Isabella and Mustafa of Baltsa (in unusually fine voice) and Raimondi, who reveals a surprising talent for comedy.

SEMIRAMIDE
Joan Sutherland, Marilyn Horne, Joseph Rouleau, John Serge, Spiro Malas. LSO/Richard Bonynge
Decca 425 481- 2 (3 CDs) R. 1966
Sutherland and Horne, great *bel canto* singers both, meet for two of the most glorious soprano–mezzo duets in Italian opera.

IL VIAGGIO A REIMS
Katia Ricciarelli, Cecilia Gasdia, Lella Cuberli, Lucia Valentini-Terrani, Francisco Araiza, Samuel Ramey, Ruggero Raimondi, Leo Nucci. Chamber Orchestra of Europe/Claudio Abbado
DG 415 498-2 (2 CDs) R. 1986
Luxury casting for Rossini's comic extravaganza, with brio from the orchestra to match.

SAINT-SAËNS
SAMSON ET DALILA
José Carreras, Agnes Baltsa, Jonathan Summers, Simon Estes. Bavarian Radio SO/Colin Davis
Philips 426 243-2 (2 CDs) R. 1989
Plausible argument for Saint-Saëns' slightly pious sensuousness, with Baltsa as an aggressive temptress.

SCHOENBERG
MOSES UND ARON
Franz Mazura, Philip Langridge, Aage Haugland, Barbara Bonney. Chicago SO/Georg Solti
Decca 414 264-2 (2 CDs) R. 1985
Clear-textured elucidation of Schoenberg's thorny dialectics from Solti and keen performance from the Chicago forces.

SMETANA
THE BARTERED BRIDE
Gabriela Beňačková, Petr Dvorský, Richard Novák, Miroslav Kopp. Czech PO/Zdeněk Košler
Supraphon 10 3511 (3 CDs) R. 1982
Lively, authentically Bohemian song and dance; the lustrous Beňačková lends a touch of class to the comedy.

SONDHEIM
SWEENEY TODD
Len Cariou, Angela Lansbury, Merle Louise, Edmund Lyndeck. Broadway Orchestra/Paul Gemingnani
RCA3379-2 RC (2 CDs) R. 1979
The cast is that of a Broadway musical, and yet the hair-raising drama of this well-produced set puts Sondheim's work firmly among the great music-theatre pieces of the 20th century.

JOHANN STRAUSS II
DIE FLEDERMAUS
Anneliese Rothenberger, Renate Holm, Nicolai Gedda, Adolf Dallapozza, Dietrich Fischer-Dieskau, Brigitte Fassbaender. Vienna SO/Willi Boskovsky
EMI CMS7 69354-2 (2 CDs) R. 1972
The most effervescent and Viennese of operetta recordings; the dialogue has been as skilfully prepared as the musical numbers.

RICHARD STRAUSS
ARIADNE AUF NAXOS
Anna Tomowa-Sintow, Kathleen Battle, Agnes Baltsa, Gary Lakes, Hermann Prey, Urban Malmberg. VPO/James Levine
DG 419 225-2 (2 CDs) R. 1986
Lively backstage repartee and luminous desert-island drama are held in fine balance. The cast has none of the weak links which spoil the Karajan, Masur and Solti recordings, though Levine's conducting is perhaps a touch grand.

CAPRICCIO
Gundula Janowitz, Dietrich Fischer-Dieskau, Peter Schreier, Hermann Prey, Tatiana Troyanos, Karl Ridderbusch. Bavarian Radio SO/Karl Böhm
DG 419 023-2GH2 (2 CDs) R. 1971
A sympathetic angle on Strauss' swansong conversation-piece from Böhm and a dedicated cast.

ELEKTRA
Birgit Nilsson, Regina Resnik, Marie Collier, Gerhard Stolze, Tom Krause. VPO/Georg Solti
Decca 417 345-2 (2 CDs) R. 1967
Red in tooth and claw, Solti's febrile conducting was highlighted by John Culshaw's 'sonicstage' tricks and manners; the sound wears well.

DIE FRAU OHNE SCHATTEN
René Kollo, Cheryl Studer, Ute Vinzing, Alfred Muff, Hanna Schwarz. Bavarian Radio SO/Wolfgang Sawallisch
EMI CDS 7 49'74-2 (3 CDs) R. 1988
Outshone in some roles by Solti's over-hyped Decca successor, Sawallisch's recording wins hands-down in the orchestral stakes and the conductor's awesome sense of pace.

DER ROSENKAVALIER
Maria Reining, Sena Jurinac, Hilde Gueden, Ludwig Weber. VPO/Erich Kleiber
Decca 425 950-2 (3 CDs) R. 1954 (m)
Erich Kleiber realizes every tic, wink and laugh in this richest of comic operas; no other rival digs so deeply. The cast is a true Viennese ensemble, charming without too much effort.

SALOME
Hildegard Behrens, José van Dam, Karl-Walter Böhm, Agnes Baltsa. VPO/Herbert von Karajan
EMI CDS7 49358 2 (2 CDs) R. 1977
Beauty outshines horror in Karajan's sensuous Salzburg-based interpretation. Behrens is a stunning and youthful-sounding Salome.

STRAVINSKY
THE RAKE'S PROGRESS
Alexander Young, Judith Raskin, John Reardon, Regina Sarfaty. RPO/Igor Stravinsky
Sony CD46299 (2 CDs) R. 1964
An incisive testament of Stravinsky's conducting genius and the expressive capabilities of the much-underrated tenor Alexander Young.

TCHAIKOVSKY
EUGENE ONEGIN
Evgeny Belov, Galina Vishnevskaya, Sergei Lemeshev, Larissa Avdeyeva, Ivan Petrov. Bolshoi Theatre/Boris Khakin
Legato Classics LCD 163-2 (2 CDs) R. 1950 (m)
Document of the high-calibre Bolshoi ensemble

in the 1950s, with Vishnevskaya at the peak of her career as a touching Tatyana.

THE QUEEN OF SPADES

Gegam Grigorian, Maria Guleghina, Nikolai Putilin, Vladimir Chernov, Irina Arkhipova. Kirov Opera/Valery Gergiev
Philips 438 141-2 (3 CDs) R. 1992
The obsession of Tchaikovsky's outsider-hero is richly characterized by the ardent Grigorian and Gergiev's hard-working Kirov orchestra; together, they make the flesh creep.

TIPPETT
KING PRIAM

Norman Bailey, Heather Harper, Thomas Allen, Felicity Palmer, Philip Langridge. London Sinfonietta/David Atherton
Decca 414 241-2 (2 CDs) R. 1981
The best of British singers present a formidable line-up for Tippett's tough Trojan War opera.

VAUGHAN WILLIAMS
THE PILGRIM'S PROGRESS

John Noble, Raimund Herincx, John Carol Case, Robert Lloyd. LPO//Adrian Boult
EMI CMS7 64212-2 (2 CDs) R. 1972
Boult brings out the visionary dimension to Vaughan Williams' 'morality' after John Bunyan's allegorical book.

VERDI
AIDA

Renata Tebaldi, Giulietta Simionato, Carlo Bergonzi, Cornell MacNeil. VPO/Herbert von Karajan
Decca 414 087-2 (3 CDs) R. 1958
An early Decca spectacular which still sounds well for its age.

UN BALLO IN MASCHERA

Margaret Price, Luciano Pavarotti, Renato Bruson, Kathleen Battle, Christa Ludwig. National PO/Georg Solti
Decca 410 210-2 (2 CDs) R. 1985
Classy casting and a fine sweep from Solti – his finest Verdi on disc.

DON CARLOS

Placido Domingo, Monserrat Caballé, Shirley Verrett, Ruggero Raimondi, Sherrill Milnes. Royal Opera/Carlo Maria Giulini
EMI 7 47701 8 (3 CDs) R. 1971
Abbado on DG offers more music from the original (French) version, but Giulini's sensible compromise has better singing right across the board and more vivid sound.

FALSTAFF

Geraint Evans, Robert Merrill, Ilva Ligabue, Mirella Freni, Alfredo Kraus, Giulietta Simionato. RCA Italiana Opera Orchestra/Georg Solti

Decca 417 168-2 (2 CDs) R. 1963
Solti's latest *Falstaff* pales by the side of this, one of his early opera recordings, striking a perfect balance between enchantment and high spirits. Freni and Kraus are outstanding as the young lovers Nannetta and Fenton.

LA FORZA DEL DESTINO

Rosalind Plowright, José Carreras, Renato Bruson, Paata Burchuladze, Agnes Baltsa. Philharmonia/Giuseppe Sinopoli
DG 419 203-2 (3 CDs) R. 1985
Forcefulness abounds in Sinopoli's epic approach to a grim masterpiece.

MACBETH

Sherrill Milnes, Fiorenza Cossotto, José Carreras, Ruggero Raimondi. New Philharmonia/Riccardo Muti
EMI CMS 7 64339 2 (2 CDs) R. 1976
Milnes keeps drama well within the notes as a powerful Macbeth, vividly complemented by Muti's highly charged conducting.

OTELLO

Placido Domingo, Renata Scotto, Sherrill Milnes. National PO/James Levine
RCA GK82951 (2 CDs) R. 1975
The best of two recordings from the finest Otello of our time, with dramatic support from Scotto, Milnes and Levine.

RIGOLETTO

Piero Cappuccilli, Ileana Cotrubas, Placido Domingo, Nicolai Ghiaurov, Elena Obraztsova. VPO/Carlo Maria Giulini
DG 415 288-2 (2 CDs) R. 1980
Polished, smoothly-sung performance which rises to the stormy heights in the last act.

SIMON BOCCANEGRA

Piero Cappuccilli, Mirella Freni, José Carreras, Nicolai Ghiaurov, José van Dam. La Scala, Milan/Claudio Abbado
DG 415 692-2 (2 CDs) R. 1977
Clear-cut, fast-moving narration of an often difficult operatic plot.

LA TRAVIATA

Ileana Cotrubas, Placido Domingo, Sherrill Milnes. Bavarian State Orchestra/Carlos Kleiber
DG 415 132-2 (2 CDs) R. 1976
Carlos Kleiber's electrifying conducting is matched by Cotrubas' deeply moving Violetta.

IL TROVATORE

Leontyne Price, Placido Domingo, Sherrill Milnes, Fiorenza Cossotto. New Philharmonia/Zubin Mehta
RCA RD86194 (2 CDs) R. 1970
Four great voices for what have been described as the four most difficult-to-cast roles in opera.

WAGNER
LOHENGRIN

Jess Thomas, Elisabeth Grümmer, Christa Ludwig, Dietrich Fischer-Dieskau, Gottlob Frick, VPO/Rudolf Kempe
EMI CDS7 49017-3 (3 CDs) R. 1964
Kempe, most natural of conductors, achieves an easy spirituality and flow in what can be Wagner's most static score.

DIE MEISTERSINGER VON NÜRNBERG

Otto Edelmann, Hans Hopf, Elisabeth Schwarzkopf, Erich Kunz, Gerhard Unger, Ira Malaniuk. Bayreuth Festival Opera/Herbert von Karajan
EMI CHS7 635000-2 (4 CDs) R. 1951 (m)
Edelmann may not be the noblest Sachs on disc – that honour goes to Norman Bailey on the otherwise disappointing Solti set – but the overall product is a Bayreuth classic, and one of Karajan's finest achievements.

PARSIFAL

René Kollo, Dietrich Fischer-Dieskau, Gottlob Frick, Christa Ludwig, Zoltan Kéléman, Hans Hotter. VPO/Georg Solti
Decca 417 143-2 (4 CDs) R. 1973
Solti's best Wagner conducting is to be found in the opera he might be expected to find least sympathetic. A magnificent cast rises to the human and spiritual challenges.

THE RING OF THE NIBELUNG

Theo Adam, Birgit Nilsson, Wolfgang Windgassen, Gustav Neidlinger, James King, Leonie Rysanek, Josef Greindl. Bayreuth Festival Opera/Karl Böhm
Philips 412 475-2 (Das Rheingold, 2 CDs);
412 478-2 (Die Walküre, 4 CDs);
412 483-2 (Siegfried, 4 CDs);
412 488-2 (Götterdämmerung, 4 CDs) R. 1967
Individual operas in Wagner's cycle, and individual performances, may be preferable on other sets – my favourite *Walküre* is the Bayreuth Centenary production, conducted by Pierre Boulez – but as an all-round testament to Bayreuth standards and a record of the finest Brünnhilde, Nilsson, this remains unbeatable.

TANNHÄUSER

Wolfgang Windgassen, Anja Silja, Grace Bumbry, Eberhard Wächter. Bayreuth Festival Opera/Wolfgang Sawallisch
Philips 434 607-2 (3 CDs) R. 1962
Yet another Bayreuth triumph: the usually level-headed Sawallisch produces electrifying orchestral results in the Venusberg orgy and Windgassen tears at the soul in Tannhäuser's Act-Three narrative.

TRISTAN AND ISOLDE

Ludwig Suthaus, Kirsten Flagstad, Blanche

Thebom, Josef Greindl, Dietrich Fischer-Dieskau. Philharmonia/Wilhelm Furtwängler
EMI CDS7 47322-8 (4 CDs) R. 1953 (m)
Furtwängler's approach to *Tristan* is symphonic rather than dramatic, but the playing of the orchestra is phenomenal and Flagstad's Isolde, if not the most beautifully sung on disc, is certainly the most awe-inspiring.

WEBER
DER FREISCHÜTZ

Gundula Janowitz, Peter Schreier, Edith Mathis, Theo Adam, Bernd Weikl. Staatskapelle Dresden/Carlos Kleiber
DG 415 432-2 (2 CDs) R. 1973
Carlos Kleiber's recordings, not to mention the number of operas he deigns to conduct, are like gold dust, so this typically febrile example should not be missed. The all-German cast is predictably idiomatic.

WEILL
THE RISE AND FALL OF THE CITY OF MAHAGONNY

Lotte Lenya, Heinz Sauerbaum, Gisela Litz, Horst Gunter. North German Radio SO/Wilhelm Brückner-Rüggeberg
CBSM2K 77341 (2 CDs) R. 1958
Adapted to the ageing Lenya's requirements, this recording is nonetheless immediate in its deliberately coarse-cut vitality.

STREET SCENE

Josephine Barstow, Samuel Ramey, Angelina Réaux, Jerry Hadley, Barbara Bonney. Scottish Opera/John Mauceri
Decca 433 371-2 (2 CDs) R. 1989
The depths of Weill's urban tragedy as well as the showbusiness kick of the brighter numbers are impressively dealt with in this sympathetic recording – the first complete version of a long-neglected masterpiece.

THE THREEPENNY OPERA

René Kollo, Ute Lemper, Milva, Helga Dernesch. RIAS Berlin Sinfonietta/John Mauceri
Decca 430 075-2 (1 CD) R. 1988
Decca's hotchpotch of vocal types – from the operatic Kollo and Dernesch to the smoky cabaret of Milva – reflects the fascination of Brecht and Weill's satirical hybrid.

ZEMLINSKY
THE BIRTHDAY OF THE INFANTA (THE DWARF)

Inga Nielsen, Kenneth Riegel, Beatrice Haldas. Berlin Radio SO/Gerd Albrecht
Schwann 314013 (1 CD) R. 1986
Poignant record of these dedicated singers' hard work in the production, seen in Hamburg and at Covent Garden, which revealed Zemlinsky's score as a work of genius.

ARIA

The aria grew out of those moments in operatic *recitative* which seemed to demand heightened expression or reflection, and developed as a set piece for solo voice. In the 18th century, when display was the order of the day, the form became that of the *da capo* aria: the singer would present the principal melody unadorned, proceed to a central section in contrasting mood, and finally return to the main theme, ornamenting it to the best of his or her abilities. In Italian opera of the early- to mid-19th century, the aria was usually divided into two parts – the *cavatina*, which provided opportunities for long, lyrical lines (usually with a simple, restrained orchestral accompaniment), followed by the *cabaletta*, a fast and often brilliant movement. Although Verdi eventually abandoned use of the *cabaletta* if the dramatic circumstances did not demand it, there is an obvious case of dramatic appositeness in his *La Traviata*, where Violetta's '*Ah, fors' è lui*' is contrasted with the hectic '*Sempre libera*'.

BARITONE

Although the original Greek means 'heavy tone', the voice falls between bass and tenor. Some rather arbitrary distinctions are made in the German system of *Fach* or vocal type – the title role in Mozart's *Don Giovanni* was originally a bass and is characterized as a *Kavalierbariton*, while Papageno in *The Magic Flute* is a *lyrischer Bariton*.

BASS

The lowest male voice. The paternal figure of Sarastro in Mozart's *The Magic Flute* (sub-classified as *basso profondo*) and the comic bass or *basso buffo* of Doctor Bartolo in Rossini's *The Barber of Seville* are two contrasting examples of the voice type. Bass-baritones combine the gravity of the *basso profondo* with a lyrical freedom in the upper reaches; Wagner's Wotan is a hard-to-cast example.

BEL CANTO

Although the definition of *bel canto* has always been imprecise (a literal translation is 'beautiful singing'), it embraces what the Italians see as the virtues of good vocal training – a fine, smooth singing line (*legato*), open tone and flawless technique.

CABALETTA

See *Aria*

CADENZA

When the music of an aria comes to rest in the cadence (or fall) before the final chord, the singer may demonstrate his or her virtuosity in a free display. Composers often provided their own cadenzas, but alternative versions to suit individual singers are still used in many cases.

CASTRATO

Male soprano castrated at puberty, originally to supply high voices for ecclesiastical purposes in the face of a Catholic edict forbidding women to sing in church. In Handel's day, the *castrato* at his brilliant best was the star of the show (see Senesino profile, page 19); last of the breed was Alessandro Moreschi, who died in 1922 but who recorded his art for posterity at the turn of the century.

CAVATINA

See *Aria*

COLORATURA

Elements in this fast, brilliant decoration of a vocal line include trills, runs and cadenzas. The word derives from the German *Koloratur*; the correct Italian word for ornamentation, which this definition tends to embrace, is *fioritura*.

CONTRALTO

The lowest female voice. Roles are fewer than for the corresponding bass category for men. The outstanding example is the earth-mother figure Erda in Wagner's *Ring*. Exponents, too, are rare (which is why Kathleen Ferrier has remained in a class of her own).

COUNTER-TENOR

High male voice produced with head tones to give a strong, vibrant sound. Britten wrote the role of Oberon in *A Midsummer Night's Dream* for the pioneering counter-tenor Alfred Deller, and the tradition remains safe in the hands of such singers as James Bowman and Michael Chance.

DA CAPO

'From the beginning' (or 'back to the beginning'): see *Aria*.

FIORITURA

'Flourish': see *Coloratura*.

MEZZO-SOPRANO

Female voice midway between soprano and contralto, though the distinction was not always noted: many of Mozart's roles which were written for sopranos have since been adopted by mezzos because their range is slightly lower. The vocal timbre is usually darker than that of a soprano, though some singers who wish to make a point describe themselves as *mezzo-contraltos*.

RECITATIVE

The form of singing, closest to natural speech, in which opera had its origins. When set pieces began to develop in the late-17th and 18th centuries, the recitative was usually used to move the action forward – *opéra comique* and *Singspiel* replaced it with spoken dialogue – although Mozart did much to break down the

artificial barriers between recitative and aria. *Recitativo accompagnato* is recitative with an orchestral accompaniment; *recitativo secco* is usually supported with harpsichord and sometimes an additional cello to fill out the bass line.

SOPRANO

Highest of the female voices, ranging from the dramatic soprano with the stamina for the part of Brünnhilde in Wagner's *Ring* and the title roles in Strauss' *Elektra* or Puccini's *Tosca* to the *coloratura* soprano capable of brilliant virtuosity, flourishing (literally) in the Italian operas of the early 19th century and given a second lease of life with the role of Zerbinetta in Strauss' *Ariadne on Naxos*. In between, much distinction is made between the straightforward

gLOSSARY

A selection of the most important basic operatic terms featured in the text. Where terms that define operatic genres, such as *opera buffa* or *opera seria*, have been explained in the main text, they have not been repeated here. Such references will easily be tracked down via the index (page 188).

lyric roles such as Mimi in *La Bohème* and those which require slightly more dramatic attack, such as Butterfly (a *lirico spinto* soprano).

SPINTO

'Pushed': see *Soprano*.

TENOR

The highest category of (natural) male voice. *Tenore* means 'holding' in Italian – an indication of the word's origin in the times when this voice was used to 'hold' the plainsong line in church services. The subdivisions are almost as striking as those within the soprano range. The *Heldentenor*, or heroic tenor, roles call for a voice of considerable strength, usually with a baritonal hue (the greatest *Heldentenor* of all, Lauritz Melchior (see page 117), began his professional career as a baritone). Lyric tenors, the best-loved breed, may just stretch to sing Verdi's *Otello*, though the *tenore di grazia* keeps within a light and graceful compass.

TESSITURA

You may hear singers discussing the suitability of a role's *tessitura* – the vocal range which the composer calls upon as it relates to the compasses of the respective voice types.

iNDEX

A list of the operas, arias, terminology and names of composers, librettists, writers, singers, conductors, etc., featured in the book. Opera titles are given in their language of origin when these are preferred in the main text and are set in italics (followed by their composer/s in brackets), as are books (followed by their author/s in brackets) and terms. Arias are set in quotation marks (followed by the opera in which they appear in brackets). Translations and explanations of all foreign-language terms and titles are given in the main text. Important basic operatic terms that are not explained in the main text (voice types, for example) are listed separately in the Glossary (page 187).

ACKNOWLEDGEMENTS

The publishers extend their thanks to the following agencies, companies and individuals who have kindly provided illustrative material for this book. The name of the supplier is credited alphabetically, followed by the page and position of the picture/s. Abbreviations: b = bottom; c = centre; l = left; r = right; t = top.

Archiv für Kunst und Geschichte, Berlin: 14, 28/9, 98/9; Catherine Ashmore/Zoë Dominic Photography: 21tr, 26/7, 38/9, 43, 83, 84/5, 133b, 136/7, 172/3b, 181b; Clive Barda/Performing Arts Library: 16, 22/3, 53, 128b, 151b, 171c; Beethoven-Haus, Bonn: 101c; Chris Bennion/Seattle Opera Association: 174t; BFI Stills: front cover, 31; Foto Ilse Buhs/Jürgen Remmler: 159t; J. L. Charmet: 12/13, 20tl, 50, 55, 60, 86, 88b, 92, 94/5, 107t, 111r, 118tl; Fritz Curzon/PAL: 135r; Erwin Döring, Dresden: 132t; Fletcher Drake/Opera Society of Washington: 154/5b; Mary Evans Picture Library: 18, 44, 78; Murrae Haynes/Santa Fé Opera: 26; Peter Krupenye/Opera Magazine: 27; Arwid Lagenpusch: 146t; Siegfried Lauterwasser: back cover, 102tl, 102/3, 104tr, 108/9, 112b, 113tr, 115b, 118br, 119t, 120b; Stuart Liff Collection: 30; Mander and Mitchenson: 19; MC Picture Library: 34, 58, 74tl; Metropolitan Opera Archives: 114tr; Metropolitan Opera, New York: 178t; Michigan Opera Theater: 180t; Alastair Muir/Opera Magazine: 144tl; Opera Magazine: 15, 40, 72, 88tl, 116t, 117b, 127c, 143tl, 147b; Photo Saporetti: 41; David Powers/San Francisco Opera Co.: 80; Bill Rafferty: 150b; Robert C Ragsdale: 175b; Royal Opera House, Covent Garden: 74b; Scala: 36; Richard Smith/Dominic Photography: 75; Society for Cooperation in Russian and Soviet Studies: 138r; Sabine Toepffer: 93.

Special thanks to Reg Wilson: title page, 17, 20br, 24, 33, 35, 42, 45, 46, 47, 48/49, 52, 56, 57, 61, 63, 64, 65, 66/7, 70/1, 76, 79, 82, 89, 91, 96c, 106tl, 123tr, 124/5b, 129r, 130tl, 131r, 134b, 140t, 141b, 144br, 145t, 148t, 152/3b, 156t, 160b, 161t, 162/3, 165b, 166t, 166b, 167t, 168r, 176t, 177b, 179b.